RAISING AN AUTISTIC CHILD

BY

Keiko Tobe

Contents

Reading Tips

With the Light: Raising an Autistic Child was originally created and published in Japanese which reads right-to-left as opposed to left-to-right as one finds with English. For the purposes of maintaining the integrity of the art and story flow of the book, that right-to-left orientation is reflected in this English language edition of *With the Light*, giving the impression that the book reads back-to-front.

For someone who has never before read a book in this fashion, it can seem disconcerting at first but is really quite easy. Simply begin reading at the upper right hand corner of the page and move through the word balloons and the panels in a right-to-left progression. The diagram below will help give you a feel for the "movement" of the story:

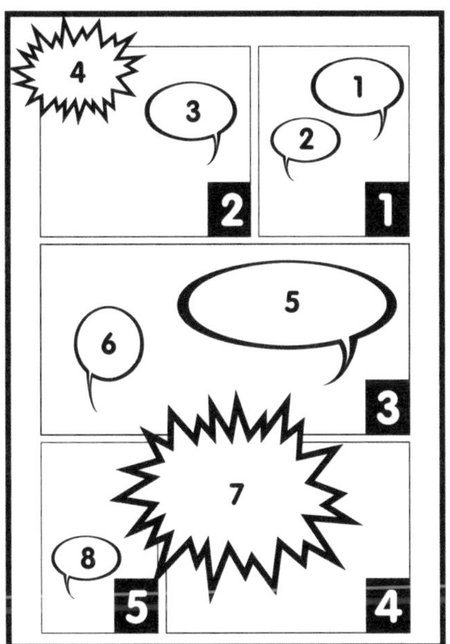

Manga, or Japanese comics, are an ubiquitous part of Japanese culture, and one finds many wonderful stories like this one dealing with all manner of topics and appealing to all walks of life. Manga presented with this orientation are becoming increasingly popular in the Western world. If this is your first exposure to manga, we are grateful for the opportunity to bring you this unique reading experience.

Cultural Notes

Autism is an affliction that doesn't observe international borders. Though the events of *With the Light: Raising an Autistic Child* take place in Japan, the experiences and emotions of the Azuma family will undoubtedly resonate with anyone who has been confronted by the disability. Despite the universality of the themes in *With the Light*, these few cultural notes will hopefully make reading this wonderful work—where cultural differences at times may seem quite foreign—a little easier.

This edition of *With the Light* attempts to remain as true to the original Japanese text as possible with respect to its translation. For any terms that may need clarification, please consult the Translation Notes at the back of the book.

Something that might help the reader better understand the text and interpersonal relationships in the book as a whole is the following chart which clarifies Japanese honorifics, terms that convey respect or affection. Maintaining the honorifics is essential because of their significance in Japanese communication as they provide an indication of the speaker's social status and/or feelings.

No honorific present	Indicates familiarity or closeness; if used without permission or reason, addressing someone in this manner would constitute an insult
-san	The Japanese equivalent of social pre-nominals such as Mr./Mrs./Miss. If a situation calls for politeness, this is the fail-safe honorific; this may be used among family members as well
-sama	Conveys great respect; may also indicate that the social status of the speaker is lower than that of the addressee
-kun	Used most often when referring to boys, this indicates affection or familiarity. Occasionally used by older men among their peers, but it may also be used by anyone referring to a person of lower standing; sometimes used to refer to girls
-chan	An affectionate honorific indicating familiarity used mostly in reference to girls; also used in reference to cute persons or animals of either gender
-sensei	A respectful term for teachers, artists, or high-level professionals; literally means "teacher"

Also, *With the Light* features sound effects like you would expect to find in any comic book. However, Japanese manga, including this one, tend to use a lot of phonetic transcription of sounds instead of actual words. Many of these words don't actually have literal translations in the English language. To simplify your reading experience, the sound effects have been subtitled with actual English words when possible.

Thank you for supporting this publication! Happy reading!

OH, IT'S THE SOUVENIR YOU GOT.
THE KALEIDO-SCOPE IS BEAUTIFUL, ISN'T IT?
MY SON, HIKARU AZUMA, IS AUTISTIC.
HE'S LIKED SPARKLY THINGS SINCE HE WAS LITTLE. ♡
ISHIDA-KUN BOUGHT IT FOR HIKARU.
I THOUGHT HIKARU-KUN WOULD LIKE THIS.
HERE YOU GO.
I THOUGHT IT WAS A SWEET MOMENT UNTIL...

Later Elementary Years
Episode 13
DANGO MARU
KORO KORO

OH NO! HIKARU TOOK IT APART!
LET'S PICK IT UP...
SCATTER
SCATTER
HE'S GONE.
ARGH! AND NOW HE'S PLAYING WITH WATER. HE'S ALL OVER THE PLACE!
LET'S GO PICK IT UP.
OWW!!

OH, DEAR, KANON STEPPED ON THE PIECES.
HIKARU GETS NERVOUS WHEN HE HEARS ME YELL.
HE UNDER-STANDS THAT SOMETHING BAD HAPPENED.
LOOK, IT CUT HER.
SHE GOT HURT BY THE PIECES YOU SCATTERED, HIKARU!
WAAAH
あ〜
HOLD ON, KANON. I'M GOING TO TAKE IT OUT, OKAY?
WAAAH
あ〜
LOOK, IT'S OUT.
THESE ARE SHARP AND DANGEROUS, HIKARU.
BLOOP
ぷ〜っ

WAAAH... IT'S BLEEDING!
HIKARU, APOLOGIZE TO KANON.
タタ
DASH
HEY, HIKARU.

I SHOULD'VE CLEANED IT ALL UP RIGHT AWAY.

BAND-AID.

HIKARU ASSOCIATES WOUNDS AND PAINS WITH BAND-AIDS.

OH...

TO HIM, THEY'RE THINGS THAT "HEAL."
BAND-AID.
THEY CAME IN HANDY WHENEVER HIKARU GOT HURT.
WAAAH
SHRIEK
THANK YOU.
LET'S SAY SORRY TO KANON.
I'M SORRY.
FORGIVE HIM.
CLUNK
HAHAHA! THAT'S GREAT.
HE MUST HAVE REMEMBERED AFTER HEARING IT SO OFTEN.
I LAUGHED SO HARD, I COULDN'T GET MAD AT HIM ANYMORE.

WHERE'S THE PRESENT ISHIDA-KUN BROUGHT BACK FOR HIKARU?
IT'S ON THE TOP SHELF IN THE CABINET. IF HE SEES IT, HE'LL DO THE SAME THING AGAIN.
IT'S BEST TO GET RID OF POTENTIAL SOURCES OF TROUBLE.
THAT'S HOW WE HANDLE IT IN THE AZUMA FAMILY.
HE STILL COMES TO ASK FOR THE KALEIDOSCOPE ONCE IN A WHILE, BUT I HAVE TO IGNORE HIM.
BEGGING POSE
STARE
HE'S PERSISTENT, BUT HE'LL ALSO JUST PLAY WITH WATER FOREVER IF I GIVE IT TO HIM.
THEN SIX MONTHS PASSED AND I'D FORGOTTEN ABOUT IT WHEN...
HELLO!
HIKARU AND KANON, HOW ARE YOU? NANA'S HERE!

HELLO, MOTHER.
HOW WAS YOUR TRIP?
HEWWO.
SFX: RUSTLE RUSTLE
IT WAS LOTS OF FUN MEETING MY OLD CLASSMATES AND GOING TO THE HOT SPRINGS.
I GOT SOUVENIRS FOR HIKARU AND KANON.
SINCE HIKARU REMEMBERS EVERYTHING ...
...I THOUGHT HE'D TAKE IT APART AGAIN.
SHAKE SHAKE
シャカ シャカ
万華鏡
万華鏡
AAAAAAH!
BAGS: KALEIDOSCOPE
SO IT'S A MARACA THIS TIME.
THAT'S NEW.
NO, HIKARU. YOU LOOK INSIDE THE KALEIDOSCOPE LIKE THIS.
LOOK IN HERE.

CAN YOU SEE?
OH...
シャカ シャカ
SHAKE SHAKE
AND HERE I THOUGHT HIKARU WOULD LIKE IT SINCE IT'S SPARKLY.
WHAT'S GOING ON?
どよーん
GLOOMY
I-DUNNO
HE DOESN'T PLAY THE USUAL WAY TO BEGIN WITH.
WE GLUED IT SHUT THAT NIGHT, SO HE CAN'T TAKE IT APART ANYMORE.
BUT DURING GOLDEN WEEK, WE HAD OTHER VISITORS.
HELLO!
HELLO, MOTHER, FATHER.
WHAT'S THE OCCASION?

WE WENT ON A TOUR.
AND WE THOUGHT HIKARU WOULD LIKE THIS.
WE BOUGHT ONE FOR KANON TOO.
......
万華鏡
万華鏡
EVERYONE THINKS ALIKE.
THEY'RE LIKE REAL MARACAS NOW THAT HE HAS TWO.
HAHA
SHAKE
シャカ
SHAKE
シャカ
SHAKE
シャカ
AUTHENTIC FORM
NICE
WELL, HOW ABOUT WE GO TO THE RESTAURANT ON THE MAIN ROAD?
YEAH.
AZUMA-SAN, ARE YOU GOING OUT?
YO.

HONDA-SAN.
MY PARENTS ARE VISITING.
WE'RE GOING OUT TO EAT.
OH, THAT'S NICE.
WE'RE TAKING A WALK.
ALTHOUGH WE JUST TAKE THE SAME ROUTE EVERY DAY.
I UNDER-STAND. WE WERE LIKE THAT TOO.
IS SHE YOUR FRIEND?
I'M SURE YOU'VE BEEN GREAT TO MY DAUGHTER AND GRAND-CHILDREN.
OH, THEY'VE BEEN GOOD TO US.
DASH
HEY, MIYU!
WAIT UP!
DART
THAT REMINDS ME OF THE OLD DAYS.
HAHA...

HIKARU'S EATING CALMLY.
WE COME HERE A LOT, SO HE'S USED TO IT.
THAT'S NOT THE ONLY REASON. YOU'VE DONE A GOOD JOB RAISING HIM.
I'M PROUD OF YOU.
SIGN: TAKEYAMA
OH, MOM.
I STILL HAVE A LONG WAY TO GO.
竹山センター
つくしんぼの会
SIGN: COUNSELING
AHAHA! YOUR HOUSE IS A KALEI-DOSCOPE MAGNET.

SOME KIDS LIKE THEM...
...BUT MAYBE HIKARU-KUN DOESN'T LIKE IT TOUCHING HIS FACE.
PSYCHOLOGIST OSAWA-SENSEI
OH, THAT MIGHT BE IT!
HAHA! I MIGHT BE WRONG TOO.
I'M JUST GUESSING AT HIS TRAIN OF THOUGHT.
OH GOSH, I DIDN'T REALIZE.
I'VE BEEN HIS MOM FOR TEN YEARS, AND I DIDN'T EVEN THINK OF THAT.
BOOK: HIKARU-KUN GAVE ME A MASSAGE. - GUNJI
光君が肩をたたいてくれました。
郡司
HOW ARE THINGS WITH GUNJI-SENSEI NOW?
DID THINGS CHANGE AFTER YOU MET WITH THE PRINCIPAL?
YES. SHE RESPONDS IN MY COM-MUNICATION NOTEBOOK NOW.
IT SEEMS LIKE IT ALL STARTED WITH HIM GIVING HER A MASSAGE.

ENVELOPE: TO THE SPECIAL EDUCATION TEACHER
SHE FINALLY READ THE LETTER YOU WROTE FOR US...
...AND THE DEVELOPMENT RECORD THAT AOKI-SENSEI HAD PREPARED.
SO IT'S A LOT DIFFERENT NOW THAN IN APRIL WHEN THINGS SEEMED HOPELESS.
障害児学級担
THAT'S GREAT...
...ESPECIALLY CONSIDERING SHE WOULDN'T LET THE PARENTS IN THE CLASSROOM BEFORE.
I THINK SO. I'D LIKE TO KEEP REMINDING HER ABOUT...
...THE CHARACTERISTICS OF AUTISM AND WHAT KIND OF THINGS LEADS TO TANTRUMS.
IT SEEMS LIKE SHE WANTS TO LEARN MORE ABOUT HIKARU-KUN.
WE ALSO DON'T HAVE DAILY CHORES AND TASKS ANYMORE.
AND I DON'T THINK SHE PLANS ANY ACTIVITIES UNLESS WE SPECIFICALLY REQUEST THEM.
I KEEP THINKING, "IF THIS WERE MR. AOKI..."
ニンジンの皮をむく
BOOK: PEEL CARROT
BOARD: DAY [TUESDAY] DATE

WELL, THE LAST TEACHER WAS SOMETHING SPECIAL...
...SO IT'S A BIT HARSH TO COMPARE THEM.
SCRATCH SCRATCH
OSAWA-SENSEI IS ALSO SOMEONE I RELY ON.
HIKARU GRADUATED FROM THE PRESCHOOL AT THE WELFARE FACILITY MANY YEARS AGO...
...BUT OSAWA-SENSEI STILL TAKES TIME TO ADVISE US DURING OUR MONTHLY COUNSELING SESSIONS.
BE SURE TO KEEP THE CURRENT TEACHER MOTIVATED...
...AND SHOW YOUR APPRECIATION. THEN YOU'LL BE ABLE TO GET EVERY-THING BACK TO THE WAY IT USED TO BE.
AUTISM ISN'T YOUR FAULT.
EACH CHILD HAS THE ABILITY TO GROW.
THOSE WORDS SAVED ME FROM A DARK PLACE.
WHEN HIKARU WAS YOUNGER...
...I DIDN'T KNOW HOW TO RAISE HIM, BUT OSAWA-SENSEI SUPPORTED ME.

WELL, SEE YOU NEXT MONTH.
ガタ
SCOOT
THANK YOU VERY MUCH.
NOW THAT WE DON'T HAVE AOKI-SENSEI ANY LONGER, I APPRECIATE HIM EVEN MORE.
HIKARU.
WHAT IS THIS?
WHAT ARE THEY DOING? IT LOOKS FUN.
IT'S A TRAIN GAME USING "VOCA."
NUMBER 350, TOBU RAILWAY, NIKKOU LINE EXPRESS.
OH, A COMMUNICATION AID?

VOCA: Voice Output Communication Aid. It's a communication aid that was developed for those who have trouble communicating audibly. There are thirty different types available on the market.

IT HELPS THOSE WHO HAVE DIFFICULTY SPEAKING, RIGHT?
NUMBER 350, TOBU RAILWAY, NIKKOU LINE EXPRESS.
THAT'S RIGHT. YOU PRE-RECORD PHRASES THAT MIGHT BE USED...
...AND YOU PUSH THE BUTTON TO REPLAY THE PHRASE WHEN YOU NEED IT.
MY HUSBAND'S COMPANY MAKES THESE IN ONE OF THEIR DEPARTMENTS.
NUMBER 100, NIKKOU LINE EXPRESS.
OH THAT'S RIGHT! HIKARU-KUN'S DAD WORKS FOR AN I.T. COMPANY, DOESN'T HE?
YES, BUT EVEN THOUGH HE WAS TRANSFERRED TO THE DEVELOPMENTAL AID DIVISION...
...HE'S WORKING IN SYSTEM MAINTENANCE SOFTWARE.
SO HE HASN'T MADE ANYTHING LIKE THIS YET.
THAT MACHINE WAS A GIFT FROM MORI-SAN.
IT'S HIGHLY RECOMMENDED FOR AUTISTIC PEOPLE.
OH, MORI-SAN WITH THE GOATEE?

I REMEMBER HIM.
WHEN I WAS PREGNANT WITH KANON, THERE WAS A TYPHOON...
...AND MORI-SAN TOOK CARE OF HIKARU AT THE SUNSHINE HOUSE.
BEARD.
HE WAS A BIG HELP.
AND HIKARU REALLY LOVED TO TOUCH HIS BEARD.
HEHE...
NOW, MORI-SAN'S A TEACHER AT THE DEVELOPMENTAL SCHOOL OF A TEACHERS' COLLEGE.
HE TAKES STUDENTS TO STORES USING VOCA.
CAN I HAVE AN ICE CREAM PLEASE?
OKAY.
THOUGH WE CAN SHOW WRITTEN WORDS TO BUY THINGS...
...THIS WAY, THE STUDENTS CAN SEE HOW COMMUNICA-TION WORKS USING SPOKEN WORDS.
IT'S BEST TO PUT IN WORDS THAT ARE BOTH USABLE AND FUN.
CAN I HAVE SOME JUICE?
PLEASE TICKLE ME.

A LOT OF THE CHILDREN WHO COME TO THE WELFARE FACILITY LIKE TRAINS...
...SO WE PUT IN TRAIN NAMES TODAY.
WE SHOW THEM HALF OF THE THE TRAIN.
HIKARU-KUN, WHAT'S THIS?
NUMBER 800.
ISEZAKI LINE EXPRESS.
PLIP
PLIP
YES, THAT'S CORRECT! ♡
...AND SO ON.
130KWx4
ア抵抗カム
LOW FRICTION.
I SEE.
YOU CAN ALSO TAKE A PART OF THE TRAIN AND ENLARGE IT.
HIKARU-KUN, WHAT'S THIS?
SOUTH AIZU EXPRESS
PLIP
THAT'S RIGHT. ♡
SOUTH AIZU EXPRESS
急行 南会津
NUMBER 350
NIKKOU LINE EXPRESS
350系
日光線急行
SMILE
YOU'RE AMAZING, HIKARU-KUN!

HIKARU-KUN, THE FIRST QUIZ IS OVER.
LET'S MIX UP THE PICTURES LIKE THIS.
AND HAVE HIKARU-KUN QUIZ US INSTEAD.
NOW IT'S OUR TURN.
PLEASE PRESS ONE.
PLIP
ピッ
NUMBER 8000, COMMUTER MODEL.
LET'S SEE...
WOW, THAT'S HARD.
I RECORDED THOSE WORDS TOO.
OH, I KNOW!
THIS ONE.
8123
HIKARU, IS IT THIS ONE?
にこっ
SMILE

WOW, THE VOLUNTEER WITH THE BEARD IS A TEACHER NOW?
THAT'S GREAT NEWS.
YEAH.
HE WAS USING DIFFERENT GADGETS ALL THE TIME.
LIKE THE QHW* AND VOCA.
HIKARU COULD UNDERSTAND THEM AND HAD LOTS OF FUN.
*QHW: QUARTER HOUR WATCH, A CLOCK THAT SHOWS TIME USING LCD DISPLAY.
NO MATTER HOW MUCH WE EXPLAIN IT IN WORDS, HE DOESN'T REALLY UNDERSTAND GAMES.
HE CAN ANSWER QUESTIONS, BUT HE CAN'T ASK THEM.
HE HAS TO CONCENTRATE REALLY HARD ON TALKING TO BEGIN WITH, SO HE PROBABLY DOESN'T HAVE THE CAPACITY TO ASK.
SO VOCA WAS HELPFUL BECAUSE HE CAN COMPREHEND JUST BY LOOKING AT IT.

FOR HIKARU, COMMUNICATING IS REALLY DIFFICULT.
IT'S LIKE THE EQUIVALENT OF ASKING US TO SPEAK IN ANOTHER LANGUAGE.
YEAH.
G! For Giraffe!
PUSHING BUTTONS TO MAKE VOICES COME OUT IS THE SAME AS THE ALPHABET BOARD, ISN'T IT?
THAT'S TRUE.
S! FOR SNAKE!
HIKARU LEARNED HIS LETTERS USING THAT.
HE WAS FASTER AT READING THAN HIS FRIENDS.

SIGN: RECOMMENDED MENU
RAMEN WITH FIVE TOPPINGS 700 YEN
SIMMERED INTESTINES 400 YEN

SO IT CONFUSED ME THAT HE COULDN'T COMMUNICATE.

REC. OM. MEN. DED.

HE CAN READ.

BUT HE CAN'T COMMUNICATE.

WHAT'S YOUR NAME?

WHAT'S YOUR NAME?

YOU WILL BE HAPPY WITH THIS OPEN SPACE.

THE ONLY WORDS HIKARU COULD MANAGE WERE REPETITIONS OF WHAT OTHER PEOPLE SAID OR COMMERCIALS HE'D HEARD.

NOW THAT I THINK ABOUT IT, HE DOESN'T UNDERSTAND THE MEANING OF WORDS.

SO HE DIDN'T DEVELOP A NEED TO EXPRESS THINGS TO OTHERS.

THROUGH EXPERIENCE, HE LEARNED TO MAKE SOME CONVERSATION.

HE LEARNED MORE DAILY CONVERSATION.

GOOD MORNING.

GOOD MORNING.

AND NOW, HE'LL MAKE REQUESTS TO A SELECT FEW WHO RESPOND TO HIM.

MOTHER, PLEASE BRUSH ME.

BUT HE DOESN'T YET HAVE THE FULL USE OF LANGUAGE...
PLEASE WAIT. PLEASE WAIT.
OH, HE WANTS TO DO SOMETHING.
...SO NOT EVERYONE UNDERSTANDS HIM.
1. 子供部屋で あそぶ
PLAY IN THE PLAY ROOM.
2. 歯みがき
BRUSH YOUR TEETH.
3. ねる
GO TO BED.
INSTEAD OF ME JUST TELLING HIM WHAT TO SAY...
YOU CAN GO NOW.
I'LL BRING A VOCA HOME FROM WORK.
IT'LL BE GOOD TO HAVE SOMETHING ELSE FOR HIKARU TO ENJOY.
...I WANT HIKARU TO BE ABLE TO EXPRESS HIMSELF MORE!
YEAH.

WE STARTED USING VOCA, AND IT CAUGHT ON.
DURING THE TWENTY MINUTE RECESS, TRAIN FANATICS GATHERED IN THE SPECIAL ED CLASS.
立 七 月 小
SIGN: SHICHIGATSU ELEMENTARY
I'LL SHOW YOU HALF. WHICH ONE IS THIS?
EIDAN HIBIYA LINE, COMMUTER MODEL.
YIKES!
HIKARU-KUN IS FAST!
SIGN: QUIZ IS OVER.
にこにこ
SMILE SMILE
HE'S TOUGH. I WON'T LOSE FOR THE ODAKYU TRAINS, THOUGH.
I DIDN'T THINK MR. GORI WAS A TRAIN FANATIC.
NEXT IS CARD PLAY.
クイズおしまい
カルタします
AND IT'S GOOD FOR HIKARU TO USE THE SAME AID BUT IN DIFFERENT WAYS.

SUNDAY
エレガンス ハイツ
SIGN: ELEGANCE HEIGHTS
SCOOT
ガタ
SCOOT
ガタッ
STAND UP.
THEY MAKE THESE WHERE MY HUSBAND WORKS.
INTERESTING EQUIPMENT.
BUT WHY DOES HIKARU-KUN NEED IT WHEN HE CAN TALK?
HIKARU USED IT IN HIS BUDDY SYSTEM CLASS TO START THE DAY.
TALKING IS DIFFICULT FOR HIKARU. IT'S LIKE RUNNING AT FULL SPEED.
MIYU-CHAN LIKES PUSHING BUTTONS, SO YOU SHOULD TRY IT TOO.
NAH, I DON'T LIKE TECHNICAL STUFF ANYWAY.
PLUS, IT LOOKS EXPENSIVE.
SCRATCH
SCRATCH
I'M CONCERNED ABOUT OUR WALKING ROUTE, THOUGH.
SHE STARTS CRYING WHEN WE CHANGE THE ROUTE JUST A LITTLE BIT.
I CAN'T EVEN STOP TO REST.

HIKARU LIKES THE "P" SIGN OF THE PARKING LOT.
SO I USED TO DISTRACT HIM BY SAYING, "THERE'S A 'P' OVER THERE."
MAP: FLOWERS, FISH
魚
花
P
AND I DREW A MAP OF THE NEIGHBOR-HOOD...
...AND TOOK SOME POLAROIDS TO SHOW HIKARU.
ONCE HE STARTED TO KNOW MORE PLACES AND GET USED TO THEM, HE WAS LESS OBSESSED.
WE HAD THE SAME PROBLEM BEFORE TOO.
THEY CRY SO MUCH IT MAKES US LOOK LIKE KIDNAPPERS.
I WISH SHE WOULDN'T GET SO OBSESSED.
ウロウロ
WADDLE WADDLE
I HEARD SOMEONE ALSO USED FIRE HYDRANTS...
HIKARU, TAKE YOUR HANDS OUT.
ゴソゴソ
RUMMAGE
RUMMAGE

WE'RE HOME.
WELCOME BACK. I HAVE SOME SNACKS READY, SO CAN YOU WASH YOUR HANDS WITH HIKARU?
AHH, WELCOME!
WELCOME!
HELLO.
KANON, LET'S EAT OVER HERE.
OKAY!
HER HUSBAND ALWAYS HELPS TAKE CARE OF THE KIDS.
HE ATTENDS SCHOOL EVENTS TOO.
AND THEIR GRANDMA SEEMED NICE.

SEE YOU TOMORROW!
AND THEY LIVE IN A NICE CONDO.
ボロッ
WORN OUT
DAMMIT, WHAT A BIG DIFFERENCE.

WE'RE HOME.
HAHAHA!
WHERE ARE YOU GOING?
TURN
NONE OF YOUR BUSINESS. LEAVE ME ALONE!
TUG
DON'T GO AROUND BORROWING MONEY, ALL RIGHT? I DON'T WANT TO MOVE AGAIN.
YOU GUYS ANNOY ME!
WHY CAN'T YOU SMILE AND WAVE ME OFF, HUH?
YOU DON'T SAY ANYTHING TO US EITHER!
SHUT UP!
HEY, DON'T KICK MIYU!
SLAM

DON'T BE BOSSY, MR. KING OF DEBT.
EEYOU.
HUH? "EEYOU"?
HE ONLY TAKES CARE OF MIYU WHEN HE'S IN A GOOD MOOD...
...AND RUNS OFF WHEN SHE GETS FUSSY.
YOU'RE MORE OF A KID THAN SHE IS, IDIOT!
SIGN: SHICHIGATSU-CHO ELEMENTARY
THE NEXT DAY
七月小学
RUMMAGE
RUMMAGE
GRAB
WHAT ARE YOU DOING!? TAKE YOUR HANDS OUT!
IT'S DIS-GUSTING!

GUNJI-SENSEI, THANK YOU FOR STOPPING HIM.
BUT PLEASE DON'T CALL IT DISGUSTING.
GASP
BUT AZUMA-SAN...
...IT'S DISGUSTING TO TOUCH HIMSELF IN FRONT OF OTHERS!
IT'S EMBAR-RASSING.
IT'S NOT STRANGE FOR CHILDREN TO TOUCH THEIR OWN BODIES.
AND HIKARU DOESN'T...
...UNDERSTAND THAT IT'S EMBARRASSING TO DO THAT IN FRONT OF OTHERS.
CAN YOU TELL HIM TO TAKE HIS HANDS OUT...
...AND DIRECT HIM TO DO SOMETHING ELSE INSTEAD, LIKE A PUZZLE?
HE HASN'T STARTED TOUCHING HIS GENITALS YET...
...SO I DON'T THINK IT'S ANYTHING LIKE THAT.
HE MIGHT HAVE A RASH.
TOUCH-ING HIS GENI-TALS...

THIS IS PROBABLY SOMETHING GUNJI-SENSEI NEVER HAD TO DEAL WITH IN HER YEARS OF TEACHING.
AND SHE ONLY HAS A DAUGHTER...
IT'S DIS-GUSTING!
THOSE ARE HORRIBLE WORDS FOR A PARENT TO HEAR.
NORMAL HUMAN BEHAVIOR IS CONSIDERED "DISGUSTING" DEPENDING ON THE PLACE.
COMBAT
MAYBE I'M THE ONE WHO'S MOST CONCERNED ABOUT HIKARU BECOMING AN ADOLESCENT.
I'VE NEVER RAISED A BOY BEFORE.

七 月 小 校
SIGN: SHICHIGATSU ELEMENTARY
WHAT HAPPENED TO YOUR FACE, HONDA-SAN?
IT WAS MY HUSBAND.
MIYU'S OBSESSED WITH SAGGING SOCKS...
...AND ZIPPERS THAT ARE PARTIALLY OPEN.
SHE'LL GO UP TO ANYONE AND FIX THEM.
ぴっ
TUG
SHE ZIPPED UP MY HUSBAND, AND IT CAUGHT THE SKIN ON HIS NECK...
...SO HE GOT UPSET AND HIT MIYU.
ヒリ ヒリ
STING STING
THIS ISN'T MY KID!

SFX: CRACK CRACK
BAM
WHY DOESN'T SHE UNDERSTAND WHAT I TELL HER!?
LOOK WHO'S TALKING!
I KICKED HIM, AND WE GOT INTO A BIG FIGHT.
PEOPLE EVEN CAME TO WATCH.
POW
WHAT DID YOU SAY!?
WOW...
SIGN: SPECIAL EDUCATION
あさがお教室
I CAN'T FORGIVE HIM.
HE ALWAYS MAKES FUN OF MIYU.
...THAT'S HOW MUCH SHE CARES ABOUT MIYU-CHAN.
GOOD MORNING.
HONDA-SAN GETS BRUISED AND BEATEN...
BADUM
GUNJI-SENSEI, HE DID HAVE A RASH.
I PUT SOME MEDICINE ON HIM, SO HE SHOULDN'T STICK HIS HANDS IN HIS PANTS ANYMORE.
WHEW
OH, THAT'S GOOD.

OH?
GUNJI-SENSEI, YOU PREPARED A BASKET FOR THE COMMUNICATION NOTEBOOK? ♡
THANK YOU SO MUCH.
SHE SEEMS RELIEVED.
I GUESS I CAN'T TALK TO HER ABOUT THESE SORTS OF THINGS.
I JUST HAVE TO PREPARE SOME-THING...
...THAT WILL HELP THEM KNOW WHAT TO DO ON SIGHT, RIGHT?
THAT'S EASY, LIKE PLANNING OUT MY KITCHEN.
YOU'RE WONDERFUL.
OH, HIKARU UNDERSTOOD AND PUT IT IN.
THE MORE HE UNDER-STANDS, THE EASIER IT IS FOR US AND FOR HIKARU.
THAT'S TRUE, WE DON'T HAVE AS MUCH TROUBLE IN THE MORNING ANYMORE, EITHER.

"WHEN"?
IF YOU INCLUDE THE "WHEN," THEN IT'S PERFECT!
BASKET: DONE
AS IN, WHEN THINGS BEGIN, AND WHEN THEY END.
HIKARU ISN'T VERY GOOD AT DETERMINING HOW FAR HE NEEDS TO GO...
...SO IT GIVES HIM AN IDEA OF HOW MUCH HE NEEDS TO DO.
おしまい
LIST: POOL 10:00 DRIVE TO 10:30 CHANGE
IN OUR FAMILY, WE CREATE SCHEDULES EVERY DAY.
I SEE.
WE DON'T KNOW WHAT'S HAPPENING EVERY DAY.
THAT'S WHY MIYU DISAPPEARS ALL THE TIME.
SPIN
SPIN
GUNJI-SENSEI! INSTEAD OF THE COMMUNICATION NOTEBOOK...
...CAN YOU MAKE A CALENDAR OR CLASS SCHEDULE?

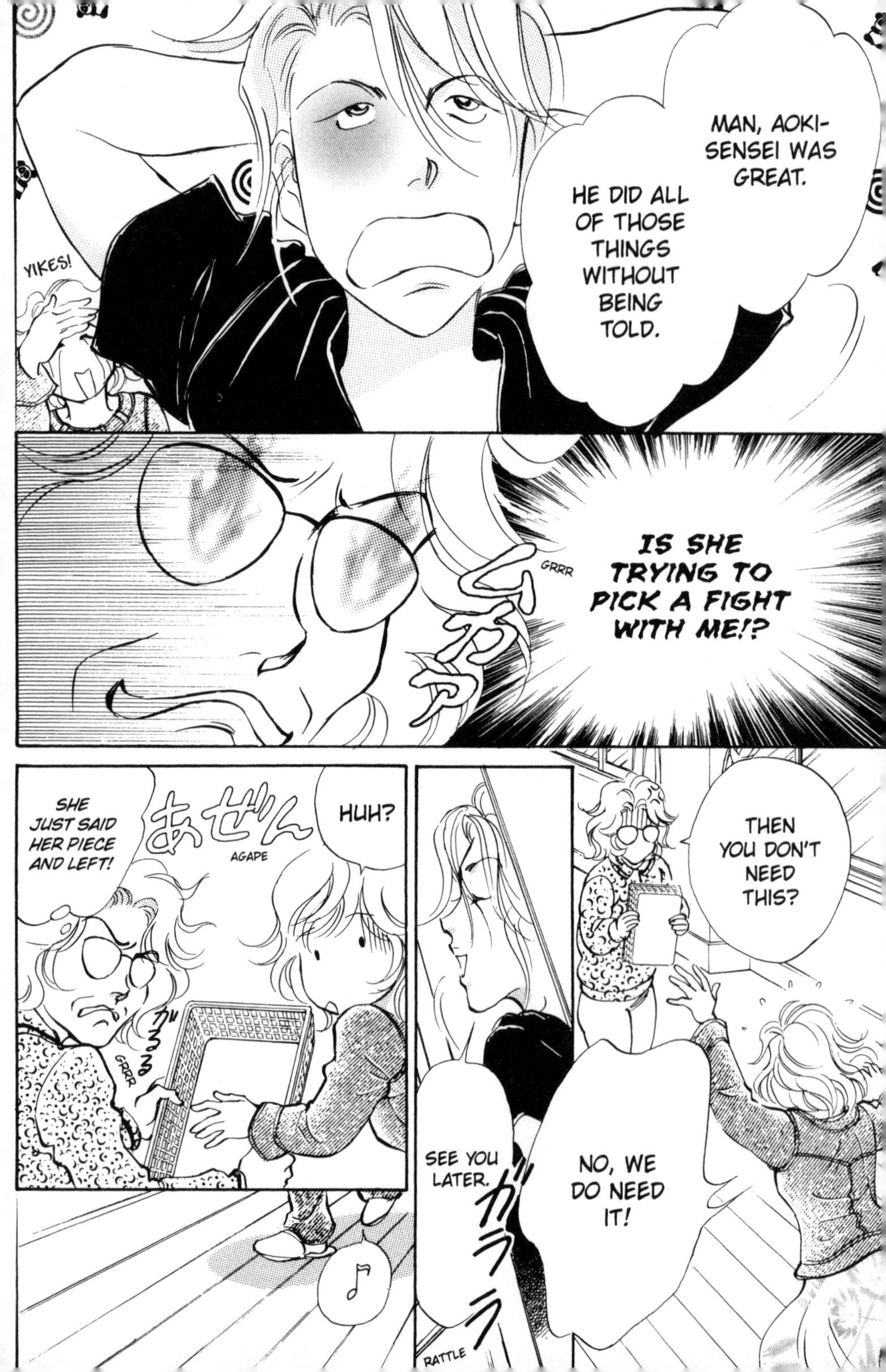
MAN, AOKI-SENSEI WAS GREAT.
HE DID ALL OF THOSE THINGS WITHOUT BEING TOLD.
YIKES!
GRRR
IS SHE TRYING TO PICK A FIGHT WITH ME!?
THEN YOU DON'T NEED THIS?
HUH?
AGAPE
SHE JUST SAID HER PIECE AND LEFT!
GRRR
NO, WE DO NEED IT!
SEE YOU LATER.
RATTLE

HEY, HONDA-SAN. PLEASE WAIT!

WHY DO YOU SAY THINGS LIKE THAT TO GUNJI-SENSEI?

YOU CAN'T COMPARE HER TO AOKI-SENSEI TO HER FACE.

BUT I'M JUST STATING THE OBVIOUS.
I'M ONLY ASKING HER TO DO WHAT TEACHERS SHOULD BE DOING!
SHE'S COMPLETELY DIFFERENT FROM AOKI-SENSEI!

IF SHE DOESN'T HAVE A SCHEDULE, SHE DOESN'T HAVE A PLAN.
SO SHE'S JUST SHOWING THEM VIDEOS ALL DAY LONG.

THAT'S NO DIFFERENT FROM BEING AT HOME.
KLUNK
THAT MAY BE TRUE...
...BUT IT'S HER FIRST TIME DEALING WITH AUTISTIC CHILDREN.

SHE'S TRYING SO HARD TO UNDERSTAND.
YOU SHOULDN'T DISCOURAGE HER.
WHAT DO YOU MEAN, "TRYING SO HARD"!?
WHY DO WE NEED TO COMPROMISE?
THIS IS THEIR JOB!
LOOKING AT YOU ANNOYS ME.
?
STOP BEING SO APOLOGETIC ABOUT EVERYTHING!
!!

......
I'M ONLY BEING POLITE BECAUSE...
...GUNJI-SENSEI IS OLDER THAN I AM.
SHE MUST BE IRRITATED BECAUSE SHE HAD A FIGHT WITH HER HUSBAND.
AND SHE'S ALSO ANXIOUS ABOUT MIYU-CHAN.
I UNDERSTAND HOW SHE FEELS.
I JUST WANT HIKARU TO BE ABLE TO LIVE AN EASIER LIFE.
ぎゅっ
SQUEEZE
HIKARU SPENDS TIME WITH GUNJI-SENSEI EVERY DAY.
I DON'T HAVE TIME TO PICK FIGHTS WITH HER.
ISN'T IT THE SAME FOR YOU?
I'D RATHER HAVE EVERYONE FEEL HAPPY IN THE PROCESS.

THOSE WHO'VE LIVED A HAPPY LIFE...
...THINK DIFFERENTLY FROM THE REST OF US.
I HAVEN'T TALKED TO MY FOLKS IN YEARS.
MY HUSBAND'S WORTHLESS AND JUST MAKES THINGS HARDER FOR ME.
SO I WANT TO AT LEAST BE ABLE TO RELY ON THE SCHOOL.
EVEN IF I HAVE TO FIGHT FOR IT, I NEED THEM TO GET BACK TO THE LEVEL THEY WERE AT LAST YEAR.
OTHERWISE IT'S TOO HARD HAVING TO DEAL WITH ALL OF THIS EVERY DAY, NOT KNOWING WHAT'S GOING TO HAPPEN.
YOU DON'T UNDERSTAND HOW IT FEELS TO HAVE NOTHING GO RIGHT, SO YOU DON'T GET HOW I FEEL, DO YOU!?
!!

IT'S NOT LIKE...
...EVERY-THING GOES RIGHT FOR ME.
I DON'T HAVE ALL THE PROBLEMS I HAD WHEN HIKARU WAS IN FIRST GRADE...
...BUT THERE ARE PROBLEMS ASSOCIATED WITH HIM BEING IN FIFTH GRADE TOO.
I DIDN'T WANT TO SAY ANYTHING SINCE YOU'RE A MOTHER OF A GIRL, BUT...
GASP
IT'S DISGUST-ING!
BLUSH
......
SORRY!
FORGET EVERYTHING I JUST SAID!

OH, I'M SO EMBAR-RASSED!
SLAM
THAT WAS EMBAR-RASS-ING!
HONDA-SAN.
EVERYONE THINKS THAT THEIR SITUATION'S THE WORST...
...WHEN IT COMES TO RAISING KIDS, WORK, EVERYTHING.
SAN
BECAUSE IN THE END...
...WE ONLY KNOW ABOUT OURSELVES.
HUH?

THIS CAN RECORD.
録る
DECK: RECORD
STUPID.
STUPID.
MAYBE I CAN USE THIS.
ちょうだい
FRIDGE: GIVE ME
おとうさん
DAD
ポリ ポリ ポリ
YAWN
ふぁ
WOBBLE
のそ…
MIYU, DAD'S GOING TO WORK.
EEYOU.

カシャ
CLICK
おとうさん
Have a good day, Dad.
HUH?
PRESS IT AGAIN, MIYU.
カシャ
CLICK
Have a good day, Dad.

MIYU...
THANKS, I WILL.
SMILE

WOW, HONDA-SAN.
I DIDN'T THINK ABOUT USING IT LIKE THIS.
I JUST RECORDED MY VOICE...
...BUT MY HUSBAND SEEMED TO BE HAPPY ANYWAY.
MIYU LIKES IT WHEN HER DAD'S NICE TO HER.
SO SHE KEEPS PUSHING THE BUTTON OVER AND OVER AGAIN.
SHE FOLLOWED HIM OUTSIDE TO PLAY THE SOUND TOO.
HAVE A GOOD DAY, DAD.
HOW CUTE. ♥
SHE'LL ONLY DO IT WHEN I SET IT UP FOR HER...
...SO MAYBE SHE JUST WANTS TO PUSH THE BUTTON.
おとうさん
もどす 聞く 録る

DECK: REWIND RECORD PLAY KNOB: LOUD - SOFT

I DON'T THINK IT'S JUST THAT.
SHE UNDERSTANDS THAT HER FATHER IS GOING TO WORK, SO SHE PUSHES IT.
AND SHE'S HAPPY THAT HE SMILES AND PATS HER HEAD...
...SO SHE WANTS TO DO IT AGAIN.
I THINK SHE UNDERSTANDS...
...THAT SHE'S SEEING HER FATHER GO TO WORK.
SHE'S BEEN SAYING "EEYOU," RIGHT?
I BET SHE WAS TRYING TO SAY "SEE YOU."
SHE WAS LISTENING TO WHAT YOU WERE SAYING, HONDA-SAN.
I HOPE SO.
...
THANKS FOR YOUR HELP.
I'M COUNTING ON YOU, SENPAI.
OH, DON'T CALL ME THAT.
キャア キャア
GIGGLE GIGGLE
SHE ACCEPTS COMPLIMENTS EASILY. SHE REALLY MUST'VE HAD A GOOD LIFE.

CARDS: JUICE / POTATO CHIPS

ジュース

ポテトチップス

HIKARU AND MIYU-CHAN HAVE THE NEED TO EXPRESS THEMSELVES.

THE PHOTOS AND CARDS THEY TAUGHT US TO USE AT THE WELFARE CENTER...

HIKARU

UNDERSTAND ME

青木先生

AOKI-SENSEI

わかってよ

UNDERSTAND ME

...THE LETTER MAGNETS THAT MR. AOKI USED...

...AND BEARDED MORI-SAN'S VOCA...

...NO MATTER WHAT THE FORMAT...

...I WANT TO ALWAYS ACCEPT THE MESSAGES FROM OUR CHILDREN.

I Love You

Later Elementary Years ⑬ / FIN

WE WILL DO THE CRAYFISH EXPERIMENT.
Later Elemen-tary Years
Episode 14
HUH?
WE'D FORGOTTEN ABOUT IT.
BUT HIKARU REMEMBERED.
THEY FISHED FOR CRAYFISH AT THE PARK EVERY YEAR.
AND THEN THEY RAISED IT IN THE CLASSROOM AND HATCHED THE EGGS.
WE CALLED IT THE CRAYFISH EXPERIMENT.

THE CRAYFISH EXPERIMENT, HUH?
THAT'S RIGHT. THEY'VE BEEN DOING IT SINCE FIRST GRADE.
I REMEMBER AOKI-SENSEI DOING THAT WITH THE KIDS.
I THOUGHT HIKARU WASN'T INTERESTED IN IT.
BUT I GUESS IT STUCK.
HE WAS ABLE TO CATCH ONE TWO YEARS AGO.
AND HE EVEN CAUGHT TWO LAST YEAR. WE HAVE IT ON VIDEO.
GIMME FOOD!
I WONDER WHERE THOSE CRAYFISH WENT.
THAT'S RIGHT. HE MUST'VE BEEN REALLY HAPPY ABOUT IT, SINCE HE WAS LOOKING AT THE AQUARIUM ALL THE TIME.
I WONDER ...

TO BECOME A CRAYFISH MASTER...

OUR SON, HIKARU AZUMA, IS AUTISTIC.

CURRENTLY TALKING TO HIMSELF

HE'S NOT VERY GOOD AT COMMUNICATING, AND WE CAN'T HOLD CONVERSATIONS WITH HIM.

WE WILL DO THE CRAYFISH EXPERIMENT.

......

IT'S IMPORTANT FOR HIKARU AND THOSE AROUND HIM THAT HE BE ABLE TO SAY, "I DON'T WANT TO DO THIS," OR "I WANT THAT."

BUT IN ORDER TO LIVE AMONG OTHERS, YOU NEED TO BE ABLE TO EXPRESS YOUR FEELINGS.

UNLESS YOU EXPRESS THEM, OTHER PEOPLE WON'T UNDERSTAND.

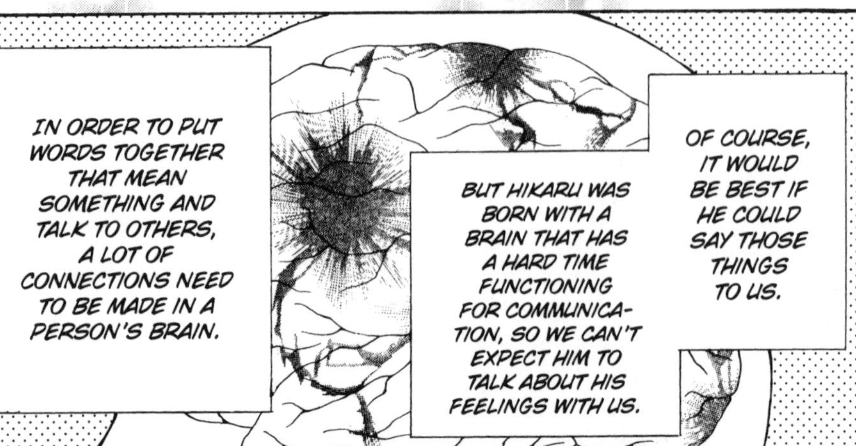

IN ORDER TO PUT WORDS TOGETHER THAT MEAN SOMETHING AND TALK TO OTHERS, A LOT OF CONNECTIONS NEED TO BE MADE IN A PERSON'S BRAIN.
OF COURSE, IT WOULD BE BEST IF HE COULD SAY THOSE THINGS TO US.
BUT HIKARU WAS BORN WITH A BRAIN THAT HAS A HARD TIME FUNCTIONING FOR COMMUNICATION, SO WE CAN'T EXPECT HIM TO TALK ABOUT HIS FEELINGS WITH US.

I DON'T MIND HOW HE COMMUNICATES...
トントン
TAP TAP
I NEED SOMETHING.
...FOR EXAMPLE, USING GESTURES...
I DON'T LIKE THAT.
PLEASE STOP.
ポテチくん
THAT.
BAG: POTATO CHIPS
...OR MAKING PHOTO AND PICTURE CARDS...
ポテチくん
...BY CUTTING OUT ACTUAL PACKAGES.
JUICE
ジュース
CAN I HAVE MORE, PLEASE?
WHETHER IT BE A COMMUNICATION BOOK OR A VOCA...
...OR LETTER MAGNETS, TEXTING, OR EMAIL... ANYTHING WILL DO...
おいしかった
PHONE: IT WAS DELICIOUS.
...AS LONG AS HIKARU DEVELOPS THE NEED TO EXPRESS HIS FEELINGS.
IF HE DOESN'T FEEL GOOD ABOUT EXPRESSING HIS FEELINGS, THEY WON'T DEVELOP.
YEAH. IN ORDER TO ENCOURAGE THAT...
...WE SHOULD DO EVERYTHING WE CAN TO MEET HIS REQUESTS.
WE WILL DO THE CRAYFISH EXPERIMENT.

5月
MAY
WOW!
GOOD JOB, HIKARU-KUN!
I WONDER WHAT HIKARU LIKES ABOUT CRAYFISH?
SIGN: SHICHIGATSU-CHO ELEMENTARY
七月小

あさがお教室
WHAT? CRAYFISH?
SIGN: SPECIAL EDUCATION
YES.
DIDN'T YOU CATCH THEM WHEN YOU WERE SMALL?
ABSO-LUTELY NOT!
BLUNTLY
きっぱり!
I HATE LOOKING AT THEM.
OH NO...
THOSE LEGS AND THAT BELLY... THEY'RE SO GROSS.
WE WILL DO THE CRAYFISH EXPERIMENT.
CRAYFISH EXPERI-MENT?
Y-YES. WE USED TO CATCH THEM AND RAISE THEM IN THE SPECIAL ED CLASS.
CRAYFISH IN MAY SEEMS TO BE STUCK IN HIKARU'S MEMORY.
I WON'T DO IT!
ガるる
GRRR
I DON'T CARE IF AOKI-SENSEI DID IT OR NOT!

I'VE PUT ALL MY ENERGY INTO...
...TEACHING ENGLISH AND MATH ALL MY LIFE!
IT WILL BE USEFUL FOR THE STUDENTS WHEN THEY ARE ADULTS.
PURE POINT
I APPRECIATE THAT FEELING...
...BUT WHAT ABOUT HIKARU'S WISH THAT HE WAS ABLE TO EXPRESS?
WE WILL DO THE CRAYFISH EXPERIMENT.
WE CAN'T JUST IGNORE IT.
MAYBE WE CAN RAISE IT AT HOME.
ぽむ
CLAP
GOOD MORNING!
れんらくちょう
エプロン
GOOD, THAT'S WHERE THE APRON GOES.
BASKET: COMMUNICATION NOTEBOOK
BAG: APRON
WHAT'S THAT, HONDA-SAN?
I'M GLAD YOU ASKED!

THERE'RE LOTS OF THINGS WE HAVE TO PUT INSIDE BAGS...
...LIKE GYM CLOTHES, APRONS, SHOES, AND CUPS.
MIYU DOESN'T KNOW WHERE THEY ALL GO.
I TAPED PHOTOS OF WHAT GOES INSIDE ON THE OUTSIDE, SO SHE CAN DO IT HERSELF.
SHE GOT IT RIGHT AWAY.
NOW SHE'LL PUT THE APRON IN THE APRON BAG.
IT'S EASIER FOR ME THIS WAY.
I'LL CHANGE THEM TO PICTURES AFTER A WHILE.
エプロン
うわぐつ
YOU'RE FULL OF GOOD IDEAS, HONDA-SAN...
...LIKE EARLIER, WHEN YOU MADE A RECORDING WITH THE CASSETTE TAPE.
I JUST WANT TO MAKE THINGS EASIER FOR MYSELF.
IF MIYU LEARNS TO DO ONE THING...
...IT'S ONE LESS THING FOR ME TO GET UPSET ABOUT.

ALL ITEMS: MIYU HONDA, BAGS: APRON, SHOES

WHAT A GOOD IDEA.
I WANT TO START SOMETHING NEW, BUT WE CAN'T START.
I CAN'T GET THEM TO FINISH ANYTHING EITHER.
HONESTLY! IT'S SO MUCH WORK!
WE HAVE SO MUCH TROUBLE GETTING READY AT THE END OF THE DAY.
I SPEND THIRTY MINUTES WITH HER, AND SHE STILL CAN'T FINISH.
SHE'S ALREADY UPSET TODAY.
......
SHE DIDN'T HAVE TIME TO THINK ABOUT THE CRAYFISH.
NO MATTER HOW MUCH SHE READS UP ON IN BOOKS OR IN THE REPORTS AOKI-SENSEI LEFT BEHIND...
...IT'S HARD TO IMPLEMENT SOLUTIONS IMMEDIATELY.
SEE YOU LATER TODAY.
RATTLE
I WISH SHE'D LEARNED SOME BASIC THINGS DURING SPRING BREAK.
SHE ONLY LEARNS THE SOLUTIONS TO PROBLEMS AFTER THEY OCCUR.
GUNJI-SENSEI'S JUST BARELY GETTING BY EVERY DAY, AND SHE'S ABOUT TO BREAK.

OH, HONDA-SAN.

THE YOUNGER STUDENTS HAVE A HALF-DAY TODAY, SO PLEASE PICK UP MIYU AFTER LUNCH.

OKAY.

SHE STILL TELLS US THE KIDS' SCHEDULES THE DAY OF, EVEN THOUGH THEY'RE PLANNED AHEAD OF TIME.

OF COURSE, SHE DOESN'T TELL THE CHILDREN IN ADVANCE EITHER.

IF SHE FORGETS TO TELL US BEFORE WE HEAD HOME, THERE'S NOTHING WE CAN DO.

MIYU-CHAN, AREN'T YOU FULL YET?

CHEW CHEW

MILK

YOUR BELLY IS FULL.

YOU SHOULD STOP EATING.

CHOMP
SHE'S SO STUBBORN.
UGH...
!!
BLEEEH
OH NO, SHE VOMITED!
STOMP STOMP
I TOLD YOU TO STOP EATING!
DASH
STOMP
WEREN'T YOU FULL ALREADY!?
WHEEZE
SIGH
HI THERE.
HONDA-SAN!
MIYU-CHAN JUST VOMITED.
IT WAS SO MUCH TROUBLE.
WHY DOESN'T SHE STOP EATING WHEN SHE'S FULL?

I DON'T KNOW WHY...
...BUT SHE FEELS LIKE SHE NEEDS TO EAT EVERYTHING ON HER PLATE...
...EVEN IF IT MAKES HER FEEL SICK AFTER-WARDS.
I DON'T THINK SHE KNOWS HOW TO STOP ON HER OWN.
AND IT'S USELESS TO JUST TELL HER TO STOP.
THEN WHAT DO YOU SUGGEST I DO?
I ONLY GIVE HER AMOUNTS SHE CAN FINISH.
IF SHE WANTS MORE, I GIVE HER MORE.
I TAUGHT HER TO ASK FOR SECONDS BY HOLDING OUT HER PLATE.
OH, I SEE.
TUG
MAYBE I PUT TOO MUCH ON HER PLATE.
I'LL GIVE HER LESS NEXT TIME.
I DON'T WANT HER TO THROW UP AGAIN.
OH.

GOOD JOB, MIYU.

YOU DID IT YOURSELF. ♡

THEY PRAISE THEIR CHILDREN TOO MUCH. I'VE NOTICED AZUMA-SAN DOES IT TOO.

WHY? THEY'RE DOING SOMETHING SO SIMPLE.

SEE YOU TOMORROW.

GASP

WHEN DID YOU PACK UP, HIKARU-KUN?

FLINCH

GRAB

IT'S NOT TIME FOR YOU TO GO HOME YET.

↑ HE'S SURPRISED BECAUSE SHE GRABBED HIM FROM BEHIND.

LOOK, YOUR MOTHER ISN'T HERE YET.

THE OLDER STUDENTS HAVE TO STAY UNTIL FIFTH PERIOD!

DASH
OH, HIKARU-KUN!
YOU CAN'T GO HOME!
SOB
SOB
OH NO! WHY ARE YOU CRYING?
I DIDN'T TOUCH YOUR NECK TODAY.
WAAAH
SIGN: NURSE'S OFFICE
保健室
HIKARU THOUGHT HE COULD GO HOME WITH MIYU-CHAN.
HE GOES HOME WITH HER ON TUESDAYS...
...AND I TOLD HIM SO THIS MORNING.
HE DIDN'T KNOW MIYU-CHAN'S SCHEDULE HAD CHANGED.

SENSEI, HIKARU CAN'T HANDLE SUDDEN CHANGES IN HIS DAILY SCHEDULE.
IT TAKES HIM A WHILE TO UNDERSTAND, SO PLEASE LET US KNOW IN ADVANCE.
TURN
WHY?
HE JUST HAS TO DO AS HE'S TOLD.
HE'S SO SELFISH.
IT'S NOT THAT HE'S SELFISH.
AUTISTIC CHILDREN CAN'T ACCEPT CHANGES EASILY.
THAT'S WHY HE'S IN THE SPECIAL ED CLASS.
NO MATTER HOW MANY BOOKS SHE READS, GUNJI-SENSEI STILL DOESN'T UNDERSTAND.
SHE THINKS HIKARU IS LAZY FOR NOT BEING ABLE TO DO SIMPLE THINGS.
DID SHE FORGET HOW MUCH IT CONFUSED HIKARU WHEN THE SPECIAL ED CLASS LOCATION CHANGED?
NO, THAT'S NOT IT.
DEEP DOWN, GENJI-SENSEI'S MENTALITY STILL HASN'T CHANGED.
ランチ

GUNJI-SENSEI.
HIKARU DOESN'T UNDERSTAND THE CONCEPT OF TIME.
WHEN YOU MAKE A SUDDEN CHANGE, HE CAN'T THINK ABOUT THE NEXT STEPS ON HIS OWN.
WOULD YOU PLEASE TELL THE CHILDREN WHAT THEIR SCHEDULE FOR THE DAY WILL BE IN THE MORNING MEETING?
IF THERE ARE ANY CHANGES, PLEASE LET THEM KNOW EACH ONE.
PLEASE GIVE THEM TIME TO TAKE IN EACH CHANGE.
SPONTANEITY IS DIFFICULT FOR THEM.
......
ALL RIGHT. IT'S A HASSLE, BUT I'LL DO IT.
I DON'T WANT HIM TO THROW A TANTRUM AGAIN LIKE HE DID TODAY.
I GET SO TIRED WHEN THEY CRY LIKE THAT.
!!
HIKARU MUST BE REALLY TIRED TOO!
THERE'S SO MUCH UNCERTAINTY EVERY DAY!

SCHEDULE: MON / TUES / WED / THURS / FRI
1 / SOCIAL STUDIES / MATH / MUSIC / SCIENCE / ENGLISH
2 / ENGLISH / SCIENCE / SOCIAL STUDIES / ENGLISH / SCIENCE
3 / MUSIC / ART / ENGLISH / MATH / SOCIAL STUDIES
4 / MATH / ART / MATH / PE / MATH
5 / PE / ENGLISH / READING / \ / PE
6 / \ / ETHICS / \ / \ / HOME EC

BOARD: MATH / SCIENCE / ART / ART

NEXT DAY

HOW'S THIS?

I WROTE DOWN TODAY'S SCHEDULE FROM THE WEEKLY CHART.

IT'S IN HIRAGANA, AND I ADDED PICTURES.

THANK YOU SO MUCH. IT'S REALLY GREAT.

BUT HIKARU UNDERSTANDS KANJI BETTER.

IF THERE'S PICTURES, HE GETS EASILY DISTRACTED.

BLAB
YEAH, AND WHY IS IT THE SAME SCHEDULE FOR BOTH KIDS?
BLAB
MIYU IS IN THE SECOND GRADE, SO WHY DOES SHE HAVE UP TO SIXTH PERIOD TODAY?

MIYU-CHAN'S SCHEDULE IS ONLY UP TO THE PART IN PINK.

SHE'S NOT GONNA UNDERSTAND THAT!

THEN WHAT IN THE WORLD DO YOU WANT FROM ME!?

EEEK

GROOOWL

UM, CAN YOU MAKE SEPARATE ONES FOR HIKARU AND MIYU-CHAN?
OTHERWISE, HIKARU MIGHT TRY TO GO HOME WITH MIYU-CHAN AGAIN.
UGH! THAT WOULD BE A PAIN...
NEXT DAY
HOW'S THIS!?
THAT'S GREAT, GUNJI-SENSEI!
CLAP CLAP
パチパチ
RIGHT: MIYU HONDA / LIVING / ENGLISH / MATH / INDEPENDENT WORK / LUNCH
WHEN THEY'RE DONE PUTTING THEIR THINGS AWAY, I'LL HAVE THEM GATHER AROUND AND READ THIS.
WOW!
WE'RE FINALLY GETTING SOMEWHERE.

IT'S GOOD TO HAVE AN IDEA OF THE DAY'S FLOW NOW.
YEP.
ALTHOUGH WHENEVER HONDA-SAN MADE REQUESTS...
...GUNJI-SENSEI WOULD GET UPSET.
BUT EVEN THOUGH SHE'S UPSET, SHE'LL STILL LISTEN.
SHE'LL ASK, "WHAT DO YOU WANT ME TO DO?"
SECONDS, PLEASE.
SECONDS, PLEASE.
IT'S GOOD TO BE ABLE TO GIVE HER SUGGESTIONS.
OH, BE CAREFUL.
THERE'S STILL HOPE AS LONG AS GUNJI-SENSEI'S COMPLAINING.
YEAH...
I'LL LISTEN TO HER GRIPE ANY DAY.
SIGN: SPECIAL EDUCATION
IT TAKES TIME FOR PEOPLE TO GROW.
あさがお教室

I SHOULDN'T GET ANXIOUS AND JUST BE PATIENT.
IF YOU WRITE IT DOWN, HE'LL COPY IT.
OH, I SEE.
TO LEARN ANOTHER PERSON'S PACE AND BE PATIENT...
...THAT'S WHAT HIKARU HAS TAUGHT ME.
SIGN: FACULTY ROOM
職員室
WHAT? COOKING CLUB?
YES, I'M THE ADVISOR.

WE MEET DURING SIXTH PERIOD ON THE FIRST THURSDAY OF EACH MONTH.
HIKARU-KUN DIDN'T PARTICIPATE IN APRIL.
WE MADE HIS FAVORITE SNACK, SO I WAS DISAPPOINTED.
SHE MARRIED THE PREVIOUS TEACHER OF THE SPECIAL EDUCATION CLASS. SHE KEPT HER MAIDEN NAME.
THIS MONTH WE'RE BAKING COOKIES.
WE'LL BE WAITING FOR HIM.
WAKA-BAYASHI-SENSEI...
BACK IN APRIL, HIKARU-KUN KEPT DISAPPEARING AND WAS ALWAYS CRYING...
...SO WE DIDN'T HAVE TIME FOR CLUBS.
BAKING COOKIES, HUH?
WHEN I WENT OVER TO HIS HOUSE, HE GAVE ME PANCAKES.
THEY WERE DELICIOUS.

THAT'S RIGHT.
HE CAN WORK ON MATH PROBLEMS LIKE THIS.
9 + 4 = 13
I THOUGHT HE WAS A STUBBORN CHILD WHO COULDN'T DO ANYTHING.
THAT DAY, I LEARNED THAT WASN'T THE CASE.
WHEN I FOLLOWED HIS MOTHER'S SUGGESTIONS ...
PUT TAPE ON THE GROUND
...HE WAS ABLE TO HELP CLEAN UP TOO.
TOY
BUT I STILL DON'T KNOW WHY HE CRIES SO SUDDENLY, LIKE LAST TIME.
HE CAN BE DIFFICULT TO HANDLE SOMETIMES.

BOOKS R-L: I WILL NOT RUN AWAY ANYMORE / IN REAL APPROACH / MYSTERIES OF
DEVELOP-MENTAL "TENDEN-CIES."
THEY GET ANXIOUS WHEN THEY DON'T KNOW WHAT'S GOING TO HAPPEN NEXT.
THEY MAY SEEM SELFISH OR LAZY...
...BUT THOSE WITH AUTISM HAVE DIFFICULTY UNDERSTANDING THE FLOW OF BOTH EVENTS AND TIME.
AND THEY CANNOT CREATE A SCHEDULE ON THEIR OWN.
HE CAN'T THINK ABOUT THE NEXT STEPS ON HIS OWN.
THIS IS A PROBLEM WITH THE FUNCTIONING OF THE BRAIN...
...AND CAN BE IMPROVED BY GIVING THE PERSON ENOUGH CONFIDENCE.
ENCOURAGE THEM TO DO WHAT THEY CAN, AND HELP THEM DO WHAT THEY CANNOT.

HUH?
ます。
次の木曜日はクラブ活動の日です。
若林先生より「クッキー作りをします。
今レシピを制作中」との伝言。
光君の予定に入れて下さい。
郡司
NEXT THURSDAY IS A DAY FOR CLUBS. WAKABAYASHI-SENSEI SAID THEY ARE BAKING COOKIES AND MAKING A RECIPE. PLEASE INCLUDE IT IN HIKARU-KUN'S SCHEDULE. - GUNJI
ALL RIGHT! ♡
I'M SO HAPPY I COULD FLY!
TO HAVE GUNJI-SENSEI TELL US ON HER OWN...!!
WE WILL DO COOKING CLUB.
LET'S PUT A CIRCLE ON THE CALENDAR.

SECOND THURSDAY IS COOKING CLUB.
5月 MAY
日 月 火 水 木 金 土
WE NEED A BANDANA AND APRON.
HE SANG THAT ALL YEAR LAST YEAR.
あさがお教室
IT'S MORNING MEETING TIME.
TODAY, MIYU-CHAN GOES HOME AFTER EATING LUNCH, UNDERSTOOD?
BLAH
HIKARU-KUN HAS COOKING CLUB DURING SIXTH PERIOD.
BLAH
BLAH
I ALREADY TOLD YOUR MOTHER, BUT YOU NEED A BANDANA AND AN APRON...
BLAH
RATTLE
SHE'S GETTING BETTER.
SHE STILL TALKS A MOUTHFUL THOUGH.
HAHA...
BUT IT'S CERTAINLY AN IMPROVEMENT.

SIGN: HOME ECONOMICS
家庭科室
THAT DAY, HIKARU WENT TO COOKING CLUB WITH GUNJI-SENSEI.
OH, IT'S HIKARU-KUN!
THERE'S ONLY ONE BOY BESIDES HIKARU-KUN.
OH, HE SURE IS POPULAR WITH THE GIRLS.
HELLO GUNJI-SENSEI.
HELLO WAKA-BAYASHI-SENSEI.
HERE'S TODAY'S RECIPE.
PLEASE SHOW THIS TO HIKARU-KUN.
クッキー
COOKIES
たまご
EGG
バター
BUTTER
こむぎこ
さとう
FLOUR, SUGAR
ふくろ
BAG
もみもみ
KNEAD
ROLL

WE'LL PREPARE AND THEN CLEAN UP ALL IN ONE HOUR.
IT'S SIMPLE COOKIE MAKING.
BUT THE RESULTS ARE DELI-CIOUS! ♡
キッチンラップ
こむぎ
さとう
I'LL CRACK THE EGGS.
ANYTHING ELSE I SHOULD BE CAREFUL ABOUT?
BOX: PLASTIC WRAP, BOWLS: FLOUR, SUGAR
WE'LL BE USING A TOASTER OVEN.
IT'S HOT ON THE OUTSIDE, SO CAN YOU BE CAREFUL WITH THAT AS WELL?
IF YOU TELL HIKARU-KUN, "IT'S HOT," HE'LL STAY AWAY.
HE'S BEEN DOING IT SINCE FOURTH GRADE, SO HE'LL BE FINE.
I'LL BE WATCHING TOO.
ALTHOUGH GUNJI-SENSEI WAS WORRIED, HIKARU WAS INTO IT.
YOU'RE GOOD AT CUTTING OUT THE COOKIES.
ぎゅっ
PRESS

HE LIKES COOKIES, SO IS THAT WHY HE CAN DO THIS WELL?
TRAINS, GARDENING AND CLEANING THE BATHTUB...
...THEY ALL STARTED FROM HIKARU'S FAVORITE THINGS.
職員室
WHAT? CRAYFISH!?
SIGN: FACULTY ROOM
YEAH.
I HAVE THE CRAYFISH FROM THE SPECIAL ED CLASS IN MY HOUSE.
I'LL BRING THEM BACK SOON.
OH, THE CHILDREN PROBABLY ALREADY FORGOT ABOUT THEM.
I DON'T THINK SO.

HIKARU-KUN ALWAYS TALKS ABOUT DOING THE CRAYFISH EXPERIMENT.
RIGHT, GORI-SENSEI?
YEAH, DURING THE TWENTY MINUTE RECESS.
THE CRAYFISH EXPERI-MENT...
...THAT WAS A GOOD SCHOOL PROJECT.
LOOKING INTO THE DISTANCE ...
IT STARTED OUT AS A SPECIAL ED CLASS PROJECT THAT THE BUDDY SYSTEM CLASS GOT INVOLVED IN.
THEN WE TOOK THE EGGS TO CLASS AND HATCHED THEM.
AND WE MADE AN OBSERVATION REPORT WITH ILLUSTRATIONS AND PRESENTED WHAT WE LEARNED.
DURING THE SCHOOL PRESENTA-TION...
...NATCHAN, WHO WAS GOOD AT CATCHING THEM, BECAME A CRAYFISH PROFESSOR TO TEACH THE OTHER STUDENTS.

BOARD: ROAD TO BECOMING A CRAYFISH MASTER
ザリガニマスター
への道
CRAYFISH TRAINERS!
HERE ARE THE KEY POINTS.
1.
POINT
OOOH!
ONE. USE CUTTLEFISH AS BAIT AND TIE TO THE END OF THE STRING.
TWO. FISH WHERE THERE ARE BUBBLES.
HIKARU-KUN TAUGHT EVERYONE HOW TO HOLD THE CRAYFISH.
LET'S DO IT AGAIN, GUNJI-SENSEI! ♡
WE CAN HAVE ALL THE GRADES PARTICIPATE THIS YEAR.
GULP
I...I CAN'T DO IT BY MYSELF. I HAVE TOO MUCH ON MY HANDS WITH WATCHING THE CHILDREN.
DON'T WORRY. WE'LL HELP TOO!
WHO'LL BE RESPONSIBLE IF SOMETHING BAD HAPPENS!?
OH...IS IT THAT YOU DON'T LIKE CRAYFISH, GUNJI-SENSEI?
BADUM
DON'T BE RUDE, GORI-SENSEI.

GUNJI-SENSEI'S GENERATION CAN CLEAN UP FISH.
SHE'S MORE USED TO LIVING CREATURES THAN ANY OF US.
RIGHT, GUNJI-SENSEI?
O-OF COURSE!
WE WERE RAISED WITH NATURE ALL AROUND US.
I'M MORE FAMILIAR WITH IT THAN YOU YOUNGSTERS.
WOW!
CRY
I SHOULDN'T HAVE BOASTED...
お知らせ
ANNOUNCEMENT
5年生 総合学習に
FIFTH GRADE SCHOOL PROJECT
「水辺の生き物
"ANIMALS BY THE RIVER"
SIGN: SPECIAL EDUCATION
あさがお教室
WE'RE GOING TO CATCH CRAYFISH?
HEH...
SEEMS SO.

THIS IS WHEN HIKARU WAS IN THE FIRST GRADE.
HE RAN AWAY PRETTY QUICKLY.
AND TAKUMI-KUN, WHO WAS IN THE FIFTH GRADE, WAS THE ONE CATCHING THE CRAYFISH.
I HAD THE TEACHERS WATCH THE VIDEOS AOKI-SENSEI GAVE US.
TAPES: CRAYFISH FOURTH GRADE, THIRD GRADE, SECOND GRADE, FIRST GRADE
IN THE SECOND GRADE, NATCHAN AND TAKUMI-KUN CAUGHT THEM...
...BUT HIKARU DIDN'T CATCH ANY.
SITTING ON HIS KNEES.
HE THREW THE FISHING ROD INTO THE RIVER.
OH MY.
HE LOOKS A BIT UPSET.
HE FINALLY CAUGHT ONE IN THIRD GRADE.
OF COURSE, AOKI-SENSEI HAD TO HELP HIM.
HIKARU-KUN LOOKS HAPPY.

HE CAUGHT TWO CRAYFISH LAST YEAR.
HE MUST WANT AOKI-SENSEI TO LOOK AT IT.
HE'S BRINGING THE FISHING ROD TO HIM.
WOW!
GOOD JOB, HIKARU-KUN.
SFX: CLAP CLAP
BEEP
OUR CLASS MIGHT LOSE.
OH NO!
I'M LOOKING FORWARD TO IT.
ME TOO.
THOSE LEGS AND BELLY.
UGH
I'LL GO TO THE RIVER ON SATURDAY AND TAKE PHOTOS.
THEN I CAN MAKE AN ITINERARY WITH MAPS ON MY COMPUTER.

WHEN SHOULD WE HAVE THE PRESENTATION?
LET'S SEE.
GORI-SENSEI...
HE WAS ALWAYS HELPING HIKARU ALONGSIDE AOKI-SENSEI.
またね
WAKA-BAYASHI-SENSEI HAS ALWAYS SUPPORTED US TOO.
WAIT UP!
I WAS SAD TO SEE AOKI-SENSEI GET TRANSFERRED.
七月小
THE BUDDY SYSTEM, THE CRAYFISH EXPERIMENT, AND THE SUPPORT OF THE TEACHERS...
...EVERYTHING WAS LAID OUT FOR US BY AOKI-SENSEI.
BUT THERE ARE PLENTY OF THINGS HE LEFT HERE FOR US.

THEY'RE STILL HELPING HIKARU DEVELOP, EVEN NOW.

IS EVERYONE READY!?
LET'S AIM TO BE A CRAYFISH MASTER!
ALL RIGHT!
YEAH!
BANANA
WOW, HIKARU-KUN. IT'S A MALE.
VULTAN ALIEN.
HAHA HA!

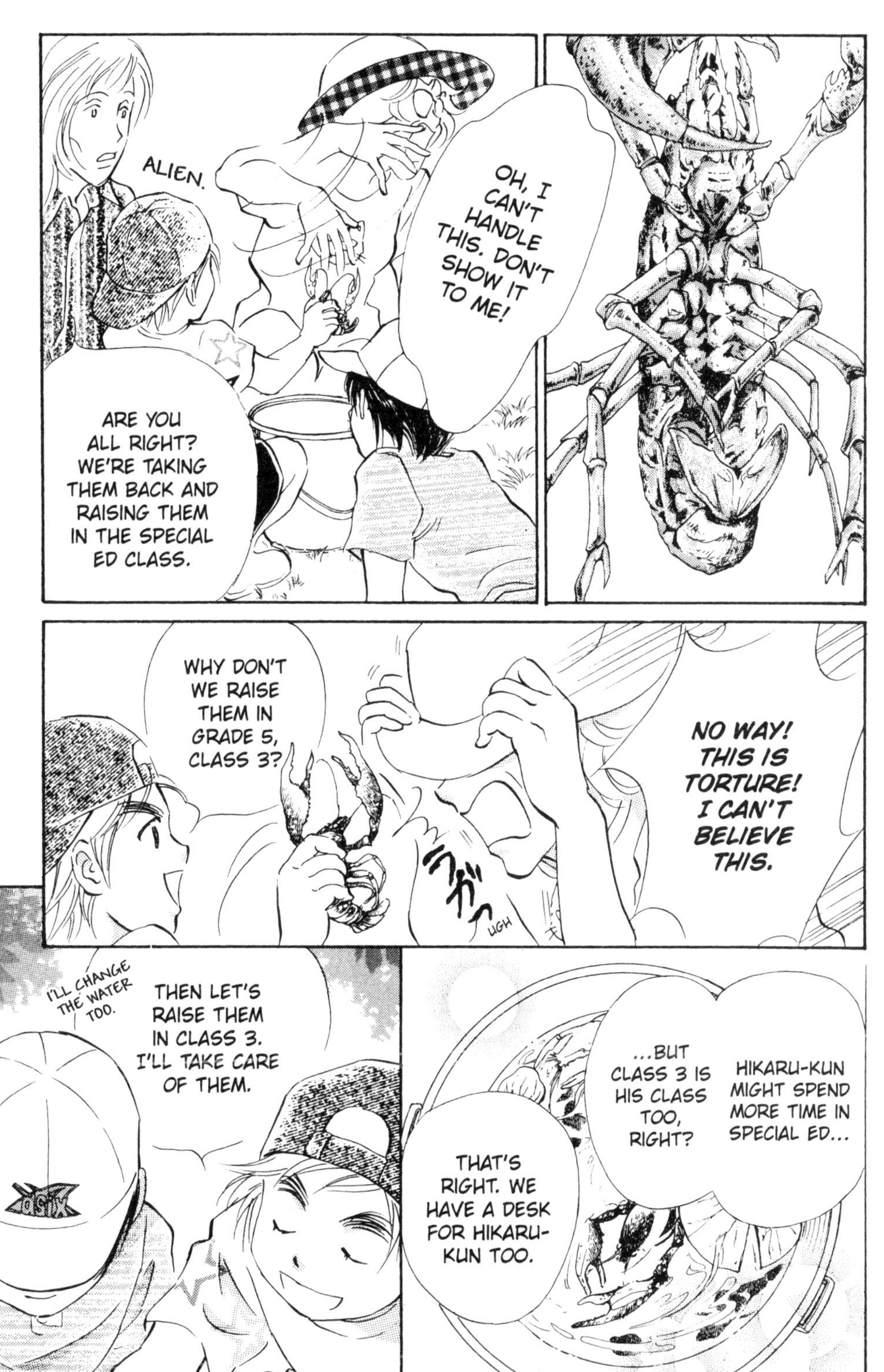
OH, I CAN'T HANDLE THIS. DON'T SHOW IT TO ME!
ALIEN.
ARE YOU ALL RIGHT? WE'RE TAKING THEM BACK AND RAISING THEM IN THE SPECIAL ED CLASS.
NO WAY! THIS IS TORTURE! I CAN'T BELIEVE THIS.
UGH
WHY DON'T WE RAISE THEM IN GRADE 5, CLASS 3?
HIKARU-KUN MIGHT SPEND MORE TIME IN SPECIAL ED...
...BUT CLASS 3 IS HIS CLASS TOO, RIGHT?
THAT'S RIGHT. WE HAVE A DESK FOR HIKARU-KUN TOO.
THEN LET'S RAISE THEM IN CLASS 3. I'LL TAKE CARE OF THEM.
I'LL CHANGE THE WATER TOO.

YOU LIKE TO LINE THINGS UP, HUH, MIYU-CHAN?
I'LL HAVE YOU HANDLE THEM, MR. NISHIWAKI.
OH, THEY'RE SO DIS-GUSTING.
WHAT DO YOU THINK, GUNJI-SENSEI?
I THINK HIKARU-KUN WOULD GET USED TO CLASS 3 FASTER THIS WAY TOO.
SPARKLE
SPARKLE
5 - 3
SO THAT'S WHY HIKARU GOES TO CLASS 3 DURING LUNCH BREAK TOO?
YES. THESE ARE THE CRAYFISH HIKARU-KUN CAUGHT.
ONE MALE AND ONE FEMALE.

NOBUAKI-KUN BRINGS HIM HERE.
IT MUST BE THE SOUND.
HE COMES INTO THE CLASS, TAKES A LOOK, AND THEN LEAVES.
IT'S LUNCH-TIME, SO HE PROBABLY DOESN'T LIKE THE CHATTER.
CHATTER
CHATTER
WHEN HE FIRST STARTED COMING TO SCHOOL, HE COULDN'T GO INTO THE GYM.
OUR PSY-CHOLOGIST TOLD US...
...THAT HIKARU'S EARS CAN HEAR...
...BUT HIS BRAIN IS UNABLE TO FOCUS ON THE SPECIFIC SOUNDS HE SHOULD LISTEN TO.
DORSAL
AUDITORY CORTEX
UNDERSTANDS SOUND
COCHLEA
COCHLEA
EAR DRUM
SOUND
CRASH
RATTLE RATTLE
THE SOUND OF A PENCIL BOX DROPPED IN THE CORNER OF THE ROOM...
COUGH COUGH
COUGH COUGH
...OR COUGHING, OR CHATTING...
...HE HEARS ALL OF THEM AT ONCE.
THAT MUST BE OVER-WHELMING.

I SEE.
IT'S ALMOST TIME FOR OPEN HOUSE.
I WAS WONDERING IF HIKARU-KUN COULD PARTICIPATE IN CLASS 3.
IF HIKARU KNOWS WHAT'S GOING ON...
...THEN HE SHOULD BE ABLE TO HANDLE IT.
I JUST DON'T WANT TO PUSH HIM TOO MUCH...
...BECAUSE IT'S JUST PAINFUL FOR HIKARU.
THAT'S TRUE.
DESK: HIKARU AZUMA
THIS IS HIKARU-KUN'S DESK.
THE REASON I BRING THIS UP IS BECAUSE...
...OF THIS DESK.
東光

SEN-SEI!
WHY DO YOU PUT THINGS ON HIKARU-KUN'S DESK!?
SORRY. IT'S ONLY FOR A LITTLE BIT.
CAN YOU MOVE THEM AFTER YOU'RE DONE?
HIKARU-KUN'S DESK ISN'T FOR STORAGE.
I HOPE HIKARU-KUN SITS HERE SOON.
OH, NOBUAKI-KUN.
TOUCHED
HE WAS IN THE SAME PRESCHOOL AS HIKARU.
HE SPEAKS HIS MIND, SO HE CLASHED WITH HIKARU A LOT INITIALLY.
SENSEI, WHY DON'T YOU GET MAD AT HIKARU-KUN!?
YOU GET MAD AT ME IF I TAKE SOMEONE'S THINGS!
IT WAS SO DIFFICULT FOR HIKARU TO SOCIALIZE BACK THEN...
...THAT HIS HAIR WOULD FALL OUT FROM THE STRESS.

BUT HIKARU LEARNED FROM THAT SITUATION.
AND NOBUAKI-KUN LEARNED HOW TO GET ALONG WITH HIKARU.
I'M SORRY.
HE FORGAVE HIKARU FOR RIPPING UP THE DRAWING OF HIS MOTHER.
NOBUAKI-KUN WAS THE FIRST PERSON HIKARU WAS ABLE TO APOLOGIZE TO.
I SEE.
I'D LIKE TO HAVE HIKARU SIT IN THIS DESK SOME DAY.
DO YOU KNOW WHAT AUTISM MEANS?
NISHIWAKI-SENSEI TALKED TO THE CLASS 3 STUDENTS ABOUT HIKARU BEFORE THE OPEN HOUSE.
DON'T WORRY. WE'LL BE QUIET.
I WANT TO PRESENT THE CRAYFISH EXPERIMENT WITH HIKARU-KUN.
BUT ON THE ACTUAL DAY...
5-3
CHATTER
CHATTER

...IT WAS THE PARENTS WHO WERE LOUD.

LOOK! IT'S TANAKA-KUN FROM JOHNNY'S JUNIORS.

CHATTER

SQUEAL

SWAY SWAY

BE QUIET YOU GUYS!

I SHOULD TAKE HIM BACK TO THE SPECIAL ED CLASS.

STOMP STOMP

WE PUT HIKARU IN THE BACK OF THE ROOM TO REDUCE STIMULATION, BUT IT BACKFIRED.

THERE'S TANAKA-KUN! ♡

TAKE A PICTURE OF HIM!

SHRIEK

FLASH

WE'RE IN THE MIDDLE OF CLASS. PLEASE STOP!

THE SUDDEN FLASH OF LIGHT...

...SENT HIKARU INTO A PANIC.

SFX: RATTLE RATTLE

Later Elementary Years ⑭ / FIN

Later Elementary Years
Episode 15
NISHIWAKI-SENSEI!
WHY DO YOU PUT THINGS ON HIKARU-KUN'S DESK!?
SORRY. IT'S ONLY FOR A LITTLE BIT.
CAN YOU MOVE THEM AFTER YOU'RE DONE?
HIKARU-KUN'S DESK ISN'T FOR STORAGE.
SURE.
CHAIR: HIKARU AZUMA
I HOPE HIKARU-KUN SITS HERE SOON.
I WISH HE COULD BE IN CLASS 3 FOOOREVER!
東光

IT STARTED OUT WITH NOBUAKI-KUN'S WORDS.
HIKARU, WHO IS AUTISTIC, WAS TO PARTICIPATE IN THE OPEN HOUSE FOR GRADE 5, CLASS 3.
5-3
BOARD: THE CRAYFISH EXPERIMENT REPORT
THE TOPIC WAS HIKARU'S CRAYFISH EXPERIMENT.
NISHIWAKI-SENSEI PREPARED HIKARU'S TURN TOO.
HE'S IN THE BACK OF THE CLASS, NEXT TO HIS CHILDHOOD FRIEND, NOBUAKI-KUN.
I HOPE HE CAN HAVE FUN DURING THIS PERIOD.
HIKARU'S CLASSMATES STAYED QUIET BECAUSE HE'S SENSITIVE TO SOUND...
SILENCE

...BUT IT WAS THE PARENTS WHO WERE LOUD.
CHATTER
ペチャクチャ
LOOK. IT'S TANAKA-KUN.
I SHOULD TAKE HIM BACK TO THE SPECIAL ED CLASS.
STOMP STOMP
バタバタ
WE PUT HIKARU IN THE BACK OF THE ROOM TO REDUCE STIMULATION, BUT IT BACKFIRED.
BE QUIET!
SHRIEK
キャーーッ
THERE'S TANAKA-KUN! ♡
TAKE A PICTURE OF HIM!
FLASH
ピカッ
RATTLE
ガラガラ
WE'RE IN THE MIDDLE OF CLASS. PLEASE STOP!
THE SUDDEN FLASH OF LIGHT...
...SENT HIKARU INTO A PANIC.
BUZZ
BUZZ

SHRIEK
OH, HE TURNED AROUND.
LET'S TAKE A PICTURE OF HIM. ♡
MUUU.
I WONDER IF HIKARU-KUN IS OKAY...
FLASH
KEEP IT DOWN!
FLASH
FLASH
BUZZ
BUZZ
LADIES, THIS IS A CLASSROOM. PLEASE ACT APPROPRIATELY.
IT'S JUST ONE PICTURE.
EXCUSE ME. PLEASE LET ME THOUGH.
BUZZ
BUZZ

HIKARU, DO YOU WANT TO GO BACK TO THE SPECIAL ED CLASS?
SHRIEK
CLATTER
STOMP STOMP
WHAT'S WITH THAT KID?
HE'S HIKARU-KUN FROM SPECIAL ED. DIDN'T YOU KNOW?
HIKARU-KUN...
SLUMP
ガックシ
THUMP
WE WERE ABLE TO GET OUT BEFORE HIKARU GOT MORE CONFUSED AND PANICKED.
BUT HIS PRESENTATION WAS CANCELLED.
I BLAMED MYSELF FOR NOT THINKING THINGS THROUGH.
THUMP

I'M SORRY, HIKARU.
I THOUGHT THE PARENTS WOULD BE QUIET DURING OPEN HOUSE.
PARENTS WHO WERE NOT QUIET.
WHAT A STRANGE BOY.
HE WAS GONE LIKE THE WIND.
YOU'RE THE ONES WHO ARE STRANGE!
WHY DO YOU SCREAM LIKE MONKEYS WHEN YOU SEE KANATA!?
MON-KEYS!?
THERE'S A CELEBRITY RIGHT THERE.
WHAT'S WRONG WITH TAKING A PICTURE?
I SHOULD'VE THOUGHT OF THIS BEFOREHAND.
I SHOULD'VE EXPECTED THIS.
PLEASE BE QUIET, EVERYONE.
I SHOULD HAVE EXPLAINED THIS EARLIER.

HIKARU AZUMA-KUN, WHO JUST LEFT FOR THE SPECIAL ED CLASS...
...HAS A DISABILITY CALLED AUTISM.
HE HAS A DIFFICULT TIME DEALING WITH DIFFERENT SITUATIONS...
...AND LOUD NOISES AND SCREAMS.
AND TANAKA-KUN MAY WORK IN THE ENTER-TAINMENT BUSINESS...
...BUT WHILE HE'S AT SHICHIGATSU-CHO ELEMENTARY, HE'S A STUDENT HERE.
PLEASE REFRAIN FROM TAKING PHOTOS OR CHATTING.
DESK: HIKARU AZUMA
東光
PLEASE COOPERATE SO ALL OF THE STUDENTS...
...INCLUDING AZUMA-KUN AND TANAKA-KUN, CAN TAKE THEIR CLASSES.

THEY'RE SO RUDE.
BAD PARENTS MAKE BAD STUDENTS.
ANNOYED
I WANT THE TEACHER TO START CLASS ALREADY.
あさがお教室
SIGN: SPECIAL EDUCATION
GUNJI-SENSEI HAD AN EXPRESSION THAT SAID, "OH, YOU'RE BACK ALREADY?"
FLASH PHOTOS AND SCREAMING?
I GUESS PARENTS THESE DAYS DON'T KNOW THEIR MANNERS.
HIKARU WAS ONLY ABLE TO STAY IN HIS COMMUNICATION CLASS FOR TEN MINUTES.
BUT IT'S NOT HIS FAULT THAT HE COULDN'T STAY LONGER.

HE MAY BE IN A BAD MOOD FOR THE REST OF THE DAY.
EEH? AGAIN?
"AGAIN"...
SFX: GRUMBLE GRUMBLE
I SHOULD STAY UNTIL HIKARU CALMS DOWN.
GEEZ.
IF I LEAVE IT UP TO GUNJI-SENSEI, I MIGHT GET CALLED BACK TO SCHOOL AGAIN.
5-3
BACK IN CLASS 3, THE STUDENTS CONTINUED...
...THE CRAYFISH REPORT WITHOUT HIKARU.
THE ROAD TO BEING A CRAYFISH MASTER.
ONE. USE CUTTLEFISH AS BAIT AND PUT IT ON A STRING.
TWO. LOOK FOR BUBBLES.
THIS IS HOW YOU TELL THE MALES AND FEMALES APART.
HERE'S HOW YOU HOLD THEM.
WE'LL REPORT FOR HIKARU-KUN.

AH, IT FELL!
ギャハハハ
HAHAHA
THE CHILDREN PRESENTED THEIR PROJECTS ON MATH, SCIENCE, SOCIAL STUDIES, ENGLISH, AND ART.
MOST OF THE PARENTS AND CHILDREN WERE PLEASED...
THE MAIN PLANTS WERE...
トイレ
TOILETS
もみじ
MAPLE
桜
CHERRY BLOSSOMS
芝生
GRASS
バードウォッチング
BIRD WATCHING
公園マップ
PARK MAP
観察日記
...EXCEPT FOR A FEW PARENTS...
NEXT IS SOEZAKI-KUN.
YES.
IT'S MY SON.
AMERICAN CRAYFISH WERE INTRODUCED FROM THE UNITED STATES AS FOOD.
THEY THRIVED SO MUCH THAT IT CHANGED THE ECO-SYSTEM.
CURRENTLY, JAPANESE CRAYFISH ARE RARE AND...
カーン
DING
コーン
DONG
PAPER: OBSERVATION REPORT
TODAY WE CAUGHT SOME CRAYFISH AT THE PARK. I WANTED TO CATCH A LOT, BUT I ONLY CAUGHT ONE. THE ROAD TO BEING A CRAYFISH MASTER IS DIFFICULT.

SOEZAKI-KUN, THANK YOU FOR YOUR RESEARCH. I'M SORRY WE RAN OUT OF TIME.
SECOND PERIOD IS OVER.
NEXT IS MUSIC, SO PLEASE HEAD OVER TO THE MUSIC ROOM.
CLATTER
SLUMP
...!!
MY CHILD WASN'T EVEN CALLED ON!
BOOK: GRADE SCHOOL MUSIC
PAT
LET'S GO, KANATA.
YOU CAN ATTEND THIRD PERIOD TOO, RIGHT?
OH... YEAH.
...
HE'S GOING TO COME OUT SOON. ♡
WE CAN TAKE PICTURES DURING BREAKS, RIGHT?
THE HALL IS FULL OF PARENTS WITH THEIR CAMERAS READY.
YEAH.
I'LL WALK IN FRONT THEN.

OVER HERE.
I'LL PROTECT THE SIDE.
ずん
STOMP
GEEZ!
WE CAN ONLY TAKE PICTURES OF HIS BACK.
BLEH!
DON'T WORRY ABOUT HIKARU-KUN.
IT'S NOT YOUR FAULT, KANATA.
THANKS, NOBUAKI.
カーン
DING
コーン
DONG
HIKARU FINALLY CALMED DOWN AFTER THE MUSIC CLASS ENDED.
I LEFT THE SPECIAL ED CLASS.
I SHOULD LET NISHIWAKI-SENSEI KNOW.

NISHIWAKI-SENSEI!
PLEASE STOP GIVING AZUMA-KUN AND TANAKA-KUN PREFERENTIAL TREATMENT!
WHAT!?
I'M NOT GIVING ANYONE PREFERENTIAL TREATMENT.
WHY DO YOU SPEND SO MUCH TIME ON THOSE TWO?
WE RAN OUT OF TIME TODAY...
...AND MY SON COULDN'T DO HIS PRE-SENTATION.
IF YOU ARE SAYING EACH STUDENT IS IMPORTANT...
...THEN PLEASE TAKE CARE OF THE CHILDREN WHO COME TO SCHOOL TO LEARN.
THAT'S RIGHT!
WE HAVE TO PREPARE FOR JUNIOR HIGH SCHOOL ENTRANCE EXAMS.
WE NEED THE SCHOOL TO TEACH OUR CHILDREN THE BASICS.
W-WE UNDER-STAND THAT...

I HOPE SO.
TURN
YES...
OH, WE'RE SO UNLUCKY TO BE IN THE BUDDY SYSTEM CLASS.
WE DON'T HAVE TIME FOR THAT.
EVEN THOUGH WE SEND OUR KIDS TO CRAM SCHOOL...
...IT'S UPSETTING WHEN YOU CONSIDER THAT SCHOOL IS A PLACE TO LEARN.
MAYBE THE KIDS WILL LEARN COMPASSION IF THEY SPEND TIME AROUND SLOWER STUDENTS.
!!
BUT I FEEL LIKE WE GOT THE SHORT END OF THE STICK.
MY CHILD'S GOING TO A LOCAL JUNIOR HIGH, SO WE'RE STUCK WITH THEM FOR GOOD!
I HAVE TO GET MY CHILD TO SURVIVE ON TOP.
BEING COMPASIONATE WILL JUST GET IN THE WAY.

TO THOSE MOTHERS, HIKARU AND TANAKA-KUN ARE JUST IN THE WAY.
THEY THINK BEING IN THE BUDDY SYSTEM CLASS IS A BAD DRAW.
IN ORDER TO GIVE HIKARU A NORMAL SCHOOL LIFE...
...WE PUT IN SO MUCH EFFORT. BUT NOW WE HAVE TO WORRY ABOUT JUNIOR HIGH.
I JUST WANT TO ENJOY HIKARU'S HAPPINESS.
I GUESS THERE WILL ALWAYS BE HURDLES TO OVERCOME.

WHAT'S WRONG, NISHIWAKI-SENSEI?
職員室
GORI-SENSEI.
SO MANY THINGS HAPPENED TODAY, MY STOMACH HURTS.
SIGN: FACULTY ROOM
I HEARD YOU GOT YELLED AT BY SOEZAKI-SAN.
GRADE 5, CLASS 3 HAS A KID IN THE ENTERTAINMENT INDUSTRY AND OTHER UNIQUE KIDS.
PLUS THERE ARE THE USUAL DIFFERENCES IN STUDENT ABILITY.
もみもみ
RUB RUB
RELAX A BIT.
THANK YOU.
BUT EACH STUDENT IS IMPORTANT TO ME.
YOU'RE TOO NAÏVE, NISHIWAKI-SENSEI.
G-GUNJI-SENSEI!

IF YOU HANDLE EACH OF THE FORTY CHILDREN, YOU'LL NEVER LAST.
T-THAT'S TRUE.
IF YOU SPEND ONE MINUTE PER STUDENT, THAT'S FORTY MINUTES.
PARENTS ONLY SEE THEIR OWN CHILDREN.
SO THEY'LL SAY ALL THEY WANT.
THEY EVEN COMPLAIN ABOUT THINGS TEACHERS CAN'T DO ANYTHING ABOUT.
YOU NEED TO DRAW A LINE SOMEWHERE.
PAR-ENTS
PICKY ONES
NORMAL
DON'T CARE
SEPARATE THE PARENTS AND STUDENTS INTO TYPES, AND LEARN TO DEAL WITH EACH TYPE...
LUNGE
...OR YOU'LL LOSE MORE WEIGHT.
YOU HAVE A LONG CAREER AHEAD OF YOU.
EEEK!
FOR TEACHING THE CLASS, PUT THE TARGET IN THE AVERAGE RANGE AND INSIST ON EVERYONE BEING THE SAME.
STOMP
OH, BUT TREAT HIKARU-KUN SPECIAL. ♡
OTHERWISE, I'LL HAVE A HARD TIME.

EVERYONE'S THE SAME...
...BUT HIKARU-KUN IS SPECIAL.
THAT'S NOT IT.
EACH CHILD IS DIFFERENT.
IF YOU WANT TO CALL ONE SPECIAL, THEY'RE ALL SPECIAL.
I NEED TO LEARN HOW TO GET EVERYONE TO SPEND TIME TOGETHER EFFECTIVELY.
I WANT TO KNOW WHAT I NEED TO DO...
...AND NOT JUST A WAY TO GET BY.
I'M TOO SCARED TO SAY THAT THOUGH.
UM, WAKABAYASHI-SENSEI.
SHOES: NISHIWAKI

OH, THAT'S TROUBLE-SOME.
WOULD YOU LIKE TO TALK TO AOKI? HE MIGHT HAVE A SUGGESTION.
HERE'S HIS CELL PHONE NUMBER.
THANK YOU, WAKA-BAYASHI-SENSEI.
GOOD. I CAN'T THINK OF ANY GOOD IDEAS WHEN IT COMES TO HIKARU-KUN.
区立島田小学校
SIGN: SHIMADA ELEMENTARY SCHOOL
LET'S SEE...
SHI-CHAN KNOWS HOW TO COUNT TO THREE...
...SO I SHOULD PUT UP THREE PINS.
KAZUNARI-KUN CAN ADD UP TO TWO MORE...
ブルル
BUZZ
THIS IS AOKI.
OH, NISHIWAKI-SENSEI. IT'S BEEN A WHILE!
YOU HAD AN OPEN HOUSE TODAY?

YES, HIKARU-KUN DOESN'T LIKE SCREAMING.
HE SEEMS TO BE OKAY WITH HIS OWN SCREAMING THOUGH.
WHEN HE COVERS HIS EARS AND STARTS MOANING...
...IS TAKING HIM BACK TO THE SPECIAL ED CLASS THE ONLY THING WE CAN DO?
YOU CAN GET RID OF THE STIMULANT...
...AND LET HIM PLACE STICKERS ON A SHEET OF PAPER.
STICKERS?
HE RELAXES WHEN THERE'S SOMETHING TO DO...
...RATHER THAN DOING NOTHING.
HE DOESN'T UNDERSTAND WHAT'S GOING ON AND DOESN'T KNOW HOW LONG IT'S GOING TO LAST.
OPEN HOUSE
参観日
SIT
1. 座る
LISTEN TO NISHIWAKI-SENSEI
2. 西脇先生お話
THE CRAYFISH EXPERIMENT
I SEE.
IS THAT WHY HIKARU-KUN'S MOTHER GIVES HIM A NOTE WITH A LIST OF TASKS?
That's right.

FROM WHAT YOU SAID, HE KNEW WHAT WAS GOING ON.
AND THE TOPIC WAS THE CRAYFISH, WHICH HE LOVES.
AND HE WAS SITTING IN THE BACK OF THE ROOM WITH HIS CHILDHOOD FRIEND, NOBUAKI-KUN.

HE SHOULD HAVE BEEN ABLE TO PARTICIPATE WITHOUT ANY PROBLEMS.

BUT UNFORTUNATELY THERE WERE THINGS THAT DISRUPTED HIM.

YES. I SHOULD HAVE BEEN MORE CAREFUL.

I FEEL SO BAD FOR THE CHILDREN.

DEPRESSED

EVEN IF HE WAS IN A DIFFERENT CLASS FROM TANAKA-KUN...

...THERE'RE ALWAYS SCREAMS AT AN ELEMENTARY SCHOOL.

WAAAH

WAAAH

MIYU-CHAN CRIES IN THE SPECIAL ED CLASS.

AND HE HAS KANON-CHAN AT HOME TOO.

SQUEAL

SQUEAL

IF THERE'S SOMETHING HE CAN RELAX WITH...
...OR A PLACE HE CAN RUN TO, THAT WOULD BE BEST.
Run to?
Yes. Hikaru-kun relaxes when there's a small space he can crawl into.
During preschool, he'd go under the table.
At home, he hides behind the couch and even inside the washing machine.
IN THE SPECIAL ED CLASS, HE WENT INTO THE LOCKER.
IT'S HOW HE PROTECTS HIMSELF FROM DIFFERENT STIMULANTS...
...SO I ALWAYS LEFT IT EMPTY.
IS IT LIKE A SHELTER?
IN THE COMMUNICATION CLASS, YOU MIGHT WANT TO FACE HIS DESK AGAINST THE WALL.
IF THAT'S STILL TOUGH FOR HIM, YOU CAN CREATE A WALL AROUND IT.
A WALL?

THERE ARE PARTIAL WALLS WHEN YOU GO TO RESTAURANTS, RIGHT...
...OR DIVIDERS?
DON'T YOU RELAX WHEN THERE'RE THINGS LIKE THAT?
YOU CAN EAT AND TALK IN COMFORT, RIGHT?
IF YOU MAKE A SPACE LIKE THAT FOR HIKARU-KUN, HE'LL RELAX TOO.
Thank you for your sugges-tions.
You've been a lot of help, Aoki-sensei.
NO PROBLEM. PLEASE CALL ME IF YOU HAVE OTHER QUESTIONS.
T-THAT WAS SUCH A RELIEF.
IT'S GREAT TO GET ADVICE FROM SOMEONE WHO KNOWS THE SITUATION.
I UNDER-STAND HOW HAVING A WALL MAKES YOU FEEL RELAXED.
I USED TO HIDE IN THE CLOSET AT BEDTIME WHEN I WAS LITTLE.

BOARD: SAT FRI THURS WED TUES MON / SAT FRI
I HAVE TO GO LOOK FOR SOME-THING...
...SOME-THING TO BE A WALL.
OH? THERE'S SOMETHING RIGHT HERE...
THAT'S PERFECT.
土金木水火月／土金
CLICK
OH, HELLO, EVERYONE.
WE WERE WONDERING IF HIKARU-KUN'S ALL RIGHT.

THANKS FOR COMING BY.
HE'S MUCH BETTER NOW. HE RELAXED A BIT AT SCHOOL.
AND HE'S IN HIS RESTING AREA.
SHH!
HE DOESN'T HIDE BEHIND THE COUCH ANYMORE?
HE'S TOO BIG FOR THAT NOW. HE LIKES IT THERE NOW.

HIKARU IS RELAXED RIGHT NOW.
BE CAREFUL GOING HOME.
OKAY!
BOW

KANATA!
I DON'T THINK THERE'S ANY PARTICULAR REASON...
...WHY NOBUAKI-KUN AND OTHERS ARE CONCERNED FOR HIKARU.
THEY JUST GREW UP THAT WAY.
AAAUGH
BWAHAHA
SHRIEK
THEY'RE WORRIED WHEN SOMETHING HAPPENS.
POKE POKE
ちょんちょん
STAND
すくっ
DING DONG

BYE, HIKARU-KUN.
HE STAYED THE WHOLE TWENTY MINUTE RECESS.
HE DIDN'T EVEN COVER HIS EARS.
THAT'S GREAT.
5-3
WHO'S DONE WITH THEIR MATH PROBLEMS?
PLEASE BRING THEM UP WHEN YOU'RE DONE.
OH, SOEZAKI-KUN'S FIRST. 100 PERCENT.
100
SIGH. I'LL BE BORED FOR THE REST OF THE PERIOD.
HERE ARE SOME MORE PROBLEMS.
THESE ARE A BIT HARDER.
NISHI-WAKI-SENSEI.

I THOUGHT STUDYING WAS ONLY FUN AT CRAM SCHOOL.
BUT I LIKE SOLVING THESE PROBLEMS TOO.
I'M ALL DONE.
HUH?
ONE OF THE DIGITS IS WRONG.
OH YEAH.
THANK YOU!
THOSE WHO ARE DONE CAN PICK THESE UP.
I PUT TOGETHER THE CRAYFISH REPORTS IN ONE BOOKLET.
ALL OF YOUR REPORTS ARE IN HERE.
BOARD: P.E. / LUNCH
BOOK: CRAYFISH
SIGN: SPECIAL EDUCATION
あさがお教室
体育
HIKARU-KUN, YOU HAVE P.E. WITH CLASS 3 NEXT.
MIYU-CHAN WILL STUDY WORDS IN HERE WITH ME.

ヒ◎ TWEE
SENSEI, HIKARU-KUN ISN'T COMING. SHOULD WE CALL HIM OVER?
SURE. TANAKA-KUN, CAN YOU GO?
ゴロ ROLL
ゴロ ROLL
SLOWLY, OKAY?
DON'T PUSH HIM TOO MUCH.
OKAY.
MUU.
MUU.
ふぃ
は◎ PLOP

MUU.
MUU.
MU...
SFX: SLIDE
TOUCH
ピト…
EEK!
HERE HE IS!
NEXT IS HIKARU-KUN'S TURN.

SMILE
SMILE
GOOD. RIGHT THERE, HIKARU-KUN.
HIKARU DOESN'T LIKE WAITING.
SO GRADE 5, CLASS 3 STUDENTS AND NISHIWAKI-SENSEI INVITE HIKARU TO JOIN IN WHEN IT'S TIME FOR HIS TURN.
WATCHING DURING AN OPEN SESSION
THEY INVITE HIKARU OVER WHEN HE SHOWS INTEREST.
HIKARU-KUN CAN DO OTHER THINGS...
...WHEN HE DOES FUN THINGS FIRST.
YEAH.
WHEN YOU TRY TO MAKE HIM DO ANNOYING STUFF FIRST...
...HE STARTS CRYING OR THROWS A TANTRUM.
YOU GUYS KNOW SO MUCH.
DING
DONG

TWEET
ピーッ
THAT'S IT FOR TODAY.
TWIRL
くる
TWIRL
くる
TWIRL
くる
TWIRL
くる
POINT
ピ
BWAHAHA! KANATA, YOU'RE FUNNY!
田中
SHIRT: TANAKA
TURN
グリ
BREAK DANCING
TWIRL
くる
TWIRL
くる
AHH! I CAN'T DO IT ANY-MORE!
田中
HOW CAN YOU SPIN SO MUCH, HIKARU-KUN??

HEE HEE!
HIKARU DOESN'T GET DIZZY FOR SOME REASON...
...NO MATTER HOW MUCH HE SPINS.
HYAH!
WHOA! YOU GOT ME!
きゃはは
AHAHAHA
HIKARU ONLY PLAYED WITH TOYS WHEN HE WAS YOUNG, BUT NOW HE CAN PLAY WITH HIS FRIENDS.
IT WARMED MY HEART, ESPECIALLY AFTER HEARING WHAT THOSE OTHER PARENTS SAID.

Later Elementary Years ⑮ / FIN

SMILE

Later
Elementary
Years
Episode
16

TODAY'S THE SWIMMING DAY THAT THE KIDS HAVE BEEN LOOKING FORWARD TO.

CAP: HIKARU AZUMA

東光
HIKARU LIKES WATER, SO IT'S A VERY FUN TIME FOR HIM.

BUT SWIM DAYS DEPEND ON THE WEATHER, RIGHT?
FOR HIKARU, WHO'S AUTISTIC, THERE ARE TIMES WHEN HE JUST CAN'T ACCEPT HOW THINGS WORK.

IT'S HARD TO TELL.
4. プール
5. 給食
6. 生活
THE LAST SWIM DAY WAS SUNNY.
SO WE KNEW THAT THERE'D BE POOL TIME, BUT TODAY IT'S HARD TO TELL.
BOARD: 4. POOL, 5. LUNCH, 6. LIVING
HIKARU IS LOOKING AT HIS SWIM BAG.
にこ
SMILE
にこ
SMILE
HAPPY!
関東地方
THERE WILL BE BRIEF SHOWERS ...
IT LOOKS LIKE IT'S GOING TO DRIZZLE.
HE KNOWS THAT SWIM DAY GETS CANCELLED WHEN IT RAINS, RIGHT?
IF HE'S EXPECTING IT AND IT GETS CALLED OFF, HE'S GOING TO HAVE A HARD TIME.
TV: EASTER REGION

CARDS: X DON'T GO TO POOL, O GO TO POOL
OF COURSE.
IN ORDER FOR HIKARU TO UNDER-STAND...
...I TAUGHT HIM ABOUT THE WEATHER.
X プール ありません
○ プール あります
TODAY IS WEDNESDAY. TODAY IS SWIM DAY.
KANON WANTS TO GO TO THE POOL TOO!
ぶん
ぶん
Good!!
SIGN: SHICHIGATSU ELEMENTARY
DID HIKARU'S WISH COME TRUE?
A BIT OF SUNSHINE BROKE THROUGH.
BUT...
七 月 小 学
SIGN: SPECIAL EDUCATION
あさがお教室
SWIMMING IS CANCELLED TODAY.

TUG
TUG
IT'S SUNNY. SUN IS SMILING.
HIKARU-KUN, THERE IS NO SWIMMING TODAY.
DO YOU UNDER-STAND?
GEEZ!
TODAY IS SUNNY, BUT IT'S TOO COLD.
THE AIR TEMPERA-TURE AND WATER TEMPERATURE HAVE TO BE ADDED AND EQUAL FIFTY DEGREES OR MORE OR YOU CAN'T GO IN.
BLAB
BLAB
IF WE'RE OFF BY EVEN ONE DEGREE, YOU CAN'T GO IN.
BLAB
YOU CAN'T GO IN EVEN IF YOU CHANGE, UNDER-STAND?
BLAB
BLAB
SEE, IT'S COLD AND THE WATER IS CHILLY TOO.
BLAB
IT'S NOT ALL DEPENDENT ON THE SUN BEING OUT.
BLAB
SHRIEK
SHRIEK
WAAAAAH
I'M EXPLAINING ALL THIS, SO WHY DON'T YOU GET IT?
FORGETTING THAT SHE NEEDS TO TALK TO HIKARU-KUN IN SHORT SENTENCES
ANNOYED

I'M GLAD THE SUN CAME OUT, SO I CAN DRY THE LAUNDRY.
NOW I CAN GET MY WORK DONE!
BUZZ
HELLO? OH, GUNJI-SENSEI.
WHAT? HIKARU IS IN HIS UNDERWEAR AND IN A PANIC?
HE'S IN THE NURSE'S OFFICE?
AAH, EVEN THOUGH THE SUN CAME OUT, SWIMMING GOT CANCELLED...
I got him to put on his clothes, but he's crying.
I UNDER-STOOD WHY THIS WAS HAPPENING.
BOOK: BOOKKEEPING
MY DEADLINE'S COMING UP, BUT I HAVE NO CHOICE.
HUFF
HUFF

保健室
SIGN: NURSE'S OFFICE
I TOLD HIM THAT IF THE SUN WAS OUT, THERE WOULD BE SWIMMING.
BUT I DIDN'T TEACH HIM HOW THE TEMPERA-TURES ARE CALCULATED.
THERE WILL BE OTHER COLD DAYS LIKE THIS.
I CAN'T HAVE HIM CARRYING ON IN HIS UNDERWEAR EVERY TIME!
I WONDER HOW HIKARU-KUN HANDLED IT BEFORE?
TSUCHIYA-SENSEI...
I'M SURE WE HAD DAYS WHERE IT WAS TOO COLD TO GO INTO THE POOL.
I DON'T THINK HE THREW A TANTRUM EVERY TIME.
HE ONLY STARTED COMING HERE IN THE FIFTH GRADE.
!!

ARE YOU SAYING I'M NOT HANDLING THINGS CORRECTLY!?
THAT'S NOT WHAT I MEAN.
THERE WAS PROBABLY SOMETHING THAT ENABLED HIKARU-KUN TO UNDERSTAND.
SOMETHING TO HELP HIKARU UNDER-STAND...
LET'S SEE... WHAT COULD IT HAVE BEEN?
GASP
OH, IT MUST'VE BEEN THE FLAG!
I THINK AOKI-SENSEI TAUGHT HIM TO LOOK AT THE FLAG TO SEE IF IT'S A POOL DAY OR NOT.
OH, THAT MAKES SENSE...

IF IT'S BLUE, WE CAN GO IN. IF IT'S RED, WE CANNOT GO IN.
THERE'S NO NEED TO LEARN HOW IT'S DETERMINED YET.
THERE'S NO NEED TO EXPLAIN THE DIFFERENCES IN TEMPERATURE.
MAOU
KNOWING WHAT THE COLORS MEAN...
...IT'S THE SAME AS TRAFFIC SIGNALS.
青
赤
FLAGS: BLUE, RED
HIKARU-KUN'S CLASSROOM AND TEACHER CHANGED.
SO HE DIDN'T HAVE A CHANCE TO CHECK THE COLOR OF THE FLAG.
ズキッ
PANG
I PACKED THE SWIM BAG AND DID EVERYTHING ELSE JUST LIKE LAST YEAR.
I FORGOT ABOUT THE FLAG TOO.
I'M SORRY, HIKARU... FOR MAKING YOU SUFFER.

食べたらみがく
IF HE'D KNOWN...
...HE WOULD'VE HAPPILY PLAYED THE PARACHUTE GAME.
EVEN IF HE COULDN'T GO INTO HIS FAVORITE POOL...
...I WANTED TO LET HIM KNOW THAT HIS OTHER FAVORITE — THE PARACHUTE GAME — WAS WAITING FOR HIM.
POSTER: BRUSH YOUR TEETH AFTER YOU EAT!
HIKARU, WHICH DO YOU WANT TO DO?
家へ帰る
学校で給食
で給食
EAT LUNCH AT SCHOOL
"GO HOME" WILL NOT BE DONE. GOOD-BYE.
家へ帰る
しません
さよなら
学校で給食
家へ帰る
GO HOME
学校で給食
EAT LUNCH AT SCHOOL
ENVELOPE: WILL NOT DO. GOOD-BYE.

WHEW.
SLIDE
スッ
GOOD. I HAD THE DEAN WATCH OVER MIYU-CHAN.
YOU'RE FAST.
タタタ...
DASH
GUNJI-SENSEI SEEMS TO THINK ALL THE PROBLEMS LIE WITH HIKARU-KUN.
SHE SHOULD CONSIDER WHY HE'S REACTING A CERTAIN WAY.
TSU-CHIYA-SENSEI.
HIKARU DOESN'T THROW TANTRUMS WHEN HE'S BY HIMSELF.
I DON'T MIND COMING TO SCHOOL SINCE WE LIVE CLOSE BY...
...BUT I HAVE A DEADLINE COMING UP, SO IT WAS A LITTLE TOUGH TODAY.
AZUMA-SAN, YOU WORK!?

保健室
WE HAVE A MORTGAGE TO PAY, AND OUR WATER BILL IS REALLY HIGH...
...SO I DO A LITTLE ACCOUNTING ON MY COMPUTER AT HOME.
I SEE. YOU SHOULD GO HOME NOW, OR IT'LL ALMOST BE TIME TO PICK HIKARU UP.
YES, PICK UP...
SIGN: NURSE'S OFFICE
HIKARU WAS ABLE TO GO TO SCHOOL ON HIS OWN WHEN AOKI-SENSEI WAS HERE.
BUT HE KEPT GETTING DISTRACTED AND CAUSED TROUBLE IN OTHER PEOPLE'S HOUSES.
HE EVEN RODE A BUS AND TRAIN ALL THE WAY TO HACHIOJI.

IT'S DANGEROUS...
...SO I STARTED DROPPING HIM OFF AND PICKING HIM UP.
HE'S BEEN TAKING THE SAME FIVE-MINUTE WALK TO SCHOOL EVERY DAY FOR THE LAST FOUR YEARS.
WE WERE THINKING OF TRYING AGAIN WHEN THE TEACHER CHANGED.
BUT HIKARU HAS GROWN UP A BIT MORE.
I THINK HE SHOULD BE OKAY ON HIS OWN SOON.
カタ CLACK
カタ CLACK
HEY!
OH, HONDA-SAN.
GASP
OH NO! IT'S THIS TIME ALREADY? I HAVE TO GO PICK HIM UP.
14:21

IT'S MY THIRD TIME GOING TO SCHOOL TODAY.
HIKARU THREW A TANTRUM BECAUSE SWIMMING WAS CANCELLED.
七月小学
SIGN: SHICHIGATSU ELEMENTARY
I BET HE STARTED CHANGING WHEN SHE TOLD HIM NO.
THAT GUNJI STILL YELLS AND TALKS IN LONG SENTENCES.
I ASKED HER TO CHANGE SO MANY TIMES, BUT IT'S NO USE.
I FORGOT ABOUT THE FLAG, SO IT'S PARTLY MY FAULT TOO.
MIYU CRIES EVEN WHEN IT RAINS AND SHE CAN'T GET INTO THE POOL.
HOW ARE THEY SUPPOSED TO LOOK AT A FLAG THAT FAR AWAY?
THIS
七月小学校
IT'S TRUE. FROM THE SPECIAL ED CLASSROOM ACROSS THE SCHOOLYARD, THE FLAG LOOKS LIKE A PEA.
SPECIAL ED CLASS
IT'S HARD TO GET THE KIDS TO NOTICE SOMETHING SO DISTANT.

THERE'S A DIFFERENCE IN WHERE WE WANT THEM TO LOOK AND WHERE THEY'RE LOOKING.

I WONDER IF THEIR FIELD OF VISION IS NARROW.

WHEN HIKARU FIRST STARTED SCHOOL...

...I THOUGHT HIS FIELD OF VISION ONLY EXTENDED FROM HERE TO HERE...

...THOUGH IT SEEMS TO BE A BIT WIDER NOW.

I THINK THAT'S WHY...

...HE GETS SURPRISED WHEN HE'S TOUCHED FROM WHERE HE CAN'T SEE.

HMMM.

I WISH THEY'D STOP CALLING US WHENEVER SOMETHING GOES WRONG.

I CAN'T GET A PART-TIME JOB THIS WAY. I HAVE DEBTS TO PAY OFF TOO.

あさがお教室

SIGN: SPECIAL EDUCATION

WE'RE HERE TO PICK UP OUR KIDS.
OH, HELLO.
YOU KNOW, YOU SHOULD HAVE MIYU-CHAN LEARN BALLET.
HUH?
SHE'S ALWAYS ON HER TOES LIKE THAT.
SHE'D LOOK CUTE IN A LEOTARD.
WHAT'S SHE TALKING ABOUT?
I WANT HER TO PUT HER FEET ON THE GROUND.
I COULDN'T CARE LESS ABOUT BALLET!
YOU SHOULD HAVE HER WEAR RUBBER SANDALS.
THE DEVEL-OPMENT CENTER TEACHER TOLD US TO...
...AND I MADE HIKARU WEAR THEM DURING THE SUMMER.
SHOES THAT GO UP TO THE ANKLE DURING THE WINTER

PUT THEM IN A SITUATION WHERE THEY HAVE TO USE THEIR HEELS...
...GET THEM USED TO WALKING WITH THEIR WHOLE FOOT.
OHHH...
I SEE.
OR MAKING THEM WALK SIDEWAYS ON A BALANCE BEAM...
...OR WALKING IN A POOL WORKS TOO.
SHE WAS IMPRESSED BY WHAT I SAID?
I WISH I COULD BE IMPRESSED INSTEAD.
I DELIVERED DIFFERENT DEVELOPMENTAL TOOLS FOR HIKARU TO GUNJI-SENSEI.
OTHERWISE, WHAT SHE PREPARED WAS TOO DIFFICULT OR TOO EASY.
GOOD-BYE.
GOOD-BYE. GOOD JOB TODAY.
Good!!
HAPPY
MEAT
6
10
8
5
PUT NUMBERS IN THE BOX.
入れてみよう
WHICH TWO ARE THE SAME?

I WON'T CRY OVER WHAT I DON'T HAVE.
I'M SURE THERE ARE THINGS THAT CAN BE ACCOMPLISHED WITH THE CURRENT SCHOOL AND TEACHERS.
楽人
多加子
WALL: GAKUTO + TAKAKO
COMMUTING ON HIS OWN, HUH?
YEAH. HE UNDERSTANDS THE TRAFFIC SIGNALS NOW.
HE'S DONE IT BEFORE, SO I THINK HE SHOULD BE OKAY.

BUT I'D HAVE TO GET IN TOUCH WITH THE TEACHERS WHO HAVE CELL PHONES...
...SO I'LL TALK TO GUNJI-SENSEI FIRST.
THAT'S TRUE. ON THE WAY HOME, YOU'D HAVE TO STAY HERE...
...AND HAVE GUNJI-SENSEI BRING HIM HOME.
YEAH. WE NEED HER TO BRING HIM RIGHT UP TO THE HOUSE...
...TO SHOW HIM THAT HE GOES HOME ON HIS OWN.
WEL-COME HOME. GOOD JOB. ♡
WE NEED TO GET HIM CONFIDENT ABOUT DOING IT ON HIS OWN...
...AND SLOWLY INCREASE THE DISTANCE.
SIGN: SHICHIGATSU-CHO ELEMENTARY
七月小学校
BUT WE WERE NAÏVE YET AGAIN.

I CAN'T DO THAT.
キッぱり
BLUNTLY
WE HAVE GROUP COMMUTING.
AND PARENTS SHOULD BE IN CHARGE OF TEACHING CHILDREN HOW TO GET HOME.
CHECKING IF THERE IS A SWIM DAY BY LOOKING AT THE FLAGS...
...IS SOMETHING THAT'S WITHIN THE CONFINES OF THE SCHOOL, SO I'LL DO IT.
BUT I CAN'T BE RESPONSIBLE FOR SOMETHING THAT'S OUTSIDE THE SCHOOL.
!?
WALKING HOME, RESTROOM TRAINING, TAKING CARE OF THEIR EATING...
...HOW MUCH ARE THEY GOING TO DEMAND?
THESE THINGS SHOULD BE TAKEN CARE OF DURING PRESCHOOL!!

OH WELL.
THERE GOES MY DREAM OF WORKING PART-TIME.
DON'T FEEL DOWN.
IF SHE CAN'T DO IT, WHY DON'T YOU ASK NOBUAKI-KUN AND THE OTHERS?
THEY WOULD PROBABLY DO IT.
......
I CAN'T.
I HAD THEM PLAY WITH HIKARU WHILE THERE WERE ADULTS SUPERVISING...
...BUT THEY'RE JUST KIDS.
IF I PUT THEM IN CHARGE...
...AND SOMETHING HAPPENS, IT WOULD BE BAD FOR EVERYONE.
YOU'RE TOO RIGID. IF IT HAPPENS, IT HAPPENS.

PLUS HIKARU SPENDS MOST OF HIS DAYS IN THE SPECIAL ED CLASS.
AND HE GOES HOME AT A DIFFERENT TIME THAN THE OTHER CLASS 3 KIDS.
IF THEY HAVE CLEANING DUTIES, AFTER SCHOOL STUDIES, OR CLUB ACTIVITIES...
...HIKARU WOULD HAVE TO WAIT OR VICE VERSA.
ON THE WAY TO SCHOOL, HE GETS LEFT BEHIND DURING THE GROUP COMMUTE.
I THINK IT'LL BE HARDER COMING HOME.
パラ
PATTER
I GUESS YOU'RE RIGHT.
I'M NOT SURE IF THEY'RE DOING IT ON PURPOSE...
...BUT SOME KIDS IGNORE MIYU COMPLETELY.
OH...
AND THERE'RE SOME KIDS WHO LOOK AFTER MIYU TOO MUCH, AND SHE DOESN'T LIKE IT.
SO WE STOPPED COMMUTING WITH THE GROUP.
SAME HERE.

SEE YA.
WHEN SOME THINGS DON'T GO RIGHT, EVERYTHING SEEMS TO GO WRONG.
TAP TAP TAP
RRR...
JUST WHEN I WAS FINALLY GETTING SOME WORK DONE TOO...
HELLO, THIS IS AZUMA.
OH, YUMI-SENSEI.
SIGN: SHICHIGATSU-CHO DAY CARE CENTER
WHAT!?
KANON HAS THE CHICKEN POX!?
七月町保育園

OH, SHE HAS THEM BY HER HAIRLINE TOO.
A LOT OF CHILDREN HAVE IT AT THE PRESCHOOL RIGHT NOW.
LIFT
ぴろ
I NOTICED A SMALL BUMP THAT LOOKED LIKE A BUG BITE THIS MORNING.
I GUESS IT'D ALREADY STARTED.
KANON, LET'S GO TO THE DOCTOR, OKAY?
SCRATCH
ポリ
SCRATCH
ポリ
I HAVE TO TAKE CARE OF IT BEFORE I GO PICK HIKARU UP.
TAKE CARE
THANK YOU.
I GUESS I'LL HAVE TO WORK LATE TONIGHT.
IT'S RAINING HARDER NOW TOO.
七月町保育園

杉田医院
SIGN: SUGITA CLINIC INTERNAL MEDICINE FOR CHILDREN
OH, IT'S CROWDED.
I SHOULD'VE MADE AN APPOINT-MENT.
ポリポリ
SCRATCH SCRATCH
コッチ
TICK
コッチ
TICK
I CAN'T MAKE IT IN TIME TO PICK HIKARU UP.
THREE GHOSTS DID...
MY HUSBAND SAID HE HAD TO WORK LATE TONIGHT.
I SHOULD'VE BROUGHT HIKARU WITH ME.
OH, I'M SO STUPID!
I'M FALLING BEHIND ON EVERYTHING!
I HAVE NO CHOICE.
BEEP
ピ。。。
職員室
SIGN: FACULTY ROOM

WHAT!?
YOU CAN'T COME TO PICK HIM UP!?
I'M SORRY. ALL OF MY FRIENDS ARE WORKING.
I DON'T HAVE ANYONE I CAN ASK AT THIS TIME.
ISN'T THERE ANYONE ELSE WHO CAN COME FOR YOU!?
I GUESS I HAVE NO CHOICE! BUT PLEASE HURRY UP!
CLACK
MY BACK'S BOTHERING ME, SO I WAS PLANNING TO GO HOME EARLY TODAY.
SIGN: TEACHER'S LOUNGE
職員室
I EVEN HAD THE JANITOR WATCH HIKARU-KUN.
SHE DOESN'T CARRY A CELL PHONE
DASH
I'M SO SORRY!
GEEZ, PARENTS THINK SCHOOLS ARE DAY CARE CENTERS.

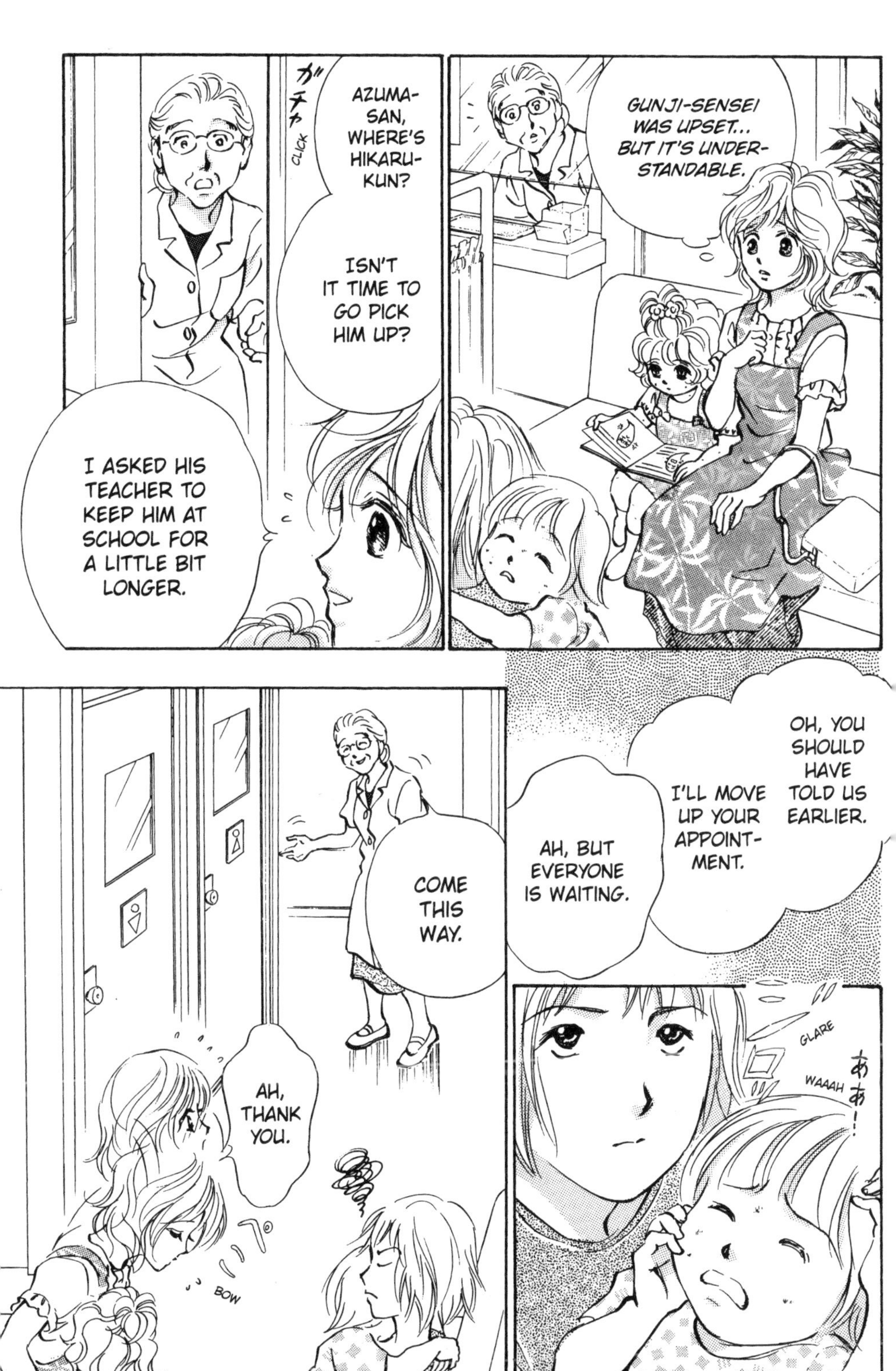
GUNJI-SENSEI WAS UPSET... BUT IT'S UNDER-STANDABLE.
ガチャ
CLICK
AZUMA-SAN, WHERE'S HIKARU-KUN?
ISN'T IT TIME TO GO PICK HIM UP?
I ASKED HIS TEACHER TO KEEP HIM AT SCHOOL FOR A LITTLE BIT LONGER.
OH, YOU SHOULD HAVE TOLD US EARLIER.
I'LL MOVE UP YOUR APPOINT-MENT.
AH, BUT EVERYONE IS WAITING.
COME THIS WAY.
AH, THANK YOU.
BOW
GLARE
ああ!!
WAAAH

SOB SOB
I FEEL BAD.
THAT GIRL PROBABLY HAS CHICKEN POX TOO.
KANON DID HAVE CHICKEN POX.
I GOT MEDICINE AT THE PHARMACY ...
...AND CALLED THE SCHOOL TO HAVE THEM BRING HIKARU TO THE GATE, AND PICKED HIM UP IN OUR CAR.
ことぶき薬局
SIGN: KOTOBUKI PHARMACY
SHRIEK SHRIEK
SCREECH
GEEZ, AZUMA-SAN, IT WAS SO MUCH TROUBLE.
I'M SO SORRY.
I DIDN'T THINK IT WOULD BE SO CROWDED AT THAT TIME.
PLEASE GO TO THE HOSPITAL WHEN IT DOESN'T OVERLAP WITH HIKARU-KUN'S PICK-UP TIME.
I DON'T WANT THIS HAPPENING EVERY DAY.

SOB グズ
SOB グズ
MOTHER ISN'T COMING.
I'M SORRY HIKARU. MOTHER IS HERE NOW.
WE DRIVE HOME NOW.
I'M SURE HIKARU DIDN'T FEEL GOOD ABOUT HIS SCHEDULE SUDDENLY CHANGING.
BUT AS SOON AS HE SAW THE CAR, HE GOT IN.
I'M GLAD I BROUGHT HIS FAVORITE BLANKET.
OH MY. HIKARU-KUN MIGHT ALREADY HAVE IT TOO.
I THINK SO TOO.
THANK YOU SO MUCH FOR TODAY.

OH, SHE'S ALL BUMPY.
WAAH...
SHE'S GOING TO HAVE A FEVER NEXT.
IT WAS A PAIN FOR GUNJI-SENSEI TOO.
AND HIKARU WAS FUSSY ALL DAY.
HE WAS FORCED TO WAIT AND HAD TO TAKE A CAR HOME.
HE PROBABLY DIDN'T FEEL GOOD ABOUT IT.
AND I'M SURE GUNJI-SENSEI HAS LOTS TO DO AFTER SCHOOL HOURS.
I KNOW.
IT LOOKS LIKE I DON'T HAVE TO TAKE KANON...
...TO PRESCHOOL FOR A WHILE NOW.
BUT CAN YOU TAKE HIKARU TO SCHOOL INSTEAD?
MEOW
I CAN'T. PRESCHOOLS HAVE EARLY HOURS...
...BUT ELEMENTARY SCHOOLS START AT 8:10 AM, RIGHT?

I WON'T GET TO WORK ON TIME.
THAT'S TRUE.
CAN YOU ASK YOUR MOTHER TO COME OVER FOR A COUPLE OF DAYS?
SHE WENT ON A TRIP TO HOKKAIDO WITH MY FATHER.
I SEE.
SHOULD I ASK MY MOM?
NO, DON'T WORRY.
I'LL TELL KANON WHERE I'M GOING AND TAKE HIM TO SCHOOL QUICKLY.
WHENEVER I SEE MY MOTHER-IN-LAW...
WHY DON'T YOU PUT KANON IN A PRESCHOOL INSTEAD OF DAY CARE?
...SHE ASKS.
YOU DON'T HAVE TO TRY TO WORK.
IF YOU SAVE MONEY HERE AND THERE, YOU'LL GET BY.
ARE YOU SACRIFICING YOUR CHILDREN FOR A LITTLE BIT OF LUXURY?

I WANT TO ASK HER FOR HELP, BUT I CAN'T.
WAAH
WAAH
BUT WORKING MOTHERS WERE UNHEARD OF IN HER GENERATION.
SO I MUST SEEM LIKE A HORRIBLE MOTHER TO HER.
I KNOW IT'S ITCHY.
OR ARE YOU THIRSTY?
AAUGH
I WANT TO USE A LITTLE BIT OF THE EXTRA MONEY TO GO OUT TO DINNER WITH MY FAMILY AND BUY NEW CLOTHES.
IT'S MY SMALL BIT OF HAPPINESS.
GULP
SO SHE MUST THINK, "WHY BOTHER?"
WAAAH
I'M GOING TO BE HERE.
BUT WE GOT THROUGH TIMES LIKE THIS.
MOMMY'S HERE.
SQUEEZE

THAT'S ALL.
THE REASON WHY I WAS ABLE TO DO IT ALL...
カタカタ
CLACK CLACK
CLACK CLACK
カタカタ
...IS BECAUSE I LOVE MY CHILDREN AND MY WORK.
SOMETIMES IT'S HIKARU. SOMETIMES IT'S KANON.
SHE WENT TO SLEEP.
IT'S BEEN TOUGH ON MY BODY AND MY TIME, BUT I'M DOING MY BEST TO RAISE THEM.
SFX: SNORE SNORE SNORE
は
GASP
I MUST'VE FALLEN ASLEEP.

GOOD MORNING. ARE YOU ALL RIGHT, SACHIKO?
あふっ
YAWN
YEAH, I FINISHED. I'LL MAKE BREAKFAST NOW.

I'LL TAKE THE TRASH OUT. IS THIS IT?
YEAH. THANKS, HONEY.

OHH, IT'S TIME FOR SCHOOL.
HE'S GOT HIS BACKPACK ON, AND HE'S ALL READY TO GO!
SNORE SNORE
スースー
SHE HAS A SLIGHT FEVER, BUT SHE'S SLEEPING SOUNDLY.
I TURNED OFF THE GAS AND PUT AWAY ANYTHING DANGEROUS.
I'LL JUST HURRY UP AND TAKE HIKARU TO SCHOOL.
I TOOK HIKARU TO THE SPECIAL ED CLASS...
...AND RUSHED BACK TO THE CONDO IN EIGHT MINUTES.
SIGN: SPECIAL EDUCATION
あさがお教室
I'M SORRY ABOUT YESTERDAY, GUNJI-SENSEI.
I LEFT KANON AT HOME, SO I'M GOING HOME NOW.
ALL RIGHT.
DASH
DASH

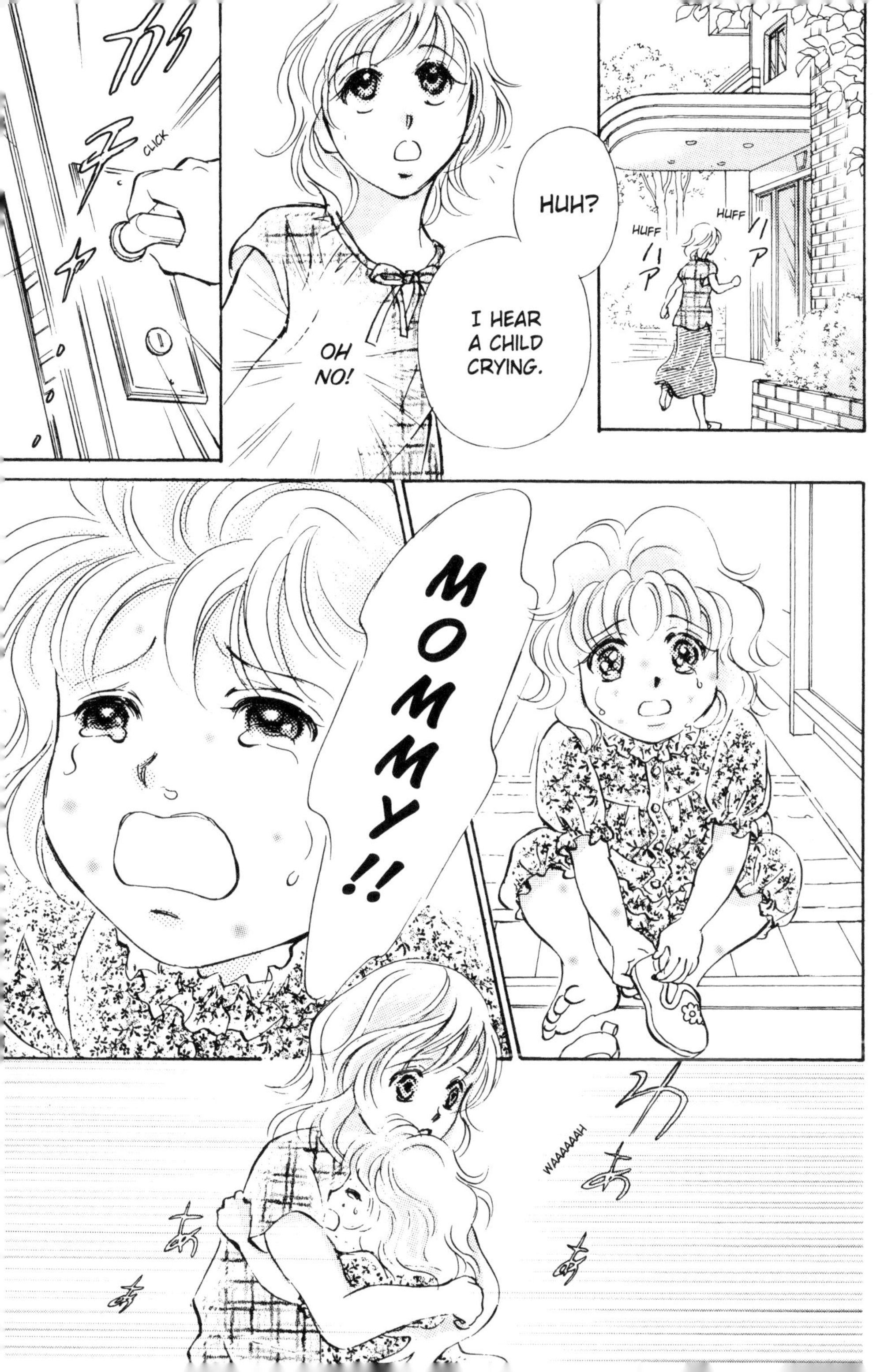
CLICK
HUFF
HUFF
HUH?
I HEAR A CHILD CRYING.
OH NO!
MOMMY!!
WAAAAAAH

KANON.
HER CRYING FACE BROKE MY HEART.
COUGH
COUGH
I'M SORRY.
I'M SO SORRY, KANON!
BECAUSE HIKARU TAKES UP MY TIME, AND I LIKE MY JOB...
...THOSE FEELINGS WERE SHATTERED AT THAT MOMENT.
I HAD MADE MY YOUNGER CHILD SUFFER SO MUCH WITHOUT REALIZING IT!!

Later Elementary Years ⑯ / FIN

Later Elementary Years
Episode 17
KANATA
たこ焼
SIGN: CANDY APPLES
SIGN: TAKOYAKI

OH?
I HEAR A CHILD CRYING. COULD IT BE...?
CLICK
ガチャ
MOMMY!!

WAAA
I WAS CRUSHED WHEN I SAW KANON CRYING.
I TOOK YOUR BROTHER TO SCHOOL...
...BECAUSE YOU WERE SLEEPING.
WHEN I WOKE UP, MOMMY WASN'T HERE!
OH, THAT'S WHY SHE DRAGGED HERSELF OUT HERE WITH HER BLANKET.
I'M SO SORRY, KANON.
HUG
SHE WAS TRYING TO GO FIND ME.
I MADE THIS SMALL CHILD WORRY SO MUCH!!

MOM'S HOME NOW, KANON.
COUGH
ゲホ
SOB
SO DON'T WORRY ANYMORE.
COME ON, LET'S WIPE YOUR FEET.
WE'LL TAKE YOUR BLANKET TOO.
SPLASH
KANON CLUNG ON AND WOULDN'T LET GO.
I WONDER IF SHE'S WORRIED THAT I'LL LEAVE HER AGAIN?
STARE

THE FLOPPY DISK WITH MY WORK FROM LAST NIGHT...
...I NEED TO DELIVER IT BEFORE NOON.
MAYBE I'LL GO DELIVER IT WITH KANON AFTER BREAKFAST.
IF I TAKE THE CAR, I CAN PARK IN FRONT OF THE OFFICE AND HAND IT TO THEM THERE.
MAYBE I'LL MAKE UDON.
SCRATCH
SCRATCH

GLANCE
GLANCE
MOMMY!?
MOMMY!
HUH? I'M RIGHT HERE.
KANON, MOMMY'S OVER HERE.
I WAS GETTING THE POT. SEE?
I'M MAKING UDON.

BAG: SANUKI UDON

USUALLY SHE'S FINE BEING AWAY FROM ME.
ベタ CLING
ベタ CLING
I'M UNRAVELING THE UDON.
BUT SHE GETS SO NEEDY WHEN SHE'S SICK.
I HAVE TO USE THE KNIFE, SO SIT HERE, OKAY?
HERE, PLAY WITH YOUR DOLLS.
ちょん BOUNCE
ちょん BOUNCE
チラ GLANCE
ヤッホー YOOHOO
くる TURN
......
CHOP
CHOP
CHOP
OH? SHE BROUGHT OVER A CHAIR. WHAT'S SHE UP TO?
KLUNK
KLUNK

MOMMY.
I WUV YOU.

OH...
SHE MIGHT BE NEEDY BECAUSE SHE'S SICK.
OR SHE MIGHT NOT WANT TO BE LEFT BEHIND LIKE BEFORE...
...AND THAT'S WHY SHE'S CLINGING TO ME.
I KNOW, SWEETIE.
BUT IT'S NOT JUST THAT.
HUG
I LOVE YOU TOO, KANON.
KANON'S FINALLY ABLE TO HAVE ME ALL TO HERSELF.

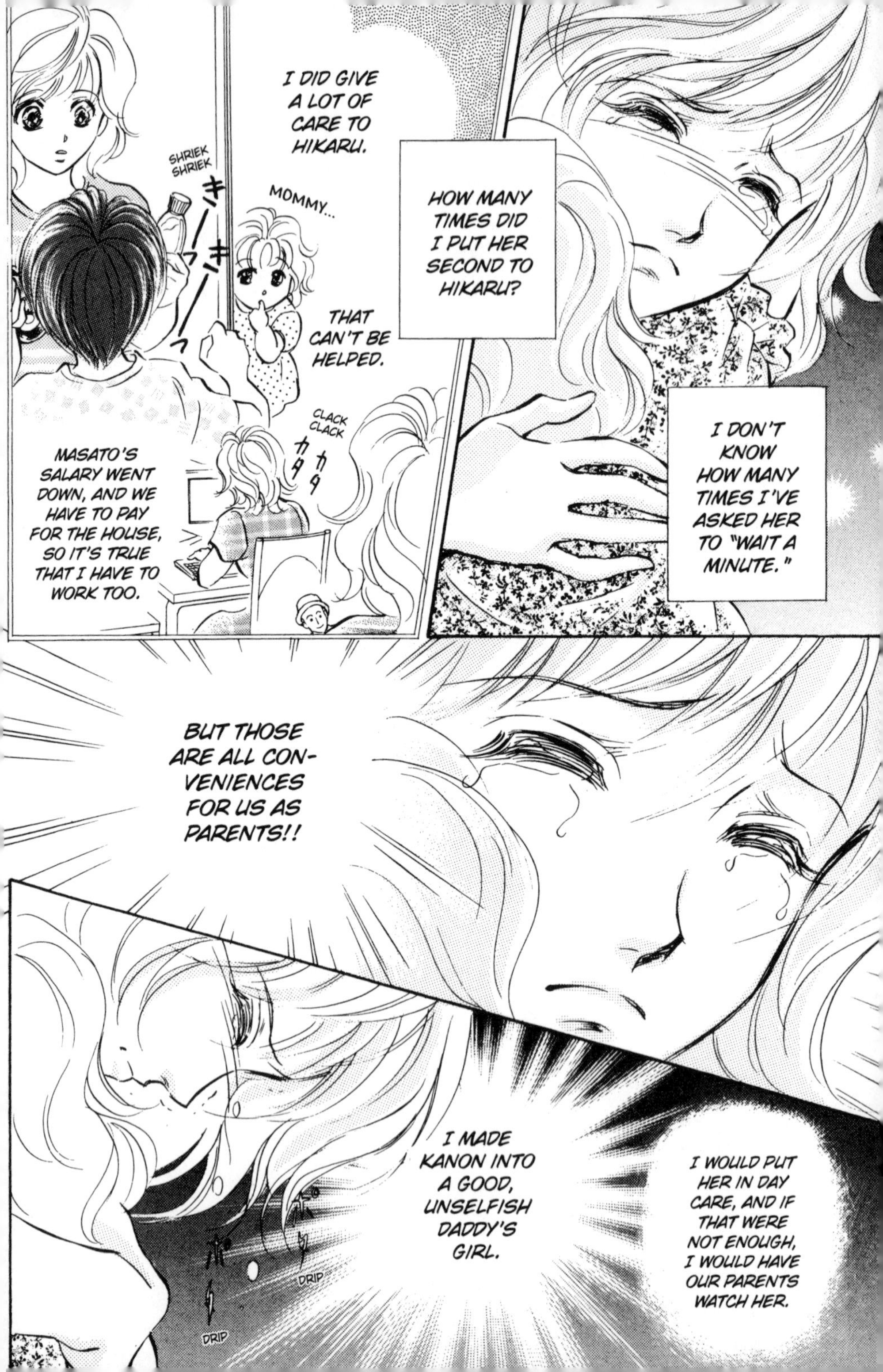

I DON'T KNOW HOW MANY TIMES I'VE ASKED HER TO "WAIT A MINUTE."
HOW MANY TIMES DID I PUT HER SECOND TO HIKARU?
I DID GIVE A LOT OF CARE TO HIKARU.
SHRIEK SHRIEK
キーキーッ
MOMMY...
THAT CAN'T BE HELPED.
CLACK CLACK
カタ カタ
MASATO'S SALARY WENT DOWN, AND WE HAVE TO PAY FOR THE HOUSE, SO IT'S TRUE THAT I HAVE TO WORK TOO.
BUT THOSE ARE ALL CON-VENIENCES FOR US AS PARENTS!!
I WOULD PUT HER IN DAY CARE, AND IF THAT WERE NOT ENOUGH, I WOULD HAVE OUR PARENTS WATCH HER.
I MADE KANON INTO A GOOD, UNSELFISH DADDY'S GIRL.
DRIP
DRIP

I THINK YOU COULD GET BY IF YOU CUT BACK.
YOU'RE SACRIFICING YOUR CHILDREN TO HAVE A LITTLE BIT OF LUXURY.
SHOULD I QUIT MY JOB, AS MY MOTHER-IN-LAW SAYS?
EVEN IF OUR INCOME DECREASED...
...SHOULD I PUT UP WITH IT TO SPEND MORE TIME WITH KANON?
BUT WOULD I REALLY BE ABLE TO SPEND THE EXTRA TIME WITH KANON?
I GET CALLS TO GO TO SCHOOL CONSTANTLY.
PLEASE COME NOW.
KANON AND HIKARU MIGHT FIGHT MORE IF THEY SPEND TOO MUCH TIME TOGETHER.
AND I HAVE MANY ERRANDS TO RUN IN THE AFTERNOON FOR HIKARU.
発達クリニック
口腔センター
つくしんぼの会
SIGNS: ORAL CAVITY CENTER
DEVELOPMENTAL CLINIC
WELFARE FACILITY
IF I'M GOING TO HAVE TO JERK HER AROUND ANYWAY...
...WOULDN'T SHE BE HAPPIER SPENDING TIME WITH HER FRIENDS IN DAY CARE?

I'M SURE IT WOULD BE BETTER TO TRY TO FIND TIME FOR THE BOTH OF US IN THIS SITUATION NOW.
BUT HOW?
HER SPOTS IN-CREASED.
HER FEVER SEEMS TO BE GETTING HIGHER TOO.
PUFF
COLLAPSE
ぐた
UGH...
I CAN'T TAKE HER OUTSIDE.
SIGN: KAWAGUCHI CERTIFIED PUBLIC ACCOUNTANT
川口公認会計事務所
WHAT, YOU'RE DONE, BUT YOU CAN'T DELIVER IT?
COME ON, AZUMA-SAN.
IT'S YOUR JOB TO DELIVER IT TO US, RIGHT?
CHICKEN POX?
IT'S NOT MY PROBLEM THAT YOUR CHILD IS SICK.
IF THAT'S THE CASE, THEN YOU SHOULD'VE BEEN A HOMEMAKER FROM THE BEGINNING.

MY CLIENT WASN'T TOO HAPPY, BUT THERE WAS NOTHING I COULD DO.

I'M REALLY SORRY!

WHEN IT COMES TO BUSINESS, THE OWNER'S REALLY STRICT...

...AND HE'S ALREADY TOLD ME THAT IF I'M LATE ONCE MORE WITH MY DEADLINES, HE WOULDN'T GIVE ME ANY MORE WORK.

ぶすっ GRUMPY

THANK YOU SO MUCH. I REALLY APPRECIATE THIS.

SLAM

BUT STILL, HE LET IT GO THIS TIME, SO I NEED TO BE GRATEFUL.

......

BOOKS: FILING RETURNS, TAXES, CORPORATION, PLEASE READ CAREFULLY

BOTH THE LAWS AND THE ACCOUNTING SOFTWARE ARE CONSTANTLY CHANGING.

IF I GET AWAY FROM IT ONCE, IT'D BE HARD TO GO BACK.

I WANT TO CONTINUE WORKING UNTIL KANON IS AT LEAST IN ELEMENTARY SCHOOL.

WAAAAH

SQUEEZE
HANG IN THERE, KANON.
IT'S OKAY.
DO YOU WANT MEDICINE?
PAT
WHIMPER WHIMPER
IT'S A TAXING PERIOD FOR BOTH OF US.
MOMMY...
I'M HERE. DON'T WORRY.
BUT WE'LL GET THROUGH IT SOON ENOUGH.
SHIBU-SAWA-SAN!
IS THE SIGN OKAY OVER HERE?
ACTUALLY, MAYBE A LITTLE MORE TO THE RIGHT.

TA-DA!
HERE?
おひさまハウス
SIGN: SUNSHINE HOUSE
YES... IT LOOKS GREAT!
OUR WORK'S ALMOST DONE.
LET'S TAKE A PICTURE.
YES, LET'S, UMINO-SAN.
EVERYONE, GATHER AROUND!
CLICK
カシャ

IT WAS TWENTY YEARS AGO WHEN I LOST MY AUTISTIC SON, YOICHI.
YAY!
IT WAS A COLD, COLD WINTER MORNING.
YOICHI...
WITH YOUR COLLEGE FUNDS, I BOUGHT STOCK...
...IN THE THEME PARK I WANTED TO TAKE YOU TO ONE DAY.
AFTER I GOT DIVORCED, I WORKED, AND IF I HAD EXTRA FUNDS, I BOUGHT MORE...
AND THE SHARES I BOUGHT IN MEMORY OF YOU SKYROCKETED IN VALUE.
SO I WAS ABLE TO BUILD THIS HOUSE. ♡
LET'S GO IN, SHALL WE?
WISH ME LUCK, YOICHI.
JINGLE

IT'S MY DREAM TO MAKE THIS HOUSE INTO A WONDERFUL PLACE FOR AUTISTIC CHILDREN.
OH...YOU CAN'T HEAR THE NEARBY CONSTRUCTION NOISE.
FILE
FILE
THE WINDOWS HERE ARE TRIPLE-PANED.
SO NO MATTER HOW MUCH NOISE WE MAKE...
...I'M SURE THE NEIGHBORS WON'T COMPLAIN.
WE HAD LOTS OF COMPLAINTS AT OUR LAST HOUSE.
THERE'S A PARK RIGHT ACROSS THE STREET...
...AND WE CAN USE THIS HOUSE FOR DAY-CARE AND OTHER ACTIVITIES.
THERE ARE BOTH WESTERN STYLE AND TRADITIONAL JAPANESE STYLE ROOMS TOO.
RRRR
OH, THE PHONE.
COULD IT BE OUR FIRST CLIENT AFTER THE MOVE?

YES, THIS IS THE NON-PROFIT SUNSHINE HOUSE.
AH, UM, THIS IS AZUMA.
I'M SORRY FOR THE LATE NOTICE, BUT I WANTED TO ASK FOR SUPPORT.
OH, SO THE YOUNGER ONE HAS CHICKEN POX...
THEN YOU WANT US TO PICK HIKARU-KUN UP AT 3?
Huh? How do you know my son's name!?
OH, HELLO. THIS IS SHIBUSAWA WITH THE CRYING MOLE.
WE MET AT AOKI-SENSEI'S WEDDING.
OH, THE SUPER-EFFICIENT SHIBUSAWA-SAN?
YOU WERE PART OF THE SUNSHINE HOUSE!?
YES, THAT'S RIGHT.
CHATTER
CHATTER
WE ACTUALLY FINISHED MOVING THE SUNSHINE HOUSE TODAY.
AND I HAVE MANY VOLUNTEERS IN FRONT OF ME, SO LET ME ASK THEM.

I'M FREE IN THE AFTERNOON.
AND I'VE PLAYED WITH HIKARU-KUN A FEW TIMES TOO.
UMINO-SAN, A STUDENT AT THE UNIVERSITY OF EDUCATION AGREED TO TAKE CARE OF HIKARU.
SHE SAID SHE COULD HELP UNTIL KANON WAS BETTER.
Then she'll arrive at your place thirty minutes beforehand to discuss the plan.
Please let Hikaru-kun's teacher know that Umino from the Sunshine House will pick him up.
OKAY.
PHEW, I'M SAVED.
OH YEAH, I HAVE UMINO-SAN'S PICTURE IN MY PHONE...
...SO I'LL SEND THIS.
SIGN: FACULTY ROOM
職員室
LUNCH-TIME
THIS IS GUNJI.
OH, HELLO, AZUMA-SAN.

SO SOMEONE ELSE IS GOING TO COME AND GET HIKARU-KUN UP?
YOU'RE SENDING HER PICTURE TO NISHIWAKI-SENSEI'S PHONE, YOU SAY? SO YOU WANT ME TO SHOW HIKARU-KUN?
OKAY.
YOUR RING TONE IS A POP SONG!
OH!
海野さんと帰ります
SHE'S CUTE. ♡
I'LL GO SHOW HIKARU-KUN.
HE'S PLAYING IN MY CLASS NOW.
FILE
FILE
I'LL GO TOO.
OH, WAIT.
IF YOU SHOW HIM NOW, HIKARU-KUN MIGHT THINK HE'S GOING HOME NOW.

CELL: GO HOME WITH UMINO-SAN.

IF THE SCHEDULE'S CHANGING, WE SHOULD SHOW HIM IN FRONT OF GUNJI-SENSEI'S WONDERFUL SCHEDULE ON THE BLACKBOARD.
OH, MY.
DING DONG
WELL, IF YOU INSIST, THEN I'LL GIVE HIM THE MESSAGE.
GIVE ME YOUR PHONE.
WHAP
AHH!
AND OFF TO CLASS.
PLEASE DON'T BREAK IT!
BUZZ
LET'S GO WATCH TOO.
BUZZ
SIGN: SPECIAL EDUCATION
あさがお教室
帰りの会
おむかえ
X お母さん
O 海野さん
BOARD: PREPARATION TO GO HOME
PICK-UP: X MOTHER
O UMINO-SAN

STARE
THIS IS UMINO-SAN.
STARE
SST
I WONDER IF HE UNDER-STOOD?
NOT SURE.
THANKS FOR THE PHONE.
OH, SURE.
UM, MAYBE YOU SHOULD CARRY A CELL PHONE TOO?
JITTERY
JITTERY
OH? SO YOU'RE GOING TO PAY FOR IT?

OH, IT'S TIME FOR CLASS...
SCURRY
HMPH!
I WOULD NEVER GET A PHONE.
NUMBER 350, TOBU RAILWAY, NIKKO LINE EXPRESS.
SIGN: ELEGANCE HEIGHTS
エレガンス ハイツ
ピ ポ
DING DONG
OH! ♡ UMINO-SAN.
THANK YOU FOR COMING. PLEASE COME IN.
HELLO.
KANON IS AT HER WORST...
WAAH
UUH
...AND SHE CRIES EVERY TIME I TRY TO LEAVE.
SO YOU CAN'T LEAVE HER HERE.

UM, THIS IS THE MAP FROM HIKARU'S SCHOOL TO OUR HOUSE.
I MADE IT LAST YEAR WHEN WE TRIED TEACHING HIKARU TO GO TO SCHOOL ON HIS OWN.
エレガンス マンション
MAP: ELEGANCE HEIGHTS
WOW!
IT HAS PICTURES IN IT.
HIKARU-KUN HAS GREAT VISUAL COMPRE-HENSION...
...SO HE MUST KNOW THE ROUTE ALREADY.
YES, HE DID GO TO SCHOOL ON HIS OWN FOR A WHILE.
BUT HE SOMETIMES STRAYS OFF...
SHIRT: UMINO
ONE TIME, HE WENT ALL THE WAY TO HACHIOJI.
THAT'S A SMALL TRIP.
HA HA...
OTHER THAN THAT, HE MIGHT SUDDENLY STOP...
...BUT I'M SURE YOU WON'T HAVE TO HOLD HIS HAND AND LEAD THE WAY.
PLEASE JUST USE YOUR BODY TO STOP HIM FROM RUNNING OUT INTO THE STREET.

OKAY, I'M OFF.
THANK YOU VERY MUCH!
THIS IS THE MAP OF THE SCHOOL, AND THIS IS THE SPECIAL EDUCATION CLASS ROOM.
OKAY.
THIS IS MY CELL PHONE NUMBER.
BEEP BEEP BEEP BEEP BEEP BEEP BEEP BEEP
I'LL TEXT YOU WHEN I GET THERE AND AGAIN BEFORE WE LEAVE.
TEARY
YOUNG PEOPLE ARE AMAZING. ♡
SHE GETS IT SO QUICKLY!
SHE HAS NIFTY FOOT-WORK TOO.
SHE'S A PRO.
SO FAST! SHE'S ALREADY AT SCHOOL.
BZZZ
I CAN USE THIS TIME TO IRON MASATO'S SHIRTS!

SIGN: SPECIAL EDUCATION
あさがお教室
ガラ ラ…
RATTLE
OH, HELLO.
HELLO, I'M UMINO.
I CAME TO PICK UP HIKARU-KUN.
NICE TO MEET YOU. I'M GUNJI.
YOU'RE GOING TO COME GET HIM UNTIL HIS SISTER'S BETTER?
YES, NICE TO MEET YOU.
ちら
GLANCE
HELLO, HIKARU-KUN. I'M UMINO.
海野

CELL: CAN WE PLAY TRAIN GAME AT HOME?
< BACK O SEND

NUMBER 350, TOBU RAILWAY, NIKKO LINE EXPRESS.

NUMBER 1800, ISEZAKI LINE EXPRESS.

GASP

I WONDER IF HE WANTS TO PLAY THE TRAIN GAME WE PLAY ALL THE TIME AT THE WELFARE FACILITY?

NUMBER 100, NIKKO LINE EXPRESS IS CORRECT.

I KNEW IT!

YOU WANT TO PLAY THE TRAIN GAME?

LET'S ASK YOUR MOTHER.

本文
家で電車クイズできますか?
◁戻る ○送信

SEND.

......

......

ピロリロリ〜ン♪
RING RING

SHE REPLIED.

I WAS RIGHT! ♡
STRIDE
STRIDE
ポカーン
STUNNED
WHAT WAS THAT ABOUT?
DASH
EVEN THOUGH A DIFFERENT PERSON PICKED HIM UP...
HE DIDN'T MAKE A FUSS.
帰りの会
おむかえ
×お母さん
○海野さん
WAS IT BECAUSE I WROTE THIS??
WE'RE HOME!
ガチャ
CLACK
YOUR TEXT WAS ABOUT THIS, RIGHT?

HIKARU CAME HOME WITH A BIG SMILE AND IMMEDIATELY SAT DOWN TO PLAY THE TRAIN GAME.
WHAT TRAIN IS THIS?
SO HIKARU WANTED TO PLAY THIS.
TODAY I WAS REALLY SAVED BY THE VOLUNTEER AND CELL PHONE PICTURES.
MOMMY...
GASP
KANON...
PLEASE GO AHEAD.
I'LL STAY HERE AND PLAY WITH HIKARU-KUN.
OH...
THE ANXIETY I FELT YESTERDAY IS GONE.
THANK YOU.
THEN I'LL LEAVE IT TO YOU.

HIKARU IS HAVING SO MUCH FUN.

KANON IS LOOKING AT ME WITH EASE.

EVERY TIME I SAW A CRYING KANON OR HIKARU THROWING A FIT, I FELT FRUSTRATED AND HELPLESS.

LET'S PUT MEDICINE ON IT.
IF YOU SCRATCH IT, BACTERIA WILL GO INSIDE.

I SHOULD'VE DONE THIS SOONER.

BUT I DIDN'T KNOW WHAT TO DO.

EVEN IF I DID, I DIDN'T DO ANYTHING.

THAT'LL BE 100 YEN.
HERE YOU GO.
I SHOULD'VE ASKED...
...PEOPLE OTHER THAN FAMILY FOR HELP SOONER.
KANON SPENT A LOT OF TIME WITH ME UNTIL SHE GOT BETTER.
OH, IT'S KANON-CHAN.
TOMO-CHAN! ♡

I'LL COME BACK LATER.
OKAY, SEE YOU SOON.
BUT WHEN SHE SAW HER FRIEND, SHE RAN TO HER WITHOUT TURNING BACK.
SLAM
THIS DAY-CARE AND YUMIKO-SENSEI WHO TOOK CARE OF HIKARU...
七月町保育園
SIGN: SHICHIGATSU-CHO DAY CARE CENTER
AND WE HAVE ANOTHER PLACE...
...DEAR TO US THAT WE CAN GO TO FOR SUPPORT.
SQUEAK

OH, AZUMA-SAN. WELCOME.
I WAS JUST WATERING THE GARDEN WITH A MEMBER OF THE ADULT GROUP.
THE SUN-SHINE HOUSE ORIGINALLY STARTED AS A GROUP OF PARENTS WITH AUTISTIC CHILDREN.
AND IT'S GROWN THIS MUCH.
SO PLEASE ASK US FOR HELP...
...WHEN YOU CAN'T TAKE CARE OF THINGS ON YOUR OWN.
I LIVE HERE, SO I CAN HELP ANYTIME.
AND WE HAVE THREE SPECIALIST STAFF MEMBERS.
STUDENTS FROM THE NEARBY UNIVERSITIES COME TO VOLUNTEER TOO.
OH, UMINO-SAN IS ONE OF THEM, RIGHT?
あそぶ
YES. HER SENIOR, MORI-SAN WITH THE GOATEE AND THE PSYCHOLOGIST, OSAWA-SENSEI, ARE BOTH ALUMNI.

SO YOU CAN LEAVE HIKARU-KUN HERE...
...WHILE YOU GO OUT WITH KANON-CHAN.
AND KANON-CHAN COULD SPEND MORE TIME WITH YOU.
IT'S A GOOD OPPORTUNITY FOR HIKARU-KUN TO INTERACT WITH PEOPLE OTHER THAN FAMILY OR CLASSMATES.
IF A MOTHER'S ALWAYS ON EDGE...
...SHE CAN'T RAISE CHILDREN WITH EASE.
RIGHT?
I'D JUST LIKE TO SEE THE CHILDREN SMILE MORE. ♡
WOW, SHE'S LIKE MOTHER THERESA, ISN'T SHE?
YEAH.
SHE TAUGHT ME THAT I DON'T HAVE TO DO EVERYTHING MYSELF.
I WAS TOUCHED.

I'D ALSO LIKE TO HELP THEM OUT...
...WITH WHATEVER SKILLS I HAVE.
LIKE HELPING THEM WITH ACCOUNTING...
THAT'S TRUE. I CAN'T ON WEEKDAYS, BUT ON WEEKENDS, I CAN HELP TOO...

OH, BY THE WAY. GUNJI-SENSEI REFUSED US, BUT THE SUNSHINE HOUSE IS WILLING TO HELP US TEACH HIKARU TO GO TO SCHOOL ON HIS OWN.

REALLY? THAT'S GREAT!

I GUESS THEY HAVE A SUPPORT FUND SYSTEM.

SUNSHINE HOUSE IS AN ORGANIZATION, SO WE CAN USE THEIR SCHOOLING SERVICES.

I'LL GO TALK TO THE COUNSELORS AT THE THE WELFARE FACILITY ABOUT IT.

SERVICE COUNSELING

SERVICE SUPPORT

RECEP-TION

REVIEW

REQUEST OF SERVICE

AGREE-MENT

USE OF SERVICE

...IS REALLY WARM LIKE SUNSHINE.
NAMEPLATE: AZUMA
THEN ONE DAY...

Later Elementary Years ⑰ / FIN

Later Elementary Years
Episode 18
YOU KNOW...
...I LOVE YOU BOTH, SO I WANT BOTH OF YOU TO BE HAPPY.
SO I'M ALWAYS THINKING ABOUT YOUR FUTURE.
I WONDER HOW...
...YOU TWO WILL DECIDE YOUR FUTURE?

MY MOTHER-IN-LAW CAME TO VISIT.
HELLO.
OH, HELLO.
PLEASE COME IN.
エレガンス ハイツ
SIGN: ELEGANCE HEIGHTS
OH... WERE YOU WORKING?
YES, WELL, KANON IS ALL BETTER NOW...
YOU KNOW, SACHIKO-SAN...KANON IS DIFFERENT FROM HIKARU.
WHY DON'T YOU PUT HER IN KINDERGARTEN AND HAVE HER LEARN PIANO OR SOMETHING?

IF YOU WANT TO WORK SO MUCH, WOULD YOU LIKE ME TO RAISE KANON?
IF WE START NOW, MAYBE KANON COULD ATTEND EIYO ACADEMY LIKE NOA.
P-PLEASE HOLD ON, MOTHER.
WHAT DO YOU MEAN BY THAT?
BESIDES, I WASN'T THINKING OF PLACING KANON IN EIYO ACADEMY...
......
YOU REALLY PUT KANON SECOND, DON'T YOU?
YOU WERE SO PASSIONATE WHEN CHOOSING HIKARU'S SCHOOL.
STING
PHEW, IT'S HOT. CAN I HAVE SOME COLD TEA?
OH... SURE...

DID SHE COME TO ASK US TO GO LIVE WITH HER?
OR DID SHE COME TO TAKE KANON AWAY FROM ME?
PAMPHLET: EIYO ACADEMY
I NEVER THOUGHT OF PUTTING KANON IN EIYO ACADEMY.
FLAP
HERE.
I WENT TO NOA'S OPEN HOUSE THE OTHER DAY.
IT'S A REALLY GOOD SCHOOL, SO PLEASE THINK ABOUT IT.
......
THIS ACADEMY FOCUSES ON MANNERS AND IS KNOWN FOR RAISING GOOD GIRLS.
AS HER NANA, I WOULD LIKE KANON TO GROW UP WITH GRACE.
I WANT HER TO BE IN A FITTING ENVIRONMENT FOR A YOUNG LADY.
ALL OF THE STUDENTS ARE GRACEFUL AND WELL-BEHAVED.

YOU KNOW...
...I DIDN'T WANT TO BRING THIS UP, BUT...
MOTHER ...
...EVER SINCE KANON'S BEEN TO DAY-CARE, HER LANGUAGE HAS GOTTEN VULGAR.
HAVEN'T YOU NOTICED?
SHE'S SAYING WORDS FROM SUPERHERO SHOWS...
...BECAUSE SHE'S WATCHING THEM WITH HIKARU.
ANNA
YUMI-SENSEI AND THE PRINCIPAL TAKE GOOD CARE OF EACH INDIVIDUAL CHILD.
YOU DON'T WANT TO?
I DON'T WANT TO EITHER!
THAT'S WHY KANON AND HER FRIENDS ARE GROWING UNCON-STRAINED.
I WOULD THINK THEY'RE TOO UNCON-STRAINED.
WHEN I HEAR "DAY CARE," I FEEL SORRY FOR KANON.

ISN'T THERE A GOOD KINDERGARTEN NEARBY?
WHEN IT WAS SUGGESTED FOR HIKARU...
...I LOOKED AT ALL THE KINDER-GARTENS NEARBY.
WE HAVE NO PRECEDENCE...
WE DON'T HAVE FUNDS TO INCREASE STAFF EITHER.
THEY MADE ALL KINDS OF EXCUSES NOT TO ACCEPT HIM.
THERE WERE TOO MANY COM-PLAINTS.
WE'RE SORRY TO NOT BE ABLE TO HELP...
英
AND THEIR SYSTEM DIDN'T SEEM VALUABLE TO ME.
IT DOESN'T SEEM LIKE THEY'VE CHANGED SINCE THEN.
EVEN IF YOU FEEL THAT THOSE KINDERGARTENS WEREN'T RIGHT FOR HIKARU...
...THEY MIGHT BE GOOD FOR KANON.
I WONDER ABOUT THAT.
IF THEY'RE NOT WILLING TO ACKNOWLEDGE THE CHILDREN THAT ARE DIFFERENT...
...I DON'T THINK THEY CAN TEACH KANON ANYTHING.

LET'S GO DRAW PICTURES.
I'M SCARED OF THOSE WHO WOULD REJECT OTHERS...
...SIMPLY BECAUSE THEY ARE DIFFERENT.
SLAM
I DON'T WANT KANON TO GROW UP WITH THEM.
I COULDN'T BEAR IT.
EVEN IF THEY ARE NICE TO KANON...
VERY GOOD.
I WENT TO THE WELFARE FACILITY...
...THE DAY CARE CENTER, AND THE ELEMENTARY SCHOOL.
I WENT TO THESE PLACES EVERYDAY AND REALIZED SOMETHING.
THE TEACHERS AND STAFF WHO TAKE GOOD CARE OF HIKARU...
...TREAT THE OTHER CHILDREN WITH THE SAME CARE.

I WOULD LIKE HIKARU AND KANON...
...TO GROW UP AMONG PEOPLE WHO ARE CONSIDERATE.
THAT WAY THEY CAN LIVE WITH EASE.
—!!
FINE, IF YOU INSIST.
SCOOT
BUT YOU SHOULD AT LEAST RESEARCH ELEMENTARY SCHOOLS.
I WANT YOU TO PUT AS MUCH ENERGY INTO LOOKING FOR A SCHOOL FOR KANON...
...AS YOU DID WITH HIKARU, THAT'S ALL.
AND MY MOTHER-IN-LAW LEFT WITH THAT.

HUH?
MOTHER CAME BY TO DROP THIS OFF?
BUT FROM MY MOTHER'S HOUSE, IT'S ONLY THIRTY MINUTES AWAY...
DOES SHE WANT US TO MOVE IN WITH HER?
EIYO, EH? IT'S POPULAR AMONG PARENTS, BUT IT'S FAR.
IT'LL TAKE AN HOUR AND A HALF OR MORE TO GET TO SCHOOL.
LET ME CALL HER.
OKAY.

OH, MOM?
YEAH... YEAH...
I SAW IT, BUT IT'S TOO FAR.
OH, BUT IT'S CLOSE FROM HERE.
IF SHE'S ACCEPTED, I CAN TAKE HER TO SCHOOL EVERY DAY! ♡
SACHIKO-SAN'S BUSY WITH WORK TOO, RIGHT?
AND IT'S NOT GOOD FOR HIKARU TO CHANGE ENVIRON-MENTS...
...SO I THOUGHT...
...I COULD TAKE IN AND RAISE KANON-CHAN FOR YOU.
I'M STILL YOUNG AND HEALTHY, SO YOU DON'T HAVE TO FEEL BAD.
Mom!

ARE YOU SERIOUS?
YOU'RE TRYING TO TAKE KANON AWAY FROM US?
DON'T MAKE IT SOUND LIKE I'M DOING SOMETHING BAD.
I'M THINKING ABOUT WHAT'S BEST FOR KANON!
SORRY, BUT NO.
WHY SHOULD A FAMILY BE SEPARATED?
...
LOOK...
...HIKARU AND KANON ARE SIBLINGS.
THEY HAVE TO GROW UP TOGETHER, JUST LIKE SIS AND I DID.
AND RIGHT NOW, KANON WANTS TO SPEND MORE TIME WITH SACHIKO.
WE'RE FIGURING OUT HOW TO MAKE IT WORK.

AND HIKARU'S AT A PLACE WHERE HE'S SPENDING MORE TIME WITH OTHERS...
...SO HE CAN BE MORE INDEPEN-DENT.
HE'S PLAYING WITH FRIENDS IN THE PARK NEARBY.
AND WE'RE LOOKING UP SCHOOLING SERVICES AND SUPPORT FOR HIM.
We're going to continue living in this city as a family.
So don't ever bring it up again... to Sachiko or to me.
OH, WAIT, MASATO...
CLICK
ガチャ
SO SHE ONLY WANTED KANON...
...AND NOT FOR US TO MOVE INTO HER HOUSE.

SHE USED TO SAY...
...I COULD GO VISIT HER IF I ONLY BROUGHT KANON AND NOT HIKARU.
UH...
ポタ
DRIP
ポタ
DRIP
SORRY, SACHIKO. I'M SORRY.
SHE COMES UP WITH BIZARRE IDEAS BECAUSE SHE ADORES HER GRAND-DAUGHTER.
YES, SHE ADORES HER GRAND-CHILD.

BUT TO MY MOTHER-IN-LAW, THE ONLY GRAND-CHILD SHE ADORES...
WHOOSH
SIGN: AZUMA
...IS KANON.
I CAN'T BELIEVE HE HUNG UP ON ME!
HOW FRUS-TRAT-ING...
I WORKED SO HARD TO RAISE HIM...
...YET HE TAKES SACHIKO-SAN'S SIDE.
CLACK!

WANDER—
WANDER—
I WAS AGAINST THEM GETTING MARRIED.
I KNEW THEY WEREN'T RIGHT FOR EACH OTHER.
SHE GREW UP DIFFERENTLY FROM MASATO.
I'M SO DISAPPOINTED THAT HE WAS TALKED INTO THIS.
SHE'S ALWAYS SAYING "HIKARU, HIKARU."
SHE CAN'T EVEN QUIT HER JOB FOR KANON.
EVEN THOUGH THEY LIVE BY A STATION THAT HAS A DIRECT ROUTE TO WORK...
...I SHOULDN'T HAVE BOUGHT THEM A CONDO IN THAT CITY.
THE PEOPLE WHO LIVE THERE...
...DON'T HAVE ANY AMBITIONS.
......
IT'S GOING TO GET HARDER TO GET AHEAD IN SOCIETY.
WHAT ARE THEY PLANNING ON DOING THEN!?

POUR
MY DAUGHTER ONLY LISTENS TO HER HUSBAND'S FAMILY.
AND MY SON JUST LISTENS TO HIS WIFE.
I LOST MY HUSBAND EARLY BUT KEPT THE FAMILY TOGETHER AND PROTECTED MY CHILDREN.
I TRIED MY BEST TOO.
AND THIS IS THE THANKS I GET?
WHEN YOU GET OLD...
...THEY ONLY COME TO YOU WHEN THEY NEED MONEY.

WHAT?
WHEN YOU NEEDED HELP, SHE IGNORED YOUR PLEAS...
...BUT NOW SHE WANTS KANON-CHAN WHEN SHE'S AT HER CUTEST!?
店米田山小
I HATE TO TALK BAD ABOUT YOUR MOTHER-IN-LAW...
...BUT THAT'S CRUEL.
YEAH.
WHEN SHE GAVE HIKARU A SCHOOL BACKPACK, I WAS SO HAPPY THAT I CRIED.
I THOUGHT SHE'D FINALLY ACCEPTED HIKARU.
SHE EVEN CAME TO SEE HIS SCHOOL PRESENTATION.
BAG: RICE
米
BUT NOW THAT KANON-CHAN'S GROWING UP...
...HER TRUE FEELINGS MUST BE COMING OUT.
SHE'S GIVING YOU ADDED STRESS.

I WONDER.
I WENT TO A PUBLIC HIGH SCHOOL...
...BUT MY HUSBAND WENT TO A PRIVATE SCHOOL.
HIS OLDER SISTER AND HER DAUGHTER NOA-CHAN GOES TO EIYO.
TO MY MOTHER-IN-LAW...
...THAT JUST SEEMS LIKE THE RIGHT THING TO DO.
CLINK
カラン…
BUT THAT DOESN'T MEAN...
...YOU HAVE TO FORCE YOUR MOTHER-IN-LAW'S DREAM...
...ONTO KANON-CHAN, RIGHT?
IS THAT EIYO ACADEMY GOOD FOR KANON-CHAN?
WHAT KIND OF SCHOOL IS WORTH TAKING A CHILD AWAY FROM HER MOTHER!?
I DON'T KNOW.
I'M SURE YOU'LL BE OKAY BECAUSE YOUR HUSBAND CARES FOR YOU.
SEE YOU LATER.

WHEN I ASKED MY HUSBAND ...
...HE SAID HE WANTED TO ENROLL KANON IN AN ALL-GIRLS SCHOOL.
I WANT TO PUT HER IN A PLACE WHERE SHE DOESN'T MEET ANY GUYS!
HE'S ALREADY IN FATHER-OF-THE-BRIDE MODE.
I'M JUST JOKING.
I'D RATHER WAIT UNTIL KANON CAN CHOOSE ON HER OWN.
LET'S GO.
YES, LET'S GO.
UNTIL THEN, WE'LL RAISE HER NEARBY.
OKAY.
ALL PARENTS DREAM OF BETTER THINGS FOR THEIR CHILDREN.
THERE ARE DIFFERENT PATHS TO THE FUTURE...
...BUT LET'S TAKE IT ONE STEP AT A TIME.

THERE'S NO NEED TO RUSH.
THE SUN JUST STARTED SHINING.
HIKARU SURE LIKES TO CLIMB...
...AND HE LIKES TO SPIN TOO.

HERE YOU GO.
キャッ キャッ
SQUEAL SQUEAL
GLANCE
チラ
DO YOU WANT TO GET ON?
WAIT YOUR TURN.
WHEN HIKARU GETS CLOSE AND SAYS "PLEASE WAIT," OR "WAIT YOUR TURN," IT MEANS HE WANTS TO GET ON.
HE'S GROWN UP.
OKAY, LET'S ASK KANON.

KANON,. YOUR BROTHER WANTS TO GET ON.
CAN YOU TRADE WITH HIM?
NO, I WANT TO STAY ON!
YEAH, I KNOW YOU WANT TO STAY ON.
WAIT YOUR TURN.
YES, WAIT YOUR TURN.
BUT YOUR BROTHER WANTS TO GET ON TOO.
SINCE YOU WERE ON A LOT...
...LET'S SING A SONG AND THEN TRADE, OKAY?
SONG?
SFX: SCRIBBLE SCRIBBLE
GOOD-BYE! EVERYONE GOES HOME! ♬
WAIT YOUR TURN.
サラサラ
HIKARU.
1. 歌をうたう
SING A SONG.
2. 光がのる
HIKARU GOES ON NEXT.

IT'S ALWAYS BEEN HARD FOR HIKARU TO WAIT HIS TURN.
SO I CARRY AROUND A PUZZLE OR TOY WITH ME.
HE'LL BREAK EXPENSIVE ONES, SO JUST THIS!
IF HE JUST HAS TO WAIT...
...THEN HE'LL SIT AND PLAY A GAME.
BUT IF THERE'S SOMETHING THAT HE WANTS TO DO THAT'S RIGHT IN FRONT OF HIM, HE CAN'T BE PATIENT.
SHRIEK SHRIEK
GOOD JOB. YOU WERE ABLE TO WAIT. ♡
NO MATTER HOW MUCH HE MAKES A FUSS, YOU HAVE TO MAKE HIM WAIT A LITTLE BIT.
AND YOU PRAISE HIM FOR WAITING, WHILE SLOWLY INCREASING THE LENGTH OF TIME HE HAS TO WAIT.
HIKARU IS WAITING UNTIL THE SONG ENDS FOR HIS TURN, WHICH MAKES ME PROUD OF HIM.
CHOMBORI, CHORORI~
HE'S ABOUT TO CRY

HE MIGHT HATE THIS SONG LATER.
CHOMBORI, CHORORI.
IT'S LOTS OF FUN.
I GO OFF. CHANGE!
ぴょん
HOP
OH?
YOUR TURN.
KANON, GOOD GIRL.
HIKARU, YOU WERE ABLE TO WAIT!

TUG
SHE'S SUCH A TOMBOY.
SHE MIGHT BE BETTER OFF...
...AT A PUBLIC SCHOOL THAN A CATHOLIC SCHOOL.
YOU NEVER KNOW.
SHE MIGHT BECOME QUITE A LADY WHEN SHE GROWS UP.
I'M LOOKING FORWARD TO THAT.
OH, SILLY.
AHAHA
I REMEMBER WHEN I CRIED AT A PARK A LONG TIME AGO.

I HAD A FIGHT WITH MY HUSBAND.
AND I CRIED IN THE PARK NEAR MY PARENTS' HOUSE.
I WAS ENVIOUS OF OTHER FAMILIES.
HIKARU WAS NEARBY, BUT I FELT SO ALONE.
BECAUSE I'D EXPECTED...
...HIKARU TO DO THINGS THAT HE COULDN'T DO.
IT MUST HAVE BEEN HARD FOR HIKARU.
HIS OWN MOTHER DIDN'T UNDERSTAND HIM.
HE WAS ALL ALONE IN THIS WORLD.

HEY, HONEY.
THEY WANT TO GET ON THIS NEXT.
HELP ME.
OH...
OKAY!
DASH
HERE YOU GO!
CREAK CREAK
THIS IS GOOD.
WE DON'T HAVE TO TAKE TURNS ON THIS ONE.
CREAK

MEMORIES GO AROUND.
EVERYONE GOES AROUND TOGETHER.
THEY'RE SMILING! THEY'RE SMILING!
WHEN EVERYONE'S HAPPY, I'M HAPPY TOO.

I'M SURE THAT THIS FEELING...
...IS WHAT THEY CALL "HAPPINESS."
TURN THE OTHER WAY.
チュン チュン…
CHIRP CHIRP
WE LIVE ON THE EDGE OF TOKYO...
...IN A CITY CALLED TAKEYAMA.

MY OLDER SON, HIKARU, HAS AUTISM.
TICK
コチ
HE WOKE UP EARLY IN THE MORNING TO LOOK FOR HIS FAVORITE DOLL.
TICK
コチ
HEY, CHOCOPI.
HEEEY!
LET ME SLEEP A LITTLE BIT LONGER.
WHAT IS IT, HIKARU?
HEY, CHOCOPI.
SSHUSH UP!
MY YOUNGER DAUGHTER KANON IS FAR FROM BEING LADYLIKE.
IF YOU HAVE SO MANY DOLLS, YOU SHOULDN'T CARE IF THERE'S ONE MISSING.
I ALWAYS HAVE TO HELP HIKARU LOOK FOR HIS TOYS.

HEEEY, CHOCOPI! HEEEEY!
WOULDN'T IT BE GREAT IF IT ACTUALLY RESPONDED?
FLIP
GASP
THAT'S RIGHT! YOU WERE PLAYING IN THE CLOSET LAST NIGHT.
SNORE
HE CAN SLEEP WITH ALL THIS SOUND. AMAZING.
HERE IT IS, HIKARU.
SEE?
WOBBLE
......

THIS IS THE INNER CITY, AND THE HOUSING COSTS ARE CHEAP.
BUT I LIKE IT HERE.
GOOD MORNING.
GOOD MORNING, HIKARU-KUN.
GOOD MORNING.
BECAUSE THIS CITY AND THE CHILDREN HERE...
...HELPED ME RAISE HIKARU.
DASH DASH
OH.
GOOD MORNING, HIKARU-KUN.
THERE WERE SOME WHO WERE MEAN, BUT THERE WERE MANY MORE WHO WERE KIND.

ISHIDA-KUN'S GREETING TIMES THREE.
CLICK
CLICK
CLICK
SMILE
にっこお

FLASH
LET'S TAKE A PICTURE.
ALWAYS BEHIND TANAKA-KUN.
FLASH
IT'S THAT CHUBBY-CHAN AGAIN!
IT'S GUARDIAN OOTA TO YOU!
THERE SHE GOES AGAIN!
HUH?
GRADE 5, CLASS 3 IS FULL OF UNIQUE KIDS.
HEHE!
HEHE!

IT'S OKAY.
HIKARU. THE SPECIAL ED CLASS IS THIS WAY.
CLASS 3 IS HIKARU-KUN'S CLASS TOO.
AND HIKARU-KUN HAS A DESK THERE TOO.
I'LL LET THE TEACHER KNOW, THEN.
CAN YOU TAKE CARE OF HIKARU FOR ME?
OF COURSE. I'M HIS BUDDY!
あさがお教室
SIGN: SPECIAL EDUCATION

OH, HE WENT OVER THERE?

I DON'T MIND.

I'LL HAVE NISHIWAKI-SENSEI TAKE CARE OF HIM DURING FIRST PERIOD.

I'LL TAKE OVER ANY WORK HE HAS FOR TODAY.

AH, HERE IT IS.

THANK YOU, GUNJI-SENSEI.

SIGN: FACULTY ROOM

職員室

OH, THANK YOU AZUMA-SAN.

WE'RE GOING TO DO WORD PROBLEMS DURING MATH CLASS TODAY.

HERE, LIKE THESE.

THEY'D BE TOO HARD, RIGHT?

HAHAHA...

Q1

1mの重さが1.7kgのパイプがあります。1.7×0.6の式になる問題を作りなさい

PAPER: THERE IS A 1.7KG PIPE THAT IS 1M LONG. MAKE A PROBLEM THAT WILL CREATE A 1.7 X 0.6 FORMULA.

THERE ARE LOTS OF KIDS WHO GET STUCK ON FIFTH GRADE MATH.
THESE MAKE THEM THINK ABOUT WHAT'S BEING ASKED BEFORE CALCULATING.
THERE'S A NEED TO UNDERSTAND WHAT THE 0.7 STANDS FOR.
EVEN THOUGH YOU CAN GET BY IN FIRST AND SECOND GRADE MATH...
...THE PROBLEMS GET HARDER AS THE KIDS GET OLDER.
SO HAVING WORK SPECIFICALLY FOR HIM WOULD MAKE HIKARU-KUN HAPPY TOO.
I'M SURE IT'LL BE HARD FOR HIKARU-KUN TO SIT THERE WITHOUT UNDER-STANDING.
AND HE MAY WANDER OFF.
OH.
HE SAYS THE SAME THING AOKI-SENSEI DOES.

IF HE DOESN'T LIKE THE SOUNDS AROUND HIM...
...HE CAN GO INTO HIS AREA TOO.
IS IT OKAY FOR HIKARU TO DO SOMETHING DIFFERENT FROM EVERYONE ELSE!?
?
I DON'T SEE WHY NOT.
I LIVED IN A MOUNTAIN VILLAGE BECAUSE OF MY FATHER'S JOB WHEN I WAS YOUNG.
THERE WAS ONLY ONE CLASS IN THE ELEMENTARY SCHOOL.
SO FIRST GRADERS AND SIXTH GRADERS STUDIED IN THE SAME CLASSROOM.
EVERY-ONE DID DIFFERENT THINGS.
DING
DONG
THAT'S FOR SURE.

SIGN: GRADE 5, CLASS 3
BOOK: ATTENDANCE
5年3組
HIKARU PARTICIPATED IN P.E. AND MUSIC IN HIS BUDDY SYSTEM CLASS...
...BUT HE JOINED THE CLASS FOR REGULAR STUDIES TOO.
I'LL EXPLAIN TO THE OTHER CHILDREN ...
...WHY HIKARU-KUN NEEDS TO DO THAT.
THANK YOU VERY MUCH.
NISHIWAKI-SENSEI, I MADE THIS.
IT WOULD BE GOOD IF HIKARU-KUN COULD WRITE DOWN WHAT HE'S FEELING...
...BUT IT'S STILL HARD FOR HIM.
みます
お絵かきします
DRAW PICTURES.
うるさいです
IT'S TOO NOISY.
あさがお教室へ行
I WANT TO GO TO THE SPECIAL ED CLASS.
トイレに行きます
I WANT TO GO TO THE RESTROOM.
はい
YES.
いいえ
NO.
BUT THIS WAY, HE CAN POINT AT WORDS AND CAN READ THEM TOO.
GREAT, NOBUAKI-KUN!
THAT'LL BE VERY HELPFUL.
I WANT TO KNOW WHAT HIKARU-KUN IS THINKING TOO.

BASKET-R: LOOK AT THE CLOCK / VACUUM THE FLOOR
SIT UNDER THE KOTATSU / SIT ON THE COUCH
BASKET-L: DONE.
おしまい
AKIKO NEE-SAN?
HE'S STUDYING WITH THEM.
ドキドキ
BADUM BADUM
LET'S DO THE SAMPLE PROBLEMS IN THE TEXTBOOK.
ONCE NISHIWAKI-SENSEI GRADED HIS PAPERS, HE HAD NOTHING TO DO.
ユラ
SWAY
I GUESS HE RAN OUT OF THINGS TO DO.
ガタン
RATTLE
ガタン
RATTLE
TEACHER, WANT ME TO ASK HIM?
HIKARU-KUN, WHAT DO YOU WANT TO DO?
READ A BOOK.
をよみます
DRAW PICTURES.
お絵かきします
IT'S TOO NOISY.
うるさいです
I WANT TO GO TO THE SPECIAL ED CLASS.
あさがお教室へ行く
I WANT TO GO TO RESTROOM.
トイレにいきます
NO.
いいえ
YES.
はい

DASH
WHOA, HIKARU-KUN'S FAST.
OH, HIKARU-KUN WANTS TO GO BACK TO THE SPECIAL ED CLASS.
WE WILL WALK.
THANK YOU, NOBUAKI-KUN. YOU CAN GO BACK TO STUDYING.
I'M SORRY, NISHIWAKI-SENSEI.
I'M SORRY TOO, AZUMA-SAN.
I COULDN'T GET HIM TO STAY FOR AN HOUR.
I'LL PLAN SOME WORK SO HE CAN WORK ON THINGS FOR THE WHOLE HOUR.
反省
REGRETFUL
I WILL GO TO THE SPECIAL ED CLASS.
SIGN: SPECIAL EDUCATION
I GUESS I HAVE TO TALK TO NISHIWAKI-SENSEI REGULARLY NOW.
あさがお教室
IT'S NOT SO BAD SPENDING SOME TIME IN THE COMMUNICATION CLASS.
THE NEXT DAY
BUZZ
ブルル

HUH? HIKARU HAS RED SPOTS TOO?
I GUESS HE GOT IT.
HELLO, THIS IS AZUMA.
OH, GUNJI-SENSEI.
SCRATCH
ポリ
SCRATCH
ポリ
HIKARU HAD GOTTEN CHICKEN POX FROM KANON.
SIGN: SUGITA CLINIC
SIGN: SPECIAL EDUCATION
I'LL TAKE HIM TO THE DOCTOR AND LET YOU KNOW.
TAKE CARE.
あさがお教室
杉田医院
HE HAS CHICKEN POX.
WE GOT THE DIAGNOSIS FROM THE DOCTOR.
HELLO?
WHAT SHOULD I DO ABOUT KANON'S PICK-UP TODAY?

OH, HIKARU-KUN GOT IT THIS TIME?
YOU NEED SOMEONE TO WATCH HIM WHILE YOU GO PICK UP KANON-CHAN, RIGHT?
BY THE WAY, DID YOU PUT IN YOUR FINANCIAL AID REQUEST?
I FINALLY WENT TO THE CITY HALL...
...AND EXPLAINED OUR FAMILY'S SITUATION TO THEM.
WE HAVE A DEVELOPMENTAL BOOK, SO IT LOOKS LIKE WE CAN GET IT.
I SEE. I KNOW SOME PEOPLE WHO COULDN'T GET COMPENSATED FOR GOING TO SCHOOL AND BACK...
...OR USED IT SO THAT THE MOTHER COULD WORK.
SO MAKE SURE YOU EXPLAIN TO THEM IN DETAIL.
BUT YOU CAN STILL USE OUR SERVICE WITHOUT THE FINANCIAL AID, SO DON'T WORRY.
RIGHT, LET'S SEE WHO'S OPEN.

BOOK: STRATEGY GUIDE
BEEP
THANK YOU SO MUCH.
SCRATCH SCRATCH
HELLO, GUNJI-SENSEI?
THIS IS AZUMA. HIKARU HAS CHICKEN POX.
SO HE'LL TAKE A FEW DAYS OFF FROM SCHOOL.
OH MY.
WE HAVE A MEETING FOR THE SCHOOL CAMP NEXT WEEK.
CALENDAR: JULY
HE'LL BE BETTER BY THEN, BUT IT'LL BE CUTTING IT CLOSE.
OH!
I FORGOT. I'LL MAKE SURE TO GO.
THAT'S RIGHT! THE SCHOOL CAMP.

I WONDER IF HIKARU WANTS TO GO?
WHAT CAN I DO TO MAKE THE EXPERIENCE PLEASANT FOR HIM?
......
I THOUGHT IT WOULD BE POSSIBLE...
...IF HE WAS WITH HIS CLASSMATES IN GRADE 5, CLASS 3.
SIGN: FACULTY ROOM
職員室
BY THE WAY, OUR FIELD TRIP IS AT THE SAME TIME AS SHIMADA ELEMENTARY, WHERE AOKI WORKS.
わあ
OOH
SO WE CAN SEE AOKI-SENSEI THERE? ALL RIGHT! ♡

Later Elementary Years ⑱ / FIN

Later Elementary Years
Episode
19
I WONDER IF HIKARU WOULD LIKE THE OCEAN? THERE ARE NO CRAYFISH, BUT THERE ARE BEACH CRABS.
AND UNLIKE THE POOL, THE WATER IN THE OCEAN IS SALTY.

Blue
sea

I WONDER IF HIKARU WOULD WANT TO GO...
...ON THE SCHOOL TRIP?
WHAT CAN I DO TO MAKE THE EXPERIENCE PLEASANT FOR HIM?
......
SIGN: FACULTY ROOM
職員室
I THOUGHT IT WOULD BE POSSIBLE...
...IF HE WAS WITH HIS CLASSMATES IN GRADE 5, CLASS 3.
BY THE WAY, OUR FIELD TRIP...
...IS AT THE SAME TIME AS SHIMADA ELEMENTARY ...
...WHERE AOKI WORKS.

あ
SO WE CAN SEE AOKI-SENSEI THERE? ALL RIGHT! ♡
わ
OOH
IT'S BEEN A WHILE.
I HAVE A LOT OF THINGS I WANT TO ASK HIM.
YOU DO TOO, RIGHT, GUNJI-SENSEI?
I'M NOT GOING.
I'LL BE IN CHARGE OF WATCHING THE POOL DURING SUMMER BREAK.
MIYU LOVES THE POOL, SO PLEASE KEEP THAT IN MIND.
BESIDES, I WAS ASKED BY THE PARENT TO DO SO.
AND I'M A WOMAN. HIKARU-KUN IS A BOY.
IT'S HARD FOR ME TO HELP HIM IF SOMETHING COMES UP IN THE RESTROOM OR WHEN HE'S IN THE BATH...
...SINCE WE'RE NOT THE SAME GENDER.

THAT'S RIGHT. YOU DID MENTION THAT AT OUR FIRST PREP MEETING.

I COMPLETELY FORGOT.

THAT'S WHY...

...I WANT YOU TO TAKE CARE OF HIKARU-KUN, NISHIWAKI-SENSEI. ♡

DRAG

SO HOW SHOULD WE GO ABOUT GUIDING HIKARU-KUN?

HE'S BEEN TO LOTS OF OUTINGS BEFORE...

...BUT THIS ONE'S THREE NIGHTS AND FOUR DAYS LONG.

AND THIS TIME, THERE'RE TRIPS TO THE OCEAN, THE MOUNTAINS, A RANCH, AND AN AQUARIUM.

OUR DISTRICT ALLOWS A VOLUNTEER STUDENT HELPER DURING SLEEPOVER CLASSES.

WHY DON'T WE ASK FOR ONE THIS TIME TOO?

MA-TSUKO-SENSEI...
BUT THE VOLUNTEER STUDENT IS MEANT TO SUPPORT THE ENTIRE CLASS, SO WE CAN'T ASK THE PERSON TO WATCH BOTH THE CLASS AND HIKARU-KUN.
YOU THINK SO?
THEN WHY DON'T WE ASK FOR ANOTHER VOLUNTEER?
THAT'S TRUE. OF COURSE, IT'S MY RESPONSIBILITY, BUT...
...I WANT EVERYONE TO HAVE A FUN AND SAFE TRIP.
I'LL ASK THE PRINCIPAL AND THE BOARD OF EDUCATION ABOUT OUR OPTIONS.
BUT HIKARU-KUN'S STILL ABSENT WITH CHICKEN POX, ISN'T HE?
WELL, I'M SURE HE'D BE BETTER BY THEN.
HAHAHA!
KIIIIII!!

SHRIEK
FLAIL
THUMP
HE'S PRETTY FRUS-TRATED.
HE SEEMS TO HAVE IT WORSE THAN KANON.
I KNOW IT'S ITCHY. LET'S BLOW ON IT.
BLOW BLOW
IT'S ITCHY? LET'S TAP IT.
TAP
TAP
バンソウコウ
HOW ABOUT WE PUT ON SOME OF THE LITTLE BAND-AIDS?
RIP
THESE TRICKS ONLY WORK FOR A FEW SECONDS...
NO MATTER WHAT YOU DO...IT'S STILL ITCHY!!

BOX: BAND-AIDS

ひ〜ん
WHIMPER
CHICKEN POX IS ITCHY, HUH?
ITCHY!
OR MAYBE HE'S SUFFERING BECAUSE HE DOESN'T KNOW WHAT'S GOING TO HAPPEN NEXT?
みずぼうそう
CHICKEN POX
かゆい ITCHY
しんどい TIRING
ポツポツが少し
LESS SPOTS
なおる
ALL BETTER
I THOUGHT HE WOULD FEEL BETTER IF HE KNEW WHEN THIS SITUATION WOULD END, SO I GAVE HIM A ROUGH ESTIMATE.
KANON IS ALL BETTER NOW.
HIKARU WILL BE BETTER IN X DAYS.
THAT'S RIGHT. I HEAR IT'S WORSE WHEN YOU'RE OLDER.
AND HE SEEMS TO HAVE MORE SPOTS THAN KANON TOO.
YEAH. SO I'M CLIPPING HIS NAILS REGULARLY.

POOR BROTHER. HE HAS CHICKEN POX.
I WAS ITCHY ALL OVER TOO. I CRIED A LOT.
YOU'RE RIGHT, IT WAS ITCHY.
HEY, KANON. IT'S BATH TIME...
WHIP
UH...
HIKARU'S GOING TO WANT TO TAKE A BATH TOO, SO DO IT DISCREETLY.
RIGHT. SORRY.

ふら～っ
WOBBLE
TIME FOR A BATH.
OH NO! HE FOUND OUT! HE HAS SUCH SHARP EARS.
GAME: THE CHOCOBI GAME I SAVED FOR THIS OCCASION
○ なおったら入ります
× 今おふろに入る
YOU'LL TAKE A BATH WHEN YOU'RE BETTER.
ぐずぐず
SNIFF SNIFF
TIME FOR A BATH!
JUST BECAUSE I TOLD HIM WHAT'S HAPPENING DOESN'T MEAN HE CAN ACCEPT IT.
LOOK, HIKARU. YOU CAN PLAY THIS!
THIS IS MY LAST RESORT.
PAPER: O BATH WHEN BETTER
X BATH RIGHT NOW
七月小学校
SIGN: SHICHIGATSU-CHO ELEMENTARY
AFTER DAYS OF PUTTING UP WITH IT, HIKARU WAS ABOUT TO GET BETTER WHEN THE PARENTS WERE CALLED IN FOR A MEETING ABOUT THE SCHOOL TRIP.
HEY, AZUMA-SAN.
AHH! HELLO, EVERYONE!

IT'S PRACTICALLY THE WHOLE CREW FROM THE DAY CARE CENTER!
I TOOK THE DAY OFF FROM WORK TODAY. IT IS THEIR FIRST CAMPING TRIP.
I LEFT EARLY TOO.
HIKARU-KUN HAS THE CHICKEN POX, RIGHT? WHO'S WATCHING HIM NOW?
I HAD MY MOM COME OVER.
THEY CAME BACK FROM THEIR TRIP.
I COULD'VE ASKED A VOLUNTEER TO HELP OUT, BUT...
...I FELT BAD BECAUSE I ALREADY ASKED THEM WHEN KANON HAD IT.
I SEE...
SIGN: MUSIC ROOM
音楽室
THIS IS WHERE THE MEETING IS, RIGHT?
YEAH.
OH, IT'S TANAKA-SAN.

WHAT'S WRONG? YOU LOOK TIRED.
OH, HEY, GUYS.
KANATA-KUN CAN GO, RIGHT?
YEAH, BECAUSE IT'S PART OF THE SCHOOL CURRICULUM.
WE TOLD OUR AGENCY AND HAD THEM FREE UP HIS SCHEDULE.
BUT HE HAS REHEARSALS FOR THE SUMMER CONCERT...
...AND HE'S REALLY TIRED.
THE OTHER DAY, HE FELL ASLEEP SITTING AGAINST THE WALL.
HE GOES TO WORK AFTER SCHOOL.
OF COURSE HE'D BE TIRED.
YEAH...
I'M JUST WORRIED ABOUT HIS HEALTH.

ORIGINALLY, HIS COUSIN SENT HIS HEADSHOTS TO THE AGENCY.
AND FOR SOME REASON HE WAS CALLED BACK FOR AUDITIONS.
OF COURSE. HE'S HANDSOME.
I THOUGHT HE COULD AUDITION JUST FOR FUN.
BUT HE HAPPENED TO PASS...
WHAT DO YOU MEAN, "HAPPENED TO?"
HE WAS GOOD, THAT'S ALL.
WHEN I WAS YOUNG, I ADORED POP STARS, BUT...
...KANATA JOINED WITHOUT KNOWING ANYTHING ABOUT IT, SO...
...WE'RE TRYING TO DECIDE...
...WHETHER OR NOT TO QUIT.
WHAAAT?
WHAT A WASTE!!
AARGH!
SORRY, BUT THERE ARE DOWN-SIDES, AS WELL!
I GET CALLS FROM FANS YEAR ROUND.
CAN I TALK TO KANATA-KUN?
UH, HE'S NOT HERE RIGHT NOW!
SOMEONE FOLLOWS US NO MATTER WHERE WE GO, AND THERE'RE GIRLS WHO STAND OUTSIDE OUR HOUSE.
AND PEOPLE RING OUR DOORBELL AND RUN AWAY EVERY DAY...
SHE'S BEEN THERE FOREVER.

SHRIEK
FLASH
FLASH
NOW I GET IT. SHE DEALS WITH THAT SITUATION ON A DAILY BASIS.
I'M SURE IT'S TOUGHER THAN WE CAN IMAGINE...
CELEBRITIES HAVE IT TOUGH, EH? NOW, NOW, RELAX.
YOU'RE FULL OF KNOTS.
OHHHH! IT FEELS SO GOOD!
REALLY... IT'S KANATA WHO'S UNDER THE MOST STRESS.
I HAVE TO HANG IN THERE FOR HIM.
IT'S HIS WORK, SO KANATA-KUN HAS TO DECIDE IN THE END.
IT MIGHT BE FRUSTRATING, BUT AS PARENTS, WE CAN ONLY STAND BACK AND WATCH.
THAT'S TRUE. THANKS, AZUMA-SAN.
OH, THE PRINCIPAL'S HERE.

HELLO, PARENTS AND GUARDIANS. I AM PRINCIPAL KOUDA.
BEFORE I BEGIN, I WOULD LIKE TO THANK YOU FOR HELPING OUT WITH THE 50TH ANNIVERSARY EVENT.

TODAY WE ARE HERE TO EXPLAIN THE NATURE CLASS SCHOOL TRIP TAKING PLACE DURING SUMMER VACATION.

THE NEARBY ELEMENTARY SCHOOLS USUALLY GO FOR THREE DAYS AND TWO NIGHTS, BUT...

...WE WILL BE GOING FOR FOUR DAYS AND THREE NIGHTS AS AN EXPERIMENTAL MODEL SCHOOL.

CHATTER ザワ

CHATTER ザワ

IT'S A LONG STAY. I'M WORRIED.

I KNOW...

KYONAN CITY, WHERE THE CHILDREN ARE STAYING, HAS MOUNTAINS AND THE OCEAN NEARBY.

THE CHILDREN WILL LEARN COOPERATION AND INDEPENDENCE AS THEY INTERACT WITH NATURE.

THEY'RE STAYING THERE? IT LOOKS NICE.

TOP SHEET: LUNCH, FLASHLIGHT, THERMOMETER, HANDKERCHIEF, PACK OF TISSUE, SHAMPOO, TARP TO SIT ON, PLASTIC BAGS
BOTTOM SHEET: GROUP ____ HEALTH CHECKLIST, GRADE ____ CLASS _____ NAME, BORN ________ , PLEASE CHECK BEFORE YOU LEAVE THE HOUSE: TEMPERATURE, DATE, MORNING, AFTERNOON, NIGHT, FOOD, ATE EVERYTHING = O, BREAKFAST, LEFT SOME = [TRIANGLE], LUNCH, DIDN'T EAT = X, DINNER, SLEEP, SLEPT WELL = O, COULDN'T SLEEP = X, REST, VERY ENERGETIC = [DOUBLE CIRCLE], NORMAL = O, TIRED

HELLO, THANK YOU FOR MEETING WITH ME.
PLEASE HAVE A SEAT.
LIKE I SAID EARLIER, THE DATES ARE 7/28 TO 7/31.
WE ARE STAYING AT THE "NOKOGIRI NATURE HOUSE."
THE FACULTY GOING INCLUDE MYSELF, TSUCHIYA-SENSEI FROM THE NURSE'S OFFICE...
5. 引率者
5. FACULTY IN CHARGE
校長 甲田徹
PRINCIPAL: TORU KOUDA
養護 土屋道子
CARE CENTER: MICHIKO TSUCHIYA
担任 五利弘 竹内松子
TEACHERS: HIROSHI GORI, MATSUKO TAKEUCH
補助員 沖山陽子
SUPPORT: YOKO OKIYAMA
...THE TEACHERS FROM EACH CLASS, AND, AS SUPPORT, ONE VOLUNTEER STUDENT FOR EACH TEACHER...
...AND AS SUPPORT FOR THE SPECIAL EDUCATION CLASS, WE WILL HAVE ONE MORE VOLUNTEER WITH A TEACHING CREDENTIAL.
HUH?
FOR THE SPECIAL EDUCATION... YOU MEAN YOU HAVE SOMEONE WHO'LL STAY WITH HIKARU?
YES.
NISHIWAKI-KUN STRONGLY SUGGESTED IT.
AND IT'S ALSO FOR SAFETY PURPOSES IF YOU CONSIDER THAT THE CHILDREN WILL BE HIKING AND SWIMMING IN THE OCEAN.

THANK YOU SO MUCH!
NO PROBLEM.
I HAVE OTHER BUSINESS TO ATTEND TO, SO PLEASE EXCUSE ME.
I CAN'T BELIEVE IT.
I THOUGHT THAT THE SCHOOL WAS GOING TO SUGGEST...
...THAT HIKARU SKIP THE TRIP BECAUSE IT'D BE TOO HARD.
AZUMA-SAN, CAN I ASK A FEW QUESTIONS?
DOES HIKARU-KUN HAVE EXPERIENCE SLEEPING OVER?

AH, YES. HE'S BEEN SLEEPING OVER AT MY PARENTS' HOUSE SINCE HE WAS A BABY.
AND DURING SUMMER BREAK, WE'VE BEEN ON TRIPS TOO.
ALSO, WHEN I GAVE BIRTH TO HIS LITTLE SISTER KANON...
...I HAD HIM STAY AT THE SUNSHINE HOUSE ALONE.
WHEN HE SLEEPS OVER, DOES HIKARU-KUN SLEEP WELL?
LET'S SEE... ACTUALLY, NO. I THINK HE GETS EXCITED.
NO MATTER WHAT TIME HE GOES TO SLEEP, HE WAKES UP EARLY. AROUND FIVE.
FIVE!?
HE DOES HAVE EXPERIENCE AT THE OCEAN. HE ONCE PUT HIS FEET IN THE LOW WAVES.
HE ENJOYED IT.
WE NEVER CLIMBED MOUNTAINS, BUT WE DID GO HIKING BEFORE.
OH? NOW THAT I THINK ABOUT IT, WE DO GO OUT A LOT.

WHAT I'M WORRIED ABOUT THE MOST...
...IS THAT HIKARU MIGHT GET TIRED BECAUSE THINGS ARE DIFFERENT FROM USUAL FOR FOUR WHOLE DAYS.
HIKARU RELIES ON ROUTINE TO GET THROUGH EACH DAY.
IF WE TELL HIM BEFOREHAND THAT THINGS WILL CHANGE, HE MIGHT BE OKAY.
BUT IF HE HAS TO EXPERIENCE SOMETHING FOR THE FIRST TIME AGAIN AND AGAIN, IT'D CAUSE HIM STRESS.
IN HIS CLASS, IT'S HIS DUTY TO WIPE DOWN ALL THE TABLES...
...SO PERHAPS HE COULD DO THAT DURING THE TRIP.
OR IF HE COULD TAKE A SECURITY ITEM WITH HIM, THAT WOULD BE GREAT.
ALSO, IF THERE'S A TIME AND PLACE WHERE HE CAN RELAX, IT WOULD HELP.

I SEE ...
THEN I'LL KEEP THAT IN MIND WHEN I ASSIGN THE ROOMS.
AND PREP-ARATION'S IMPORTANT!
MAP: FROM SHICHIGATSU-CHO ELEMENTARY, MAP: RECREATION ROOM, GIRLS, BOYS
七月小学校から
3 階
JUST AS WE DID FOR THE CRAYFISH RESEARCH...
...NISHIWAKI-SENSEI AND I WILL MAKE AN INSTRUCTIONAL GUIDE.
AND WHEN WE FINISH EDITING THE VIDEO, WE'LL MAKE YOU A COPY.
THANK YOU SO MUCH!
YOU KNOW...
...THIS IS FROM MY EXPERIENCE RAISING HIKARU, BUT...
...WHEN WE TRY TO START SOMETHING NEW...
...IF HIKARU'S NOT INTERESTED, THERE'S NOTHING I CAN DO.
EVEN IF WE TRY VARIOUS TACTICS TO MAKE HIM DO IT, IT SEEMS FORCED.

BUT IF HE IS INTERESTED ...
...HE CAN ACCOMPLISH ANYTHING.
IF YOU CONSIDER HIKARU'S FEELINGS...
...WHAT HE'S INTERESTED IN...
...OR IF HE'S TIRED FROM TRYING TOO HARD...
...I CAN WAIT FOR HIS RETURN WITH EASE.
THIS IS OUR FIRST TIME TAKING A TRIP WITH AN AUTISTIC CHILD...
...BUT WE HOPE TO WORK TOGETHER TO PREPARE FOR IT.
THANK YOU VERY MUCH.

I WAS SO HAPPY WITH THE TEACHERS' CONSIDERATION.
NOW IT'S UP TO HIKARU WHAT HE WANTS TO DO.
I'M HOME...
ONE SUNNY DAY~
I MET A BEAR~
ONE SUNNY DAY~
I MET A BEAR~
OH NO, IT'S "ONE SUNNY DAY."
MOM'S STUCK!

OUT IN THE WOODS A WAY OUT THERE~
OKAY, HIKARU-KUN. WE'RE DONE.
GOOD JOB.
OH, SACHIKO! YOU'RE FINALLY HOME.
HE MADE ME SING THE SONG OVER THIRTY TIMES! MY THROAT HURTS.
OUCH.
HIKARU'S HOOKED ON "ONE SUNNY DAY."
HERE YOU GO.
HE POPPED HIS HEAD IN AND SAID, "ONE SUNNY DAY."
SO I ECHOED HIM, AND WE SANG FOREVER AFTER THAT...
YOU HAVE TO TELL HIM, "ONE LAST TIME," OR HE WON'T FINISH.
I KNOW.
AND HE FINISHES BY SAYING, "GOOD JOB."

CHICKEN POX IS A HASSLE BECAUSE HE CAN'T GO OUTSIDE UNLESS THE DOCTOR ALLOWS IT, RIGHT?
HE HAS SO MUCH PENT-UP ENERGY.
THAT'S RIGHT.
I GUESS IT'S TIME FOR THE OBSTACLE COURSE.
GARDEN NET
IT'S A GOOD SOLUTION, EVEN IF HE SWEATS A LITTLE.
SHOULDN'T IT BE OKAY FOR HIM TO SHOWER NOW?
THE AZUMA HOUSE OBSTACLE COURSE-FOR DAYS WE CAN'T GO OUT.
BOUNCE
BOUNCE

BUT IT'S REALLY GREAT...
...TO SEE THE TEACHERS TAKING TIME TO LISTEN TO OUR REQUESTS.
"ONE SUNNY DAY."
I'M SORRY, BUT I CAN'T. WE'RE TALKING RIGHT NOW.
AND IT'S NOT JUST US.
THEY'RE OFFERING SUPPORT FOR KIDS WITH VARIOUS ISSUES...
...LIKE...
...KIDS WITH ECZEMA, KIDS WITH ASTHMA...
...AND GIRLS WHO'VE STARTED THEIR PERIODS. YOU JUST HAVE TO ASK.

THE FIFTH GRADE TEACHERS ARE THOROUGH THIS YEAR.
PLUS, THE PRINCIPAL IS REALLY INTO THIS TRIP...
...BECAUSE IT'S AN EXPERIMENTAL MODEL FOR FOUR DAYS AND THREE NIGHTS.
"ONE SUNNY DAY."
I'M SORRY, BUT I CAN'T.
MOM, THIS WAS A GIFT, BUT IT'S DAD'S FAVORITE SNACK.
OH, THANKS.
スタ
STEP
スタ
STEP
"ONE SUNNY DAY."

WELL, I'M GOING HOME SOON...
...SO JUST ONCE.
ONE TIME.
ONE SUNNY DAY~
ONE SUNNY DAY~
OUT IN THE WOODS~
OUT IN THE WOODS~
HIKARU USED TO CRY JUST BECAUSE SOMEONE LEFT THE ROOM.
THIS WAS BECAUSE HE COULDN'T ACCEPT THE CHANGE.
I MET A BEAR~
I MET A BEAR~
A WAY OUT THERE~
A WAY OUT THERE~
OKAY, WE'RE DONE.
GOOD JOB, HIKARU-KUN. YOU FINISHED.
IT WAS A LONG ROAD TO GET THIS FAR.
BUH-BYE, GRAMMA. COME AGAIN!
GOOD JOB.
THANK YOU, HIKARU-KUN AND KANON-CHAN.
IT'S NICE WHEN HE CAN UNDERSTAND, "IT'S OVER" OR "GOOD-BYE." ♡

SACHIKO, CALL ME ANYTIME IF YOU NEED ME AGAIN.

THANKS, MOM.
AND THANKS FOR TAKING HER HOME, MASATO.
NO PROBLEM.

MY MOTHER HAS SUPPORTED ME FROM THE START, AND I COULD NEVER THANK HER ENOUGH.
GRAMMA WENT HOME.
VROOM
RAISING KIDS STILL BRINGS ONE PROBLEM AFTER ANOTHER, BUT...

SIGN: SUGITA CLINIC

...I THINK I'M SLOWLY GETTING BETTER.

杉田医院

HIKARU-KUN, YOU'RE ALL BETTER.

YOU CAN GO TO SCHOOL NOW.

YAY! ♡

診断書

HEALTH REPORT

I GOT THE OKAY TO GO TO SCHOOL FROM THE DOCTOR.
SO WE CAN GO OUTSIDE TOO.
I'LL ASK HIKARU WHAT HE WANTS TO DO. ♡
HIKARU, WHAT DO YOU WANT TO DO?
BOARD: HOME TURTLE PARK TAKEYAMA PET
竹山ペット
カメ公園
家
TURTLE PARK?
WE WON'T DO THE OTHER TWO. GOOD-BYE TO THEM.
PAPER: TURTLE PARK
ENVELOPE: WON'T DO GOOD-BYE
WHOOSH
I'M GLAD HE'S HAVING FUN.

OH?
ブスのくせ!
なにが守護神だ
ナマイキなんだよ
太田はただのデブー
GRAFFITI: YOU'RE UGLY! / GUARDIAN? GIVE ME A BREAK. / OOTA IS JUST A FAT PIG!
HOW MEAN...
THIS IS PROBABLY THE OOTA-SAN I KNOW.
SHE'S VERY SWEET.
SOME GIRLS MUST BE JEALOUS BECAUSE SHE GETS ALONG WITH KANATA-KUN.
SHOE: NISHIYAMA (SACHIKO'S MAIDEN NAME)
WHEN I WAS YOUNG...
...I WAS PICKED ON TOO.
西山
A GIRL'S WORLD IS TOUGH TO LIVE IN...
...ONCE SOMEONE'S JEALOUS OF YOU.

5-3
WHEN HIKARU RETURNED TO SCHOOL...
...HE STARTED SPENDING MORE TIME IN CLASS 5-3.

THE BOYS STILL SEEM YOUNG...
...BUT THE GIRLS ARE GETTING MATURE.
ARGH! I HAVE MILK COMING OUT OF MY NOSE!
BEING AKIKO-SAN FROM BEHIND THE DOOR♪

CUP: ALMOND PUDDING

チラ GLANCE

I DON'T WANT THIS.

THAT'S WHY YOU'RE SO SKINNY.

杏仁

ヒソ WHISPER

OOTA-SAN...

...DOESN'T NOTICE.

AHAHA!

SLAP SLAP

OUCH!

職員室
SIGN: FACULTY ROOM
BOOK: HIKARU AZUMA
NISHIWAKI-SENSEI, I BROUGHT THE SUPPORT BOOK.
東光
OH, SO THIS IS IT?
I SEE. IT HAS HIKARU-KUN'S PROFILE AND HOW TO INTERACT WITH HIM.
THIS HELPS ME A LOT.
I SHOULDN'T TOUCH HIS NECK OR PULL HIS EARS.
OH? HE ONLY EATS KOSHIHIKARI RICE?
HE EATS THE PLAIN RICE SERVED AT SCHOOL.
REALLY? THEN IT'S JUST AT HOME.
I KEEP ORDERING THE SAME RICE, SO I JUST ASSUMED.
I'M GLAD YOU TOLD ME, BECAUSE NOW I CAN STOP ORDERING IT.
HA HA HA...
I'LL GIVE THIS BOOK TO THE VOLUNTEER TEACHER BECAUSE HE'S COMING TO MEET HIKARU-KUN...
...THE DAY AFTER TOMORROW.
AND THIS IS FROM GORI-SENSEI.

THANK YOU.
OH, AND THIS MAY BE NONE OF MY BUSINESS...
...BUT I SAW SOME GRAFFITI THE OTHER DAY THAT BOTHERED ME.
ブスのくせ!
なにが守護神だ
ナマイキなんだよ
太田はただのデブー
SIGH
はあ…
THANK YOU FOR TELLING ME. THAT'S HORRIBLE.
I JUST HOPE IT'S NOT KIDS FROM MY CLASS.
ACTUALLY, MY CLASS'S GIRLS ARE DIVIDED RIGHT NOW.
THERE'S THE GIRLY GROUP...
...AND THEN THERE'RE THE GIRLS WHO HANG OUT WITH THE BOYS.
I WANT THEM TO...
...GET ALONG AND NOT BE HOSTILE TOWARDS EACH OTHER...
I SEE. GIRLS THAT AGE ARE ALREADY SPLIT UP INTO GROUPS?
YEAH. IT'S TOUGH BEING A GIRL.

PAPER: GROUP 7 / NOBUAKI, OOTA / TANAKA, SAORI
LOOK.
THIS IS HIKARU'S GROUP DURING THE TRIP.
EVERYONE EXCEPT FOR SAORI-CHAN SAID THEY WANTED TO BE IN HIKARU'S GROUP.
THAT'S GREAT.
SO IS MOE-CHAN THE GIRLY ONE?
SHE LOOKS GIRLY, BUT HER PERSONALITY IS MORE FRANK AND BOYISH.
OOTA-SAN'S THE TYPE THAT HANGS OUT WITH THE BOYS.
SAORI-CHAN IS THE TYPE THAT NEEDS HER GIRL-FRIENDS...
...TO DO ANYTHING, EVEN GO TO THE BATHROOM.
TV: COME COME SEA WORLD
WOW, YOU'RE REALLY OBSERVANT.
IT'S A HABIT. I LIVED LIKE THIS ALL MY LIFE.
AND COMPARED TO THAT, HIKARU DOESN'T CARE.
HE COULDN'T CARE LESS ABOUT THE PROBLEMS OF THE GIRLS' WORLD.

SPLASH
BOUNCE
ぴょん
ぴょん
HE SEEMS TO LIKE THE DOLPHIN SHOW AT *COME COME SEA WORLD.*
AND HE KEEPS WATCHING THE CRABS.
IT'S TO BE EXPECTED FROM HIS LOVE FOR CRAYFISH.
FLIER: FATHER RANCH
ファザー牧場
I'M WORRIED ABOUT THE FATHER RANCH ON THE SECOND DAY.
HIKARU'S SCARED OF ANIMALS.

TRUE.
HE'S EVEN SCARED OF A DOG A HUNDRED METERS AWAY FROM HIM.
WE SHOULD LET THE TEACHERS KNOW.
HIKARU WAS EXCITED ABOUT GOING...
...AND OBLIVIOUS TO OUR WORRIES.
チュ
CHIRP
チュ
CHIRP
ON JULY 28, I WILL GO ON A CAMPING TRIP!
JUMP
JUMP
HE'S SUPPOSED TO BE A DOLPHIN.
WOW.
FOUR DAYS AND THREE NIGHTS IS LONG.
MIYU WILL GET TO GO TOO WHEN SHE'S A FIFTH GRADER, EH?
I CAN'T IMAGINE.
ACTUALLY, I CAN'T BELIEVE IT MYSELF.
BUT HIKARU'S WILLING TO GO...
...AND I'VE DONE WHAT I CAN.

OH YEAH, SHIMADA ELEMENTARY'S GOING TO BE THERE TOO.
IT'S WHERE AOKI-SENSEI WAS TRANSFERRED!
OOH!
SO HIKARU-KUN MIGHT SEE HIM THERE?
I'M SURE HIKARU REMEMBERS HIM...
...SO I'M EXCITED. ♡ I WISH I COULD GO TOO.
I KNOW.
SIGN: SPECIAL EDUCATION
あさがお教室
GOOD MORNING!
GOOD MORNING, MIYU-CHAN.
HIKARU-KUN, WHERE DO YOU WANT TO LEARN TODAY?
PAPER: REPORT CARD
GRADE 5, CLASS 3
HIKARU AZUMA
通知表
BZZZ
BZZZ

MARY HAD A LITTLE LAMB~
TEMPERATURE IS OKAY.
35.9°C
TODAY IS JULY 28. I WILL GO CAMPING.
YES, YOU'RE GOING.
IT'S ONLY 5 A.M.
LOOKING FORWARD TO THE DOLPHINS.

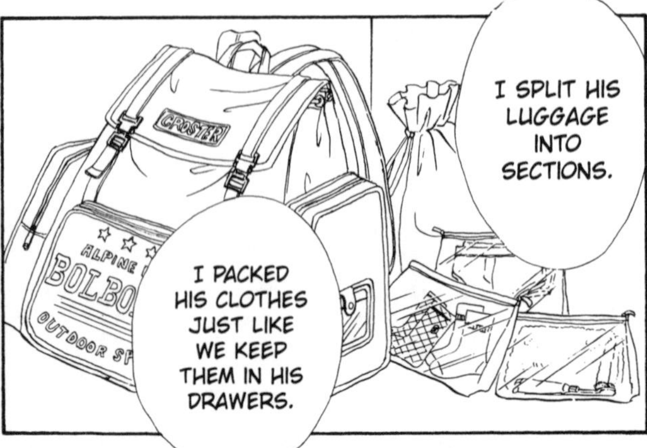

WE'RE OFF!
WOW, THEY'RE GOING ON THOSE BUSES.
入れます
EQUIPMENT
BOLBOLETA
OUTDOOR SPORTS
BAG: PUT IN
AZUMA-SAN!
OH, NAKAJIMA-SAN. YOU CAME TO SEND HER OFF?
YEAH, BUT I HAVE TO LEAVE.
I'M GOING TO BE LATE.
ALL RIGHT, MOE. HAVE FUN.
OKAY.

PLEASE LINE UP IN YOUR GROUP WITH YOUR CLASS.
GOOD MORNING, AZUMA-SAN, HIKARU-KUN.
I'M KURI-BAYA-SHI.
AH, YOU'LL BE SUP-PORTING HIKARU.
THANK YOU VERY MUCH.
WHOA, HE'S COM-PLETELY HIKARU'S TYPE!
I HOPE HIKARU DOESN'T PLAY WITH HIS SHORT-CROPPED HEAD.
OKAY, LET'S EXCHANGE OUR E-MAIL ADDRESSES.
BEEP BOOP
BEEP BEEP BOOP
THANK YOU.
I'LL SEND YOU UPDATES ON HOW HIKARU-KUN IS DOING.
I MAY ASK YOU FOR ADVICE IN CERTAIN SITUATIONS TOO.
JINGLE
CELL: SAVED
登録

THEY LOOK GOOD TOGETHER. ♡
GLANCE
GROUP 7, PLEASE TAKE CARE OF HIKARU!
LEAVE IT TO US!
GLANCE
OH, IT'S SAORI-CHAN.
SHE'S GOSSIPING LIKE USUAL.
MORNING, AZUMA-SAN.
THE PRINCIPAL'S SPEECH IS LONG, AS USUAL.
YEAH, IT IS.
GOOD MORNING!
SFX: WHISPER WHISPER

ENVELOPE: ORDER FORM FOR PICTURES
_______-SAN
CANDID PICTURES ____ YEN/PHOTO

SFX: SHRIEK SHRIEK SHRIEK

WHAT'S THAT? THEY'RE PARENTS FROM OTHER GRADES.
TANAKA-KUN!
キャーッ
キャー
キャー
THEY'RE HERE JUST TO SEE TANAKA-KUN?
NOBUAKI SAID THEY'RE BAD, BUT NOW I SEE IT'S TRUE.
I WAS ASKED...
...TO ORDER TRIP PICTURES WITH TANAKA-KUN IN THEM.
I GUESS THEY'RE PRECIOUS PICTURES OF HIM. WOULD THEY SELL IN HARAJUKU?
MAYBE I WANT SOME TOO.

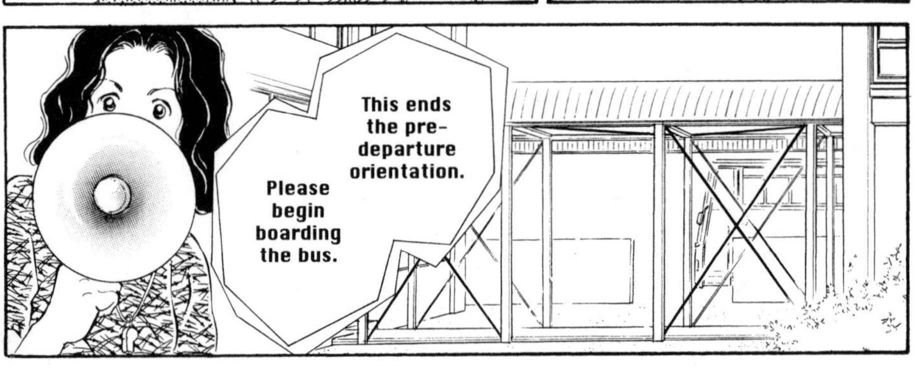

This ends the pre-departure orientation.
Please begin boarding the bus.

LOOK, THE SUPPORTING TEACHERS...
...THEY'RE HOLDING BUCKETS.
IT'S FOR WHEN KIDS THROW UP.
HOW SAD.
HAVE FUN!
ONCE THE KIDS PACKED THEIR LARGE BACKPACKS INTO THE BUS, THEY GOT ON ONE BY ONE.

LABEL: PUT IN

CARD: BUS #1

HIKARU GOT ON THE BUS, JUST LIKE EVERYONE ELSE.

HIKARU WON'T EVEN LOOK THIS WAY.

NOBUAKI'S LOOKING, THOUGH...

...AND DOING STUPID THINGS.

VROOM
VROOM
OH, THEY'RE LEAVING.
ARE THEY REALLY GOING?
BYE-BYE!
COME BACK SAFELY!

IT'S TOUGHER ON US TO WATCH THEM GO.
THE KIDS ARE ALL SMILING.
VROOM
JUST LIKE THIS, THE KIDS WE RAISED SLOWLY START GROWING UP AND AWAY FROM US.
THAT'S HOW THEY BECOME ADULTS.
WE HAVE TO GRADUALLY LET GO OF THEIR HANDS FOR THEM TO GROW...
...BUT, AS PARENTS, WE'RE RELUCTANT...

...BECAUSE THE INSTANT OF LETTING GO IS JUST TOO HARSH.
OH NO, THEY'RE GONE!
WHOA-OH!
EVEN THOUGH DEEP DOWN, WE KNOW THAT WE HAVE TO LET GO ONE DAY.
I WONDER IF OUR PARENTS FELT THIS WAY?
YOU KNOW?
YOU KNOW, I'M ALWAYS WORKING...
...SO I FEEL A LITTLE GUILTY THAT I DIDN'T...
...PAY MORE ATTENTION TO HIM.
BUT HE ALREADY HAS THE FACE OF A FIFTH GRADER.
KIDS ARE AMAZING, AREN'T THEY?

HE'S A POP IDOL NOW.
IT'S SO TRUE.
THE LITTLE TODDLERS WE KNEW ARE ALL GROWN UP.
HIKARU HAD THE FACE OF A FIFTH GRADER TOO.
SO WE'RE MEETING AT SIX FOR DINNER, OKAY?
SEE YOU THEN!

CARD: ICHIHARA RESTROOM ENVELOPE: ALL DONE, GOOD JOB.

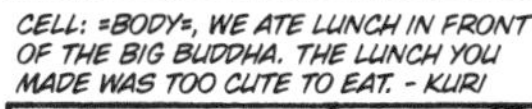
CELL: =BODY=, WE ATE LUNCH IN FRONT OF THE BIG BUDDHA. THE LUNCH YOU MADE WAS TOO CUTE TO EAT. - KURI

EVEN THOUGH WE WERE APART, KURIBAYASHI-SENSEI'S E-MAILS LET ME KNOW WHAT WAS GOING ON AND REASSURED ME.

公衆
=本文=
大仏広場でお
を食べました
食べるのがもった
いないくらいかわ
いいお弁当ですね
くり

I HOPE HE LIKED THE CHOCOBI LUNCH I MADE.
HIKARU ONLY ATE TOMATOES WHEN HE WAS LITTLE.
NOW HE EATS A WIDE VARIETY OF FOODS.
THUD
ド
Shichi-gatsu-cho Elementary students, please gather round.
HIKARU-KUN...

Later Elementary Years ⑲ / FIN

Later Elementary Years
Episode 20
MOM ALWAYS THINKS ABOUT YOU AND WONDERS WHAT YOU'RE DOING EVEN WHEN WE'RE APART.
I DO FEEL REASSURED WITH THE E-MAILS KURIBAYASHI-SENSEI'S BEEN SENDING ME.
I MISS YOU, BUT YOU PROBABLY DON'T MISS ME AS MUCH.
Shichi-gatsu-cho Elementary students, please gather round.
ドン
THUD

HIKARU-KUN...

......

HE'S WONDERING WHY I'M HERE.

PASS

GROUP 7, OVER HERE!

7

JUMP

YOU HAVE A SUPPORT TEACHER WITH YOU.

I'M GLAD YOU'RE DOING WELL.

AOKI-SENSEI, THERE ARE UNICORN BEETLES...
...BUT NO GRIFFIN BEETLES.
TOMOYA-KUN'S BUDDY.
THAT'S TRUE, TOMOYA-KUN.
THERE ARE MAMAKARI, BUT NO PAPAKARI.
YOU'RE RIGHT.
HEY, ISN'T THAT AOKI-SENSEI?
IT IS!
AOKI-SENSEI!
HIKARU-KUN, LOOK. AOKI-SENSEI IS OVER THERE.

HIKARU-KUN DOESN'T REALLY LOOK WHERE YOU POINT.
THAT'S RIGHT. WHEN WE LOOK AT TRAFFIC SIGNALS, HE HARDLY PAYS ATTENTION.
YOU SHOULDN'T FORCE HIM.
HIKARU-KUN DOESN'T LIKE IT.
OH, REALLY?
DARN, HE'S GONE NOW.
I WANTED TO TALK TO HIM.
I HEARD HE'S STAYING IN THE SAME PLACE AS WE ARE.
SO WE'LL SEE HIM AGAIN.
BUT I WONDER IF HIKARU-KUN FORGOT AOKI-SENSEI.
NO WAY. HE REMEMBERS EVERYTHING.
THAT'S WHAT HIS MOM SAID.
I CAN'T JOIN IN ON THE CONVERSATION.
I DON'T KNOW MUCH ABOUT HIKARU-KUN.

SIGH
はぁ～
I WISH MIKA-CHAN WAS IN MY GROUP.
GROUP 1 IS ALL HERE.
GROUP 5 IS HERE TOO.
Everyone's here, so we're going back to the bus!
JUST LIKE HIKARU-KUN'S MOTHER AND NISHIWAKI-SENSEI TOLD ME...
...HIKARU-KUN HAS NO PROBLEM WITH MOVING AROUND.
HIKARU'S SUPPORT TEACHER FOR THE TRIP KURIBAYASHI-SENSEI
BANANA

HE ALWAYS SEEMS TO WALK BEHIND THAT HANDSOME BOY...
...NAMED TANAKA-KUN.
YOU'RE COMPLETELY RELAXED TODAY.
YOU THINK?
I GUESS I AM... I WONDER WHY?
I KNOW WHY.
IT'S BECAUSE THERE ISN'T ANY SCREAMING OR PICTURE TAKING.
IT'S REALLY QUIET.

BUT ISN'T IT BAD FOR AN IDOL TO BE WALKING AROUND...
...AND NOT BE NOTICED?
KANATA! YOU HAVE TO GET MORE FAMOUS!!
I'D RATHER STAY THIS WAY.
WHY? YOU NEED TO BECOME A SUPER-CELEBRITY.
WOW. I GET TOO NERVOUS...
...TO TALK TO TANAKA-KUN LIKE THAT.
FIDGET
もじもじ
FIDGET
BUT I DON'T WANT TO BE ALONE IN THIS GROUP.
MAYBE I'LL TRY TALKING TO MY GROUP MEMBERS MORE.

HEY, NAKAJIMA-SAN. WHO DO YOU LIKE MOST AMONG JOHNNY'S JUNIORS?
DON'T YOU THINK SOTOUMI-KUN IS CUTE?
I'M SORRY. I DON'T KNOW MUCH ABOUT THEM.
WHAT? YOU DON'T WATCH MUSIC SHOWS ON TV?
NOPE. MY GRANDMA WATCHES MURDER MYSTERIES...
...AND MY MOM WATCHES PROFESSIONAL BASEBALL AND KICKBOXING.
I USUALLY WATCH "THE SATO FAMILY DINNER TABLE."
OH... I SEE.
AND THE CONVERSATION ENDS...
CAW
カア
OOTA-SAN ALWAYS WEARS CUTE CLOTHES.
I'LL TRY AGAIN!

YOUR T-SHIRT'S CUTE.
WHERE DID YOU GET IT?
OH, THIS? I DON'T KNOW.
MY MOM JUST BOUGHT IT FOR ME.
I KNOW IT DOESN'T LOOK GOOD ON ME, BUT I LIKE IT BECAUSE IT'S COLORFUL.
JUST BECAUSE IT'S COLOR-FUL?
SHE DOESN'T CARE ABOUT FASHION!?
DON'T YOU READ "PETITE TEEN" OR ANYTHING?
THEY INTRODUCE CUTE BRAND-NAME CLOTHES.
LIKE MEZZO MEZZO OR PINK POMME.
SORRY, I DON'T KNOW.
OH... OKAY...
AND THE CONVERSATION ENDS...
CAW
I CAN'T GET ALONG WITH THEM!
THIS IS BORING. I WANT TO BE WITH MY FRIENDS.
THUD
THUD

We've arrived at the Nokogiri Nature House.

This is where we're staying.

WOW, IT'S HUGE!

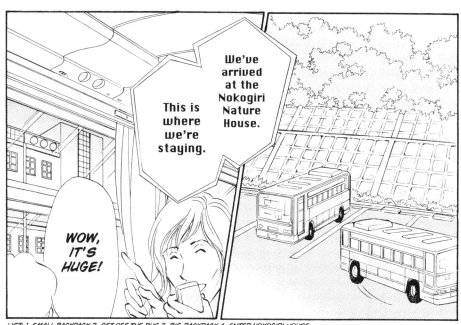

LIST: 1. SMALL BACKPACK 2. GET OFF THE BUS 3. BIG BACKPACK 4. ENTER NOKOGIRI HOUSE

Once you get off the bus, you will get your luggage and enter the house.

Got it?

OKAY!

小さいリュック
2 バスを下りる
3 大きいリュック
4 鋸ハウスに入る

THIS IS NOKOGIRI HOUSE.

CARD: HIKARU AZUMA

WE WILL TAKE OFF OUR SHOES.

I'M SUPPOSED TO PUT THIS IN THE SHOE BOX.

THE CORNER IS HIKARU-KUN'S FAVORITE SPOT.

東 光

GOOD JOB, HIKARU-KUN.

WE'LL TAKE OUT OUR INSIDE SHOES.

Gather in the lobby!
Line up by your respective room numbers.
THE GIRLS FROM GROUP 7 AND GROUP 8 ARE IN ROOM 307!
YAY, SAORI!
I MISSED YOU GUYS!
3F
315
HIKARU-KUN AND I ARE IN ROOM 315.
Shichigatsu-cho Elementary will be staying on the third floor. Follow me to the stairs.

TRUDGE
TRUDGE
ROOM 315. THAT'S THIS ROOM. IT'S RIGHT NEXT TO THE STAIRS.
315
SIGN: ROOM 315
STICK
ぺた
315号室
SLIDE
ガララ…
WOW, WHAT A BIG ROOM.
IT'S TOO BIG FOR JUST THE TWO OF US.
STICK
ぺた
上ばきを
ぬぎま
PAPER: TAKE OFF YOUR INSIDE SHOES
PHEW, WE MADE IT, HIKARU-KUN.
LET'S PUT AWAY OUR STUFF.
ドサ
THUD

OH YEAH.
I HAD TO SAY SOMETHING EVERY TIME WE FINISH AN ACTIVITY.
WE ARRIVED AT ROOM 315. GOOD JOB.
GOOD JOB.
はーっ
SIGH
HIKARU-KUN, YOU'RE GREAT.
WE HAVEN'T HAD ANY PROBLEMS SO FAR.
TEARY
うるうる
KNOCK KNOCK
コンコン
KURIBAYASHI-SENSEI, GOOD JOB.
EVERYTHING WENT SMOOTHLY.
HI, NISHIWAKI-SENSEI. YEAH, I'M VERY RELIEVED.
HAHAHA! IT'S ONLY THE FIRST DAY.

MAP: ESCAPE ROUTE FOR 3RD FLOOR
PAPER: TAKE OFF YOUR INSIDE SHOES
THE EVACUATION DRILL'S ABOUT TO START...
...BUT HIKARU-KUN LOOKS TIRED, SO HE CAN SKIP IT.
OH, OKAY.
3F避難
315
THIS ROOM IS THE CLOSEST TO THE ESCAPE ROUTE, AND I KNOW IT ALREADY.
IF THERE'S A FIRE OR AN EARTHQUAKE, I'LL GRAB HIKARU-KUN AND ESCAPE!
AFTER THE DRILL IS THE AREA TOUR, RIGHT?
WE'RE MEETING IN THE LOBBY AT THREE FOR THAT.
WANDER
WANDER
I WONDER IF HE'S RESTLESS?
HUH?
WHOOSH

HE'S CLOSING ALL OF THE CURTAINS?
シャ
WHOOSH
ずん
SLIDE
ずん
SLIDE
ゴロ
ROLL
ゴロ
ROLL
HE WANTED TO SLEEP.
I GUESS I'LL PREPARE FOR THE TOUR THEN.
OH, BUT I SHOULD EMAIL AZUMA-SAN FIRST.

OH, IT'S 3 O'CLOCK ALREADY. I HAVE TO GO PICK HIKARU UP...
TOOT TOOT
KERCHUNK KERCHUNK
KERCHUNK KERCHUNK
THEY'VE HAD THIS CLOCK FOR 9 YEARS.
OH, RIGHT. HIKARU'S NOT AT SCHOOL.
I WAS ACTING OUT OF HABIT...
THEN I CAN CONTINUE TO WORK UNTIL I HAVE TO PICK UP KANON.
THIS IS LIKE A DREAM.

MAYBE I'LL MAKE COFFEE AND TAKE A BREAK.
BLUB
コポ
IT SMELLS SO GOOD.
I HAVEN'T HAD A RELAXING AFTERNOON IN A LONG TIME.
ブルル
BUZZ
OH, MY PHONE.
IT'S FROM KURIBAYASHI-SENSEI.
栗林
Subject
鋸ハウス到着
本文
無事鋸ハウスに
着きました。
光君はテーブルの
下にもぐって昼寝
ました。
CELL: KURIBAYASHI. SUBJECT: ARRIVED AT NOKOGIRI HOUSE. BODY: WE ARRIVED SAFELY AT NOKOGIRI HOUSE. HIKARU-KUN WENT UNDER THE COFFEE TABLE AND SLEPT.
CHUCKLE
GEEZ, HIKARU GOES UNDER THE TABLE NO MATTER WHERE HE GOES.
I SHOULD RESPOND.
IF HE SLEEPS TOO MUCH, YOU MIGHT HAVE TROUBLE PUTTING HIM TO SLEEP AT NIGHT.
PLEASE WAKE HIM UP IN ABOUT TWENTY MINUTES OR SO... AND, SEND.
ピ BEEP
ピ BEEP
ピ BEEP
ピ BEEP
ピ BEEP
ピ BEEP
ピ BEEP

I CAN ENJOY A COFFEE BREAK LIKE THIS...
...BECAUSE I KNOW HIKARU IS SAFE.
KURIBAYASHI-SENSEI, NISHIWAKI-SENSEI...
...AND EVERYONE FROM GROUP 7...
...PLEASE CONTINUE TO...
...TAKE CARE OF HIKARU FOR ME.

307
IT'S ALMOST THREE. LET'S HEAD TO THE LOBBY.
OKAY!
I WANT TO GO TO THE BATHROOM.
THEN LET'S ALL GO.
LET'S GO.
MAN, WE HAVE TO GO BACK TO OUR GROUPS NOW.
I WISH THEY'D LET US STAY WITH OUR ROOMMATES INSTEAD.
YOU'VE GOT BAD LUCK, SAORI, GETTING STUCK IN THAT GROUP.

Please line up with your groups.
DARN.

WHISPER
WHISPER

SEE YOU LATER.
YEP.

HEY, YOU THREE DANGO SISTERS. GET IN YOUR GROUPS!
WOW, THAT WAS CORNY.
NISHIWAKI-SENSEI, THAT'S SO FIFTY YEARS AGO.

SANO-SAN, I'VE BEEN MEANING TO MENTION THIS.
YOU SHOULDN'T WHISPER AMONGST YOURSELVES LIKE THAT.
IT DOESN'T MAKE A GOOD IMPRESSION.
GEEZ, NISHIWAKI-SENSEI'S SO MEAN!
HE DIDN'T HAVE TO SCOLD ME IN FRONT OF EVERYONE!
OH NO...
THAT NISHIWAKI-SENSEI.
HE NEEDS TO BE MORE SENSITIVE.
There are three things to be careful of.
The area is large. Don't go near dangerous places such as cliffs or lakes.
There may be snakes and poisonous insects, so be careful in the bushes.
Don't damage nature.

STARE
じっ
I MADE THIS.
OH?
THAT CERTAINLY MAKES IT CLEAR...
Then we'll go in order. Class 1's Group 1 goes first.
THIS IS THE CLIFF NISHIWAKI-SENSEI WAS TALKING ABOUT.
HOW SCARY.
IN THE SHOWS GRANDMA WATCHES, CORPSES ARE SUNK INTO LAKES LIKE THIS.
I SEE.
WHOA, A GORILLA!?

THERE'S EVEN AN OBSERVATION DECK.
YAHOOO!
LOOK, A TRAIN.
THE ATHLETIC FIELD WE JUST PLAYED IN LOOKS TINY FROM UP HERE.
We visited two places with a nice view today, didn't we?
Let's take baths once we get back to the house...
...since we're all dirty now.
If your whole group is here, go back to your rooms and prepare for your bath.
OKAY!

STUPID!
YAHOOO!
にこお
SMILE
HIKARU-KUN?
SHRIEK
キー
SHRIEK
キー
DOES HE LIKE THE ECHO?
KURIBAYASHI-SENSEI, I'M GOING AHEAD.
I NEED TO PREPARE THE BATH FOR THREE WHOLE CLASSES.
I'LL LEAVE HIKARU-KUN TO YOU.
OH, OKAY.
WHAT SHOULD I DO? THE STUDENTS FROM CLASS 3 LEFT ALREADY.

PAD: 3 O'CLOCK TOUR / 4 O'CLOCK ROOM 315 / 4:30 BATH

HIKARU-KUN, LET'S GO. WE NEED TO TAKE A BATH.

3時庭を歩く
4時 315号室
4時30分お風

WE HAVE TO GO BACK TO ROOM 315 AT FOUR.

......

SNIFF SNIFF

IS HE GOING TO COME?

I HAVE TO TAKE HIS TEMPERATURE AND PREPARE FOR BATH.

TEXT: 4 O'CLOCK ROOM 315

SHRIEK
き～

4 O'CLOCK, ROOM 315!

PAPER: MAP
THIS IS SOMETHING I HEARD LATER, BUT...
...HIKARU KEPT TURNING BACK TO LOOK AT THE TUNNEL.
地図
MAP: OBSERVATION AREA
SEE, WE'RE HERE NOW.
てんぼう台
THIS IS THE HOUSE.
BUT SINCE THE GROUP HAD TO STAY TOGETHER...
...KURIBAYASHI-SENSEI MADE AN EFFORT TO BRING HIKARU BACK TO THE HOUSE.
HEY!
WATERBOYS?
PUBLIC BATH
ASTRO BOY!
GOR
HEY, CAN YOU GUYS BE QUIETER?
HIKARU-KUN'S COVERING HIS EARS.
SPLASH
WE'RE SORRY!

CAFETERIA
We are sharing the Nokogiri House...
...between Shimada Elementary and Shichigatsu-cho Elementary.
Please cooperate with one another to make this a fun experience for all of us.
HEY! TAKE SHOWERS SITTING DOWN!
SORRY HIKARU KUN.
I CAN'T FIND MY UNDER-WEAR.
I CAN'T FIND MY TOWEL.
YOU FORGOT THEM IN YOUR ROOM?
MUST BE TOUGH...
SFX: DRIP DRIP
LOOK, AOKI-SENSEI'S HERE.
YOU'RE RIGHT. I CAN'T BELIEVE IT.
THERE IS NOKOGIRI HOUSE BUT NO HAMMER HOUSE.
YEAH, THERE'S NO HAMMER HOUSE.
青木
SHIRT: AOKI
Okay, let's give thanks for our food. Itadakimasu!
ITADAKIMASU!

I THINK THE SUPPORT BOOK SAID HIKARU-KUN LOVES CURRY.
CLANK
カチャン
UGH, I GOT A HUGE PIECE OF CARROT.
OW. YOU'RE KICKING ME.
BLAB BLAB
ペチャクチャ
CLATTER
ガタ
KU-
UKE
SO
OD.
CLINK CLINK
カチャカチャ
U HAVE
RRY ON
UR CHIN.
GULP GULP
ぱしぱし
ガタタ
CLATTER
HIKARU-KUN, WHERE ARE YOU GOING? YOU HAVE TO CLEAN UP.

WAIT FOR ME!
OH, THEY BOTH DASHED OUT.
IT WAS PROBABLY TOO NOISY FOR HIKARU-KUN.
HE COULD BARELY STAND THE NOISE DURING LUNCH BREAK AT SCHOOL.
AND WE SHOULDN'T HAVE BEEN SO ROWDY IN THE BATH.
I'LL CLEAN UP HIKARU-KUN'S PLATES.
THANKS. I'LL GO CHECK UP ON THEM.
......
THANK YOU FOR THE FOOD.
OH, SAORI FINISHED EATING.
WE SHOULD GO TOO.
カタ
SCOOT

PAPER: IT'S NOISY / PLEASE GO AWAY / GO TO THE BATHROOM I'M THIRSTY / IT'S HOT / YES / NO

WHAT? HOW MEAN!
NISHI-WAKI-SENSEI SAID THAT?
YEAH.
HE SAID TO STOP WHISPERING WITH YOU GUYS...
...THAT IT DOESN'T MAKE A GOOD IMPRESSION.
WHY CAN'T WE? IT'S NOT LIKE WE'RE SAYING ANYTHING BAD.
THAT'S RIGHT. IT'S BECAUSE IT'S NOTHING IMPORTANT THAT WE'RE SPEAKING IN LOW VOICES!
I CAN'T TAKE IT ANYMORE. I WANT TO BE IN YOUR GROUP.
SAORI... DON'T CRY!

WHAT'S WRONG, SANO-SAN?
NISHI-WAKI-SENSEI!
IT'S YOUR FAULT SHE'S CRYING!!
GLARE
HUH? WHAT DID I DO?
SHRIEK
YOU TOUCHED SAORI!
THAT'S SEXUAL HARASS-MENT!!
STOP IT. I DIDN'T MEAN IT THAT WAY.
HIKARU-KUN!?
OH, NISHIWAKI-SENSEI...
KURIBAYASHI-SENSEI? WHY ARE YOU ALONE?

I...I'M SO SORRY! I LOST SIGHT OF HIKARU-KUN!
HE'S NOT IN THE BATHROOM, AND I CAN'T FIND HIM ANYWHERE!
WHAT!?
OH NO...
WE SHOULD GO LOOK FOR HIM.
AUGH!
CAN YOU GIRLS HELP TOO?
WE CAN TALK ABOUT THIS LATER.
WHAT DO YOU WANT TO DO?
I'LL HELP.
THIS IS NO TIME TO BE CRYING.
THANK YOU! THEN COULD YOU GO TO ROOM 3A AND TELL THE OTHER TEACHERS?
OKAY!

LET'S CHECK THE ENTRANCE FIRST.
R-RIGHT!
I JUST HOPE HE DIDN'T GO OUTSIDE!
HEY, AOKI-SENSEI. LET'S GO TO HIKARU-KUN'S ROOM.
I WANT TO SEE HIKARU-KUN'S HAPPY FACE.
THANK YOU...
...BUT I'LL PASS.
I'M NOT HIS TEACHER ANYMORE.
SO I WANT HIKARU-KUN TO GET ALONG WITH HIS CURRENT TEACHER.
青木

AND I HAVE MY OWN STUDENT.
HE'S PLAYING CARDS WITH HIS BUDDY RIGHT NOW.
I SEE...
I GUESS IF YOU'RE GOING TO VISIT SOMEONE, IT WOULD BE HIM.
I SAW HIM WITH YOU AT LUNCH TODAY.
YEAH. HIS NAME IS TOMOYA-KUN, AND HE LIKES TO PLAY WITH WORDS.
STOMP
バタ
STOMP
バタ
THAT SO?
WHAT'S UP, NISHIWAKI-SENSEI?
OH, NOBUAKI-KUN. AND AOKI-SENSEI.
ACTUALLY, HIKARU-KUN'S MISSING RIGHT NOW.
HAVE YOU SEEN HIM!?
!!
青木

I ASKED MY HUSBAND TO WATCH KANON TONIGHT, SINCE I'M WATCHING HER ALL DAY TOMORROW.
SIGH
は～っ
うまいもん
SIGN: DELICIOUS STORE
I HAVEN'T GONE OUT DRINKING IN A LONG TIME.
SO BRING ON THE BEER!
YOU HAD TWO CASES OF THE CHICKEN POX ONE AFTER ANOTHER.
YOU DESERVE THIS BREAK.
THANKS.
I'M JUST GLAD THEY BOTH GOT IT OVER WITH.
THAT'S TRUE. IF YOU GET IT WHEN YOU'RE AN ADULT, YOU HAVE TO BE HOSPITALIZED.
I WONDER IF OUR KIDS ARE EATING DINNER NOW TOO.
IT'S 6, SO MAYBE THEY'RE JUST ABOUT DONE.
REALLY?
I HAVEN'T GOTTEN AN E-MAIL FROM KURIBAYASHI-SENSEI SINCE.

MAYBE HIKARU'S PLAYING WITH NOBUAKI-KUN AND THE GANG.
I'M SURE IT JUST MEANS THEY'RE DOING WELL.
SIGN: SHOE CLOSET
下足室
NISHIWAKI-SENSEI! HIKARU-KUN'S SHOES AREN'T HERE.
WHAT!?
AND THE FRONT DOOR'S UNLOCKED.
HE PROBABLY WENT OUTSIDE.
DREAD
I'M SURE HE'S COULDN'T HAVE GONE TOO FAR.
LET'S SPREAD OUT AND LOOK FOR HIM!

HIKARU-KUN!
HIKARU-KUN, WHERE ARE YOU?
WHAT SHOULD I DO!? IT'S ALL MY FAULT!
WHAT IF SOMETHING HAPPENS TO HIKARU-KUN!?
THERE ARE CLIFFS...
...LAKES...
...AND WORSE YET, TRAINS NEARBY!!

Later Elementary Years 20 / FIN

Later Elementary Years

Episode 21

カンパーイ
CHEERS!
うまいもん
IT'S SO GOOD.
I'M GLAD KANON-CHAN AND HIKARU-KUN GOT OVER THEIR CHICKEN POX.
MY SON, HIKARU AZUMA, IS AUTISTIC.
HE'S CURRENTLY OUT ON A SCHOOL TRIP, SO THE OTHER MOTHERS AND I GOT TOGETHER FOR A DRINK.
THEY'VE PROBABLY FINISHED DINNER BY NOW.
I WAS OUT HAVING FUN AT HOME...
I'M SURE THEY'RE DOING FINE.
...WHILE THE TEACHERS WERE PANICKING ON THE TRIP...

HIKARU-KUUUN!
HIKARU-KUUUN, WHERE ARE YOU?
TEACHER OF GRADE 5, CLASS 3 NISHIWAKI-SENSEI
HIKARU'S SUPPORT TEACHER DURING THE TRIP KURIBAYASHI-SENSEI
I'LL SEARCH THE OBSERVATION AREA, SO CAN YOU SEARCH ON THE OPPOSITE SIDE?
YES!
WHAT SHOULD I DO!? IT'S ALL MY FAULT!
THERE ARE CLIFFS, LAKES, AND TRAINS NEARBY...
WHAT IF SOMETHING HAPPENS TO HIKARU-KUN!?
青木

MAYBE I'LL SEARCH NEAR THE BUILDING.

HIKARU-KUN DOESN'T LIKE DARK PLACES.
EVEN IF HE CAME OUTSIDE, I WONDER IF HE'D GO OUT THAT WAY.

I SHOULD LEAVE IT UP TO HIS TEACHERS.

青木

THERE HE IS.

THIS IS NISHIWAKI.
YOU FOUND HIKARU-KUN!?

A PEACH-COLORED...

I...I'M SO RELIEVED...
THANK YOU SO MUCH, AOKI-SENSEI.
I'LL LET KURIBAYASHI-SENSEI KNOW, AND WE'LL BOTH HEAD BACK THAT WAY.

I HAVEN'T TALKED TO HIM YET.
SORRY FOR CAUSING YOU SO MUCH TROUBLE!
I'M SO GLAD, HIKARU-KUN!!
OH...
HIKARU-KUN, YOU CAN'T GO OUTSIDE ALONE...

I DIDN'T KNOW THEY HAD FIREFLIES AROUND HERE.

PHEW. I'M SO RELIEVED, I'M WEAK IN THE KNEES.
I'M SO GLAD YOU'RE SAFE...
SNEAK SNEAK
コソ コソ
HIKARU-KUN KNOWS HE'S GOING TO GET SCOLDED.
THAT WAS REALLY DANGEROUS, SO I HAVE TO BE STRICT.
HIKARU-KUN.
WEAR A SCARY FACE.
AND ONLY SCOLD HIM FOR ONE THING.
YOU CAN'T GO OUTSIDE ALONE!
I AM SORRY.

OKAY, LET'S RETURN TO ROOM 315.
HE WENT OUTSIDE ALONE WHEN HE WAS SUPPOSED TO STAY IN HIS ROOM.
AND HE MADE EVERYONE WORRY, SO OF COURSE HE SHOULD SAY SORRY.
BUT WHY DID HE GO OUTSIDE IN THE FIRST PLACE?
HE TOOK THE TROUBLE TO CHANGE HIS SHOES AND UNLOCK THE DOOR...
光
WE SAW FIREFLIES THERE FOR THE FIRST TIME TOO.
SO I DON'T THINK HIKARU-KUN WENT OUT TO SEE THEM.
青木

OH, IT'S HIKARU-KUN. SO HE DID GO OUTSIDE.

THANK GOODNESS HE WAS FOUND SO SOON.

THEY WERE WORRIED.

DOESN'T HIKARU-KUN LOOK LIKE HE DID SOMETHING TERRIBLE?

HE'S PROBABLY SCARED HE'S GOING TO GET IN TROUBLE.

LET'S GO BACK TO OUR ROOM THEN.

WE HAVE TO PLAN OUR SKIT FOR THE BONFIRE.

WE SHOULD INVITE THE GIRLS TOO.

HIKARU-KUN!

HAVE YOU SEEN HIKARU-KUN?

THANK YOU, SANO-SAN.
WE FOUND HIKARU-KUN.
OH, GOOD!
わあ
CHEERING
I KNOW.
SANO-SAN, LET'S PRACTICE OUR SKIT.
COME ON, GO!
ドキドキ
BADUM BADUM
OH, OKAY.
にこにこ
SMILE SMILE
YOU MADE HER CRY!!
THAT'S SEXUAL HARASS-MENT!
SO WHAT WAS THAT ALL ABOUT?

WHY DO YOU LOOK PUZZLED?
OH, TSUCHIYA-SENSEI.
I DON'T UNDERSTAND GIRLS' FEELINGS AT ALL.
BUT HALF OF YOUR CLASS IS GIRLS.
I KNOW SANO-SAN BECAUSE SHE HELPS OUT AT THE NURSE'S OFFICE.
SHE'S A GOOD GIRL.
BUT SHE'S NOT VERY CONFIDENT ...
...SO SHE TENDS TO DECIDE THINGS AFTER DISCUSSING IT WITH HER FRIENDS.
I KNOW THE WHISPERING DOES GIVE A BAD IMPRESSION, THOUGH.
BUT SHE CARES ABOUT WHAT OTHERS THINK...
...SO SHE'D PROBABLY PREFER BEING SCOLDED WHEN NO ONE'S AROUND.
OHHHH!
YOU SHOULDN'T WHISPER AMONGST YOUR-SELVES.
THAT'S WHY SHE WAS MAD...
UM...
THERE'S ONE MORE UPSET PERSON WAITING FOR YOU.

3 A
NISHI-WAKI-SENSEI!
IT WAS GOOD THAT WE FOUND HIM...
...BUT WHAT IF AN ACCIDENT HAPPENED!?
WE HIRED A SUPPORT TEACHER FOR SAFETY.
SO WHY WAS HE LET OUTSIDE ALONE!?
HONESTLY, WE DON'T KNOW YET.
BANG
THAT'S NOT AN EXCUSE!!
ANYWAY, MAKE SURE THIS DOESN'T HAPPEN AGAIN.
I DON'T WANT ANY ACCIDENTS!!
YES, SIR...

THAT WAS A ROUGH ONE.
HAHA.
THE STUDENTS ARE UNDER OUR CARE, SO IT'S TO BE EXPECTED.
I'M GOING TO ASK KURIBAYASHI-SENSEI FOR DETAILS.
I WONDER IF HE'S GOING TO BE OKAY.
I THINK SO.
HIKARU-KUN'S MOTHER ...
...ALWAYS TOLD ME WHEN SHE CAME BY THE NURSE'S OFFICE...
"...YOU CAN FIGURE IT OUT WHEN YOU KNOW WHAT HAPPENED BEFORE AND AFTER."
SO...
WELL, IF SOMETHING ELSE COMES UP, LET'S LEND HIM A HAND.
I HAVE TO GO TALK TO STUDENTS WITH ASTHMA BEFORE THEY GO TO BED.
HMM. TSUCHIYA-SENSEI IS REALLY HELPFUL.

315号室
TWIRL
くる
くる
TWIRL
DROOP
どよ〜ん
DON'T BE SO DOWN.
CAN YOU TELL ME MORE ABOUT THE INCIDENT?
YES...
ACTUALLY, HIKARU-KUN SAID, "LET'S GO," BEFOREHAND.
LET'S GO.
HUH? WHERE?
SO HE DIDN'T LEAVE WITHOUT SAYING ANYTHING.
BUT I DIDN'T KNOW WHERE HE WANTED TO GO.
I SHOWED HIM THE PAPER I ALWAYS USE, BUT I GUESS THE OPTION WASN'T ON THERE.
さい
っちへ行って
トイレに行きます
のどがかわいた
あついです
はい
い
HE PROBABLY GOT IMPATIENT BECAUSE I WAS TAKING TOO LONG.
SO HE JUST TOOK OFF SUDDENLY.
RIED CHASE M, BUT RIPPED.

SO YOU LOST HIM, AND WHILE YOU BUMPED INTO ME...
...HIKARU-KUN HAD GONE OUTSIDE TO WATCH THE FIREFLIES.
HMMM...
OH!
DIDN'T HIKARU-KUN'S SUPPORT BOOK SAY THAT HE'S AFRAID OF THE DARK?
FLIP FLIP
IT SAID THAT HE'D PROBABLY ...
...GET SCARED DURING THE BONFIRE.
OH, RIGHT!
I READ THAT, EVEN AT HOME, THEY KEEP A NIGHT-LIGHT ON.
SO WHEN HE WENT OUTSIDE, IT WAS TOO DARK FOR HIM TO GO ANY FURTHER.
AND HE WAS WANDERING AROUND LOST...
...WHEN HE SAW A FIREFLY.
THAT MAY BE IT, NISHIWAKI-SENSEI!

キー SHRIEK
キー SHRIEK
BUT WE STILL DON'T KNOW WHY HE WENT OUTSIDE.
キー SHRIEK
キー SHRIEK
OH!
HE WANTED TO GO BACK TO THE TUNNEL!
I'M SURE THAT'S IT.
HE LOOKED REALLY HAPPY THERE.
PAPER: MAP
HIKARU-KUN WANTED TO STAY A BIT LONGER, BUT I HAD TO BRING HIM BACK...
...BECAUSE I WANTED TO MAKE SURE HE BATHED ON SCHEDULE.
地図
OH, I REMEMBER NOW.
HE PROBABLY WANTED TO SAY, "LET'S GO TO THE TUNNEL."
BUT HE COULDN'T BECAUSE HE DIDN'T KNOW THE WORD "TUNNEL."

SIGNS: BATH HOUSE
< WOMEN MEN >
大浴室
女湯←
男湯→
THAT'S POSSIBLE.
I ALSO DON'T THINK THAT HE WENT OUTSIDE TO GO WATCH FIREFLIES.
WHAT SHOULD I DO, AOKI-SENSEI?
DO YOU THINK HE'LL FORGET ABOUT THE TUNNEL AFTER A WHILE?
NO, IN FACT HE'D REMEMBER IT WELL...
...ESPECIALLY IF HE WAS INTERESTED IN IT.
AUTISTIC PEOPLE REMEMBER MANY THINGS.
I KNOW OF A PERSON WHO TRAVELED FAR AWAY...
..JUST TO EAT A CURRY DISH HE'D MISSED OUT ON MANY YEARS BEFORE.

ANOTHER EXAMPLE IS OF SOMEONE WHO EXPERIENCED...
...SOMETHING BAD WHEN RIDING THE BUS AND REMEMBERED IT EVERY TIME ON THE BUS THEREAFTER.
SHE WOULD GET AGITATED AND START EXPLAINING HER EXPERIENCE, SO THAT'S HOW I KNEW.
THE MEAN THINGS OTHERS DO TO THEM, POORLY EXECUTED MATTERS...
...THINGS THEY DIDN'T GET TO DO, THINGS THEY HAD TO DO, UNFINISHED BUSINESS...
カレーライス
SIGN: CURRY
...I'M SURE AUTISTIC CHILDREN REMEMBER ALL OF THESE THINGS.
ザザ
SPLASH
THEY ESPECIALLY CAN'T FORGET UNPLEASANT INCIDENTS...
...SO I WONDER HOW HAPPY THEY WOULD BE IF THEY COULD EXPERIENCE THE SAME THING AGAIN BUT THIS TIME PLEASANTLY.
IF THEY COULD ONLY KNOW...
...THAT "THIS INCIDENT IS OVER WITH."
I SEE...

THINGS ABOUT WHICH WE COULD SAY "OH DARN," OR "AW SHUCKS"...
...AND THEN JUST LET THEM GO...
...ARE THINGS HIKARU-KUN WON'T EVER FORGET.
I GUESS HIS PARENTS WOULD WORRY...
...IF HE GOES HOME AND ASKS TO GO TO A TUNNEL.
ACTUALLY, HE MAY...
...TRY TO GO ALONE AGAIN TOMORROW.
WHAT SHOULD I DO, AOKI-SENSEI!?
CHUCKLE
クス…
YOU SHOULD ASK HIKARU-KUN AND NOT ME.
HIKARU-KUN WOULD ANSWER YOU.
THE INTERACTION YOU HAVE WITH EACH OTHER IS FINE.

315号室
HOW IS HIKARU-KUN DOING?
HE WAS TWIRLING A TOWEL EARLIER...
...BUT HE'S ASLEEP NOW.
OH MY, HE'S UNDER THE TABLE.
HE LIKES IT THERE.
I'LL MOVE IT LATER.
OH YEAH, I SPOKE TO AOKI-SENSEI IN THE BATH.
HE'S THE TEACHER WHO FOUND HIKARU-KUN FOR US.
HE WAS HIKARU-KUN'S TEACHER UNTIL LAST YEAR, AND I GO TO HIM FOR ADVICE.
ANYWAY, HE SAID THAT WE SHOULDN'T IGNORE THIS MATTER.
LET'S ASK HIKARU-KUN IF HE WANTS TO GO TO THE TUNNEL.
HE SHOULD POINT TO IT IF WE PUT IT ON PAPER.

THAT'S RIGHT. I FORGOT WHY I CARRY AROUND A PEN AND PAPER.
I WAS FOCUSED ON GETTING MY MESSAGES ACROSS AND FORGOT TO ASK HIM.
WE'RE BOTH NEWBIES AT THIS.
IF HE WOULD LIKE TO GO...
...PLEASE TAKE HIM THERE DURING FREE TIME.
OKAY.
THAT'S A GOOD IDEA, GO AHEAD.
PHEW, I FINALLY FEEL LIKE TAKING A BATH.
WHEN YOU GET BACK, WE CAN MOVE THIS TABLE.
SURE.
I HOPE YOU CAN GO AND ENJOY YOURSELF, HIKARU-KUN.

THERE'S NO ONE AROUND.
THEN LET'S DO IT.
LET'S NOT. IT'S CHILDISH.
WHUMP
ばふ、
LET'S GET READY TO RUMBLE!
HEY! BE QUIET IN THERE!!

AND SO THIS IS HOW EVERYONE SPENT THE NIGHT...
IT'S FROM YOUR PILLOW FIGHT.
GASP GASP
WHEEZE WHEEZE
I WON'T DO IT AGAIN.
AND THE SUN ROSE...
...ALONG WITH ONE OTHER PERSON...
CHIRP
CHIRP
HEEEEY.
HEEEEY.
GASP
LET'S GO.
OH, HIKARU-KUN'S THE TYPE TO SLEEP AT NINE AND WAKE UP AT FIVE.

トンネルへ行く
GO TO THE TUNNEL.
はい
YES.
いいえ
NO.
SONIC SPEED
1. TAKE TEMPERATURE.
1. 検温
2. WASH FACE.
2. 顔を洗う
3. CHANGE CLOTHES.
3. 着がえ
4. TUNNEL.
4. トンネル
MARY HAD A LITTLE LAMB~

HOO
HOO
YAHOOO!
SMILE
にこーっ
HE LOOKS HAPPY. I SHOULD'VE LET HIM STAY UNTIL HE WAS SATISFIED.
FLAP
ぱた
FLAP
ぱた
THEN YESTERDAY'S INCIDENT COULD'VE BEEN AVOIDED.
THAT TIME, I FELT PRESSURED TO LEAVE...
...BECAUSE EVERYONE ELSE HAD LEFT.
I FELT THAT HIKARU-KUN NEEDED TO TAKE A BATH ACCORDING TO THE SCHEDULE...
BUT IT WAS ACTUALLY WORSE BECAUSE IT WAS TOO ROWDY...
...AND IT WOULD'VE BEEN BETTER TO DELAY OUR BATHTIME ANYWAY.
ASTRO BOY!

BUZZ
ザワ
CLINK CLINK
BUZZ
ザワ
YAY.
AND THE CAFETERIA WAS NOISY TOO. IT MUST'VE BEEN HARD ON HIM.

ONCE HE CAME BACK TO THE QUIET ROOM...
...HE CALMED DOWN AND REMEM-BERED THE TUNNEL, SO HE...
??
LET'S GO.
...BUT I DIDN'T UNDER-STAND.

THAT'S WHY HE WENT ALONE.
AND HE WAS SCOLDED BY HIS TEACHER...

I AM SORRY.

...EVEN THOUGH IT WAS MY FAULT FOR RUSHING HIM TO LEAVE.
SORRY, HIKARU-KUN.
青木先生のアドバイ
スもあり、トンネル
にリトライ！光君も
すっきりした顔です
これからは光君の様
子をよく見て柔軟に
対応したいです。
くり
I SEE.
SO THEY HAD QUITE AN ADVENTURE LAST NIGHT.
I DIDN'T KNOW EITHER AND WAS DRINKING AWAY.
CELL: I TOOK AOKI-SENSEI'S ADVICE AND WE RETURNED TO THE TUNNEL! HIKARU-KUN LOOKS VERY SATISFIED. FROM NOW ON I'LL TRY TO OBSERVE HIKARU-KUN MORE AND RESPOND FLEXIBLY.
I KNOW THERE ARE TIMES WHEN YOU CAN'T BUDGE...
...LIKE WHEN YOU'RE CATCHING THE BUS OR RIDING THE FERRY...
...BUT WE'D LIKE HIKARU TO BE AS SATISFIED AS POSSIBLE...
...AS LONG AS IT DOESN'T TROUBLE ANYONE.

I AGREE. BUT THIS SUPPORT TEACHER IS VERY UNDER-STANDING.
USUALLY, A TEACHER WOULD JUST SCOLD HIKARU FOR GOING OUT ALONE, END OF STORY.
AND THEY'D CONCLUDE THAT HIKARU'S TROUBLE.
YEAH,
THEY MIGHT JUST LOOK AT THE RESULT.
CAN YOU MAKE SURE TO INCLUDE MY NAME WHEN YOU SEND HIM A "THANK YOU" TEXT?
WELL, I'M OFF. I DON'T NEED DINNER TONIGHT.
BYE!
OKAY. DON'T WORK TOO HARD.
I'M TAKING YOU TO DAY CARE TODAY.
YAAAY!
POKE POKE
BUT BEFORE WE GO, I SHOULD SEND A MESSAGE BACK...
BEEP BEEP BEEP BEEP BEEP
...SENT!
BEEP BEEP
Kuribayashi-sensei, Thank you so much for going back to the tunnel. Please continue to watch him for three more days. <(__)>
- Hikaru's Mom and Dad
YES, I'LL DO MY BEST.

SO HE WENT BACK TO THE TUNNEL?
THAT'S GOOD.
TWIRL
くる
くる
TWIRL
YES, HE SEEMS TO BE REALLY SATISFIED.
I LEARNED A LOT FROM THIS EXPERI-ENCE.
I'D LIKE TO ASK HIKARU-KUN HOW HE FEELS AND ACT DEPENDING ON HIS REQUESTS.
ESPECIALLY SINCE THERE IS A LOT OF FREE TIME TODAY.
HE'S REALLY GOOD. IS HE YOUR STUDENT?
YES.
TOMOYA-KUN KNOWS MANY DIFFICULT KANJI AND PROVERBS.
BUT HE DOESN'T KNOW HOW TO INTERACT WITH OTHERS AND IS OFTEN MISUNDER-STOOD.
青木

HOW SO?
HE'S TOO HONEST, I GUESS.
HE'D CALL A CHUBBY FRIEND FAT, WITHOUT ANY MALICIOUS INTENT.
EVEN IF HIS FRIEND GOT MAD, HE WOULDN'T BE ABLE TO READ THEIR EXPRESSION.
HE'S NOT INTELLECTU-ALLY INFERIOR, SO I WANT HIM TO BE IN THE NORMAL CLASS...
...BUT THERE WERE PROBLEMS, SO HE'S IN MY CLASS RIGHT NOW.
OH, WE SHOULD GO SOON.
LET'S GO, HIKARU-KUN.
チラ...
GLANCE

青木
TOUCH
タッチ
SO HIKARU-KUN DOES REMEMBER ME.
IT'S JUST LIKE YOU TO BE NON-CHALANT.

FATHER RANCH
カチーン
FROZEN
HIKARU-KUN IS SO NERVOUS.
IS HE GOING TO BE OKAY? WE'RE GOING TO THE PETTING AREA SOON.
PAPER: TOUCH RABBITS / YES / NO
Rabbit
PLEASE STOP.
HE'S STAYING BACK.
BUT THEY'RE SO CUTE.
HIS MOTHER SAID HE'S SCARED OF DOGS A HUNDRED METERS AWAY, AND SHE'S RIGHT.
GOATS, RABBITS, AND GUINEA PIGS ARE ALL OUT OF THE QUESTION.
うさぎにさわる
はい
いいえ

SIGN: THIS WAY.
Pony
⇨こちら
PONIES, EH? BUT HE'S SCARED OF RABBITS, SO I DON'T THINK HE COULD RIDE A PONY...
ずん ZIP
ずん ZIP
HUH?
GETTING TOO CLOSE.
HIKARU-KUN, YOU HAVE TO GET IN LINE.
HEY, DON'T PUSH!

にこお
SMILE
Pony
YOU LOOK COOL!
パシャ
CLICK

TODAY IT'S JUST ME AND KANON.
MAYBE I'LL MAKE OMURICE.
BUZZ
ブルル
OH, MY CELL.

Hikaru-kun was scared and only came because he was going to be rewarded with ice cream. But he really enjoyed the pony ride. (^_^)V

- Kuri

OH...

HIKARU LOOKS REALLY HAPPY.
広告の品
牛ヒレ
680円
THE MEAT SECTION WAS CHILLY, BUT MY HEART WAS WARM.
Later Elementary Years ㉑ / FIN

SIGNS: AS ADVERTISED BEEF FILET 680¥ / PORK CHUCK 580¥

Episode 22

WE DON'T SUDDENLY BECOME PARENTS JUST BY GIVING BIRTH TO CHILDREN.

IN FACT, WE JUST DO THE BEST WE CAN, AND WHEN WE REALIZE IT, WE'VE GROWN. OUR CHILDREN TAUGHT US THAT.

I'M SURE MY FEELINGS AS A PARENT WON'T GO AWAY. EVEN WHEN WE LET OUR CHILDREN GO, THEY DON'T DISAPPEAR.

MY SON, HIKARU AZUMA, IS AUTISTIC.
HE LEFT FOR A SCHOOL TRIP YESTERDAY.
THERE WAS AN INCIDENT WHERE HE WENT OUT ALONE AT NIGHT...
...BUT IT WAS RESOLVED WITH THE HELP OF THE TEACHERS.
I'LL SAVE THE PICTURES KURIBAYASHI-SENSEI SENT ME ON MY COMPUTER.
BEEP BEEP
BEEP BEEP
HIS FACE WHEN HE'S EATING THE ICE CREAM...
SFX: GIGGLE

I HOPE YOU CONTINUE TO ENJOY YOUR TRIP.
I'LL BE WORKING HARD AT HOME TOO.

SIGN: SUBWAY / NANDAKANDA STATION

HEY, TANIGAWA-KUN. IT'S BEEN A WHILE.

I WAS TRANSFERRED TO THE TAMA OFFICE STARTING ON THE 9TH.
I JUST STOPPED BY THE MAIN OFFICE TO TRAIN MY SUCCESSOR.
I SEE...IF YOU HAVE TIME, WOULD YOU LIKE TO GET SOME COFFEE?

SIGN: STAR BECKHAM

I'M AMAZED YOU WERE ABLE TO STAY ON IN THE MAIN OFFICE.
I GUESS IT WAS EXPECTED.

I'M IN THE TOURISM DEPARTMENT. I FEEL SO OUT OF PLACE. I GRADUATED FROM A TECHNICAL UNIVERSITY, AND THIS IS WHAT I GET?
BUT WE JUST HAD OUR SECOND CHILD, SO I CAN'T QUIT.
AND IT'S HARD TO FIND A JOB ELSEWHERE TOO.
OUR COMPANY'S NO DIFFERENT.
THE ENTIRE I.T. INDUSTRY IS CUTTING BACK. THERE ARE MERGERS AND REORGANIZA-TIONS GALORE.
SO THERE'S DOWN-SIZING EVERY-WHERE.
YEAH, THEY'RE DONE LAYING OFF PEOPLE IN THEIR FIFTIES.
NOW THEY'RE AFTER PEOPLE IN THEIR THIRTIES WHO JOINED THE COMPANY DURING THE BUBBLE.
IT'S FRUSTRATING, BUT YOU CAN'T CHOOSE WHERE TO BE TRANSFERRED.
NEW!
BUT AZUMA-SAN, YOU SUC-CESSFULLY STARTED A BIG PROJECT...
...AND YOU'RE HIGHLY REGARDED IN YOUR CURRENT DEPARTMENT, SO YOU'RE SAFE, RIGHT?
NO, I'M A TARGET TOO.
I WAS CALLED IN BY MANAGER USUI THE OTHER DAY.
HUH?
THAT CAN'T BE!

HE TOLD ME TO TRANSFER TO A DEPARTMENT THAT'S RUMORED TO SHUT DOWN SOON.
SO HE'S PROBABLY GOING TO BOOT ME AT THE SAME TIME.
THAT WOULD BE A LOSS FOR THE COMPANY!
I KNOW I ACCOMPLISHED A LOT.
THE NUMBERS PROVE IT.
BUT MY DIRECT SUPERVISOR IS STILL TRYING TO BOOT ME.
SO IT'S NOT ABOUT ABILITY ANYMORE.
......
RECEPTACLE: PAPER, PLASTIC
STAR BEKKAMU COFFE
AZUMA-SAN, YOU OBVIOUSLY DECLINED THE TRANSFER, RIGHT?
YEAH.
I HAVE A FAMILY, SO I CAN'T LOSE MY JOB NOW.
HE PICKS ON ME IN VARIOUS WAYS EVERY DAY.
BUT I'M MAKING SURE I DON'T LOSE MY TEMPER.
I UNDERSTAND. I WAS LIKE THAT TOO.
紙
プラスチック

IF YOU GET UPSET AND QUIT...
...THAT'S EXACTLY WHAT THEY WANT.
OH, BUT YOU HAVE TO DEAL WITH USUI-SAN, HUH?
UNLIKE YOU, AN ENGINEER...
...HE'S THE TYPE TO MOVE UP THE LADDER JUST BY KNOWING THE RIGHT PEOPLE AND BEING A PLAGUE IN OFFICE POLITICS.
I KNEW THAT HE DIDN'T LIKE ME FROM THE START.
BUT I HAD TO AVOID CONFLICT IN ORDER TO RESOLVE OUR CLIENTS' ISSUES.
MY JOB IS TO PROVIDE SOLUTIONS TO THEIR SYSTEMS.
AZUMA-SAN, MY COLLEAGUE WHO JUST QUIT TOLD ME THIS...
HE WAS ALSO THE TYPE THAT WAS DISLIKED BY HIS SUPERIORS.
THEY KNOW THAT PROMOTIONS BASED ON SENIORITY ARE DISAPPEARING, AND A MERIT-BASED SYSTEM WILL EVENTUALLY TAKE THEIR PLACE.
THAT'S WHY THEY'RE GETTING RID OF PEOPLE WHO'LL THREATEN THEIR POSITIONS.
IT'S BECAUSE THEY DON'T WANT TO BE UNDER A FORMER SUBORDINATE.

ガーッ
SLIDE
PLEASE DON'T LOSE TO USUI-SAN!
THANKS, TANIGAWA-KUN. I HOPE YOU GET USED TO YOUR NEW DUTIES SOON.
LET'S BOTH WORK HARD FOR THE SAKE OF OUR FAMILIES.
BUILDING: JAPANET CO.
BUSINESS SOLUTION DEPARTMENT, MEDICAL AND WELFARE DIVISION
CHIEF? MANAGER USUI WOULD LIKE TO SEE YOU IN THE CONFERENCE ROOM.
OKAY, I'LL BE RIGHT THERE.
I WONDER HOW HE PLANS TO PICK ON ME TODAY?
ガチャ
CLICK
EXCUSE ME.

YOU'VE REFUSED ALL OF MY SUGGESTIONS UNTIL NOW.
YOU KNOW, PEOPLE GET FIRED FOR TURNING DOWN A SIX-MONTH BUSINESS TRIP IN THIS COMPANY.
CREAK
I DON'T KNOW WHY YOU WOULD BE SO UNCOOP-ERATIVE.
THIS IS YOUR LAST CHANCE.
GO TO BAHRAIN, OR BE TRANSFERRED TO A SUBSIDIARY WITHIN JAPAN.
GIVE ME YOUR DECISION IN TWO HOURS.
—!!

DON'T BE SO UPSET.
YOU'RE ACTUALLY ALLOWED TO DRINK ALCOHOL THERE.
THOUGH IT DOES GET HOT DURING SUMMER...
...BUT YOU'RE YOUNG. YOU'LL GET USED TO IT.
PAT PAT
ポンポン
WELL... I'LL SEE YOU IN TWO HOURS.
SLAM
NO MATTER WHICH OPTION HE CHOOSES, THE RESULT WILL BE THE SAME.
SACHIKO...
HEH HEH HEH...
ADULTS CAN BE SO CRUEL.
IN THE END, HE'S GOING TO HAVE TO QUIT.
HEH HEH HEH...
I KNOW HE'S NOT GOING TO STOP UNTIL I GIVE UP.
KANON'S PROBABLY TAKING A NAP AT DAY CARE RIGHT NOW...

...AND HIKARU...
CAP: AZUMA
ピ
TWEET
It's time for a break. Everyone from Shichigatsu-cho Elementary, are you with your buddy?

HIKARU-KUN.
CAP: KANAZAWA
MY BUDDY!!

GOOD LUCK, SAORI!
GO TO THE RIGHT!
CAP: NEE
CAP: SOU
WOBBLE
SHE MISSED!
SFX: SWOOP
DARN IT.
HERE.
YOU WERE CLOSE.
HIKARU-KUN, YOU'RE UP.
CAP: GOZARU
I'LL BLINDFOLD YOU.
OH!
NISHIWAKI-SENSEI, I HEARD FROM HIS MOTHER THAT HE DOESN'T LIKE BLINDFOLDS.
HE DOESN'T LIKE THINGS ON HIS FACE.
WHEN SOMEONE WAS PLAYING AROUND AND COVERED HIS EYES FROM BEHIND, HE THREW A TANTRUM.

OH, OKAY.
THEN YOU DON'T NEED TO DO IT.
HIKARU-KUN, HIT THE WATER-MELON.
GOOD LUCK, HIKARU-KUN!
WHOOSH
OOH!
TAP
OH NO.
THAT WON'T BREAK THE WATER-MELON.
ガク
WOBBLE
ポイ
PLOP
HE DOESN'T SEEM THAT INTERESTED.

THEN NEXT UP IS TANAKA.
SHRIEK
キャー
SHRIEK
キャー
GOOD LUCK!
THEY SCREAM NO MATTER WHAT HE DOES.
くるくる
SPIN
くる
SPIN
SPIN
田中
WHOOSH
びゅっ
田中
TAKE THAT!
THUNK
ズサ
YOU TOTALLY MISSED!
CAP: OOTA
CAP: TANAKA
田中
YOU'RE ON, OOTA-SAN.
RIGHT ON!
太田
GLINT
キラーン

CAP: NAKAJIMA
OOTA-SAN, A LITTLE BIT MORE TO THE RIGHT!
SST すす
HER FORM IS PERFECT, ISN'T IT?
RIGHT THERE! GO FOR IT!
HYAAAAAH!
CRUSH
WOOOW!
AMAZING. NOTHING LESS TO BE EXPECTED FROM YOUR BODYGUARD.
WHOA...
SHE TAKES KENDO CLASSES AT THE TAKEYAMA POLICE STATION.
NO WONDER.

IT WAS CRUSHED. OH NO, IT WAS CRUSHED.
東
そわそわ
FIDGET FIDGET
WHAT'S WRONG, HIKARU-KUN?
HIKARU-KUN HATES IT WHEN THINGS BREAK.
IT'S FUNNY BECAUSE HE BREAKS A LOT OF THINGS WHEN HE THROWS A TANTRUM.
HE CRIED WHEN SOMEONE ELSE DROPPED AN EGG DURING HOME EC CLASS TOO.
I WONDER IF HE THINKS IT'S HIS FAULT?
OH NO, IT'S BAD.
OR MAYBE THE IMAGE OF SOMETHING BREAKING STICKS IN HIS MIND AND HE CAN'T GET RID OF IT.
IT WAS CRUSHED.
MAYBE IT'S BECAUSE WE CRUSHED IT INSTEAD OF CUTTING IT. HIKARU-KUN MIGHT THINK A WATERMELON IS TO BE CUT, NOT CRUSHED.
中島
HE PROBABLY DOESN'T UNDERSTAND THAT WE'RE CRUSHING IT FOR FUN.
I'M NOT SURE.
THESE KIDS ARE PRETTY AMAZING...

GLANCE
チラ・・・
SLICE
サク
SLICE
サク
HE MIGHT RELAX IF YOU CUT IT AND EAT IT IN FRONT OF HIM.
THAT'S TRUE.
LOOKS YUMMY!
IT'S SO SWEET!
IT'S GOOD!
THAT'S RIGHT, HIKARU-KUN CAN'T ASK FOR THINGS THAT EASILY.

TAP TAP
トトト
NISHIWAKI-SENSEI, CAN I HAVE SOME WATERMELON?
にこっ
SMILE
HERE YOU GO, HIKARU-KUN.
にこお
SMILE
GOOD JOB! ♡

SPLASH
ザ
PICK PICK
ほじ
ほじ
YOU'RE THOROUGH, AREN'T YOU?
SPIT SPIT SPIT
ぶぶぶ
SPIT SPIT
ぶぶ
WHEN WE WERE YOUNGER, HE USED TO EAT THE SEEDS TOO.
OH, NO.
HE'S PUSHING THE SEEDS FARTHER INSIDE THE MELON.
LASH
ザザ
HIKARU-KUN EXPERIENCED A LOT OF NEW THINGS TODAY.
HE RODE A PONY, SWAM IN THE OCEAN, AND ATE CRUSHED WATERMELON.
SIGN: SCHOOL TRIP
SPLASH SPLASH
I'M SURE IT'S TIRING...
...SO LET'S ALLOW HIM TO MOVE AT HIS OWN PACE.
I AGREE.

SO YOU'LL TAKE THE OFFER?

GOOD CHOICE, AZUMA-KUN.

I CHOSE A PLACE IN KOSHIKAWA, NEAR YOUR HOUSE...

...SO YOU COULD SLEEP IN A LITTLE LONGER.

OKAY?

ギ...

CREAK

YOU'LL BE GOING TO THE KOSHIKAWA OFFICE STARTING NEXT WEEK.

SO HAVE YOUR SUCCESSOR TAKE OVER YOUR DUTIES BY THE END OF THIS WEEK.

ポンポン

PAT PAT

I HAD NO OTHER CHOICE.

SLAM

IF I GO TO BAHRAIN, THERE'S NO GUARANTEE I CAN COME BACK.
WHAT WOULD HAPPEN TO MY FAMILY THEN?
I CAN'T TAKE THEM WITH ME. HIKARU CAN'T DEAL WITH CHANGE. IT WOULD BE TOO STRENUOUS FOR HIM.
WE'LL ALSO LOSE THE SUPPORT WE HAVE IN OUR COMMUNITY.
EVEN IF I KNOW THAT CLEANING AND WATCHING THE WAREHOUSE IS WHAT AWAITS ME...
...I HAVE TO CHOOSE IT SO I CAN STAY IN JAPAN.
DAMNED IF I DO, AND DAMNED IF I DON'T.
HE SHOULD TRY BEING IN MY SHOES...

HUH? WHAT DO YOU MEAN?
YOU SHOULD TRY BEING IN THEIR SHOES.
IT WAS AN AGONIZING DECISION FOR HIM.
BROCCOLI, WHICH HE HATES.
BELL PEPPER, WHICH HE REALLY HATES.
HE HAD NO FUN CHOOSING.
THIS IS A MISTAKE I MADE BEFORE.
I WANTED A BOY TO DO SOMETHING HE DIDN'T LIKE. SO I GROUPED IT WITH ANOTHER CHOICE HE LIKED EVEN LESS...
...AND MADE HIM CHOOSE ONE.
I REALIZED MY MISTAKE QUICKLY, SO I STOPPED RIGHT AWAY, BUT I STILL REGRETTED IT.
I WANTED HIM TO ACT ON HIS WILL BY LETTING HIM CHOOSE.
BUT INSTEAD I WAS MANIPULATING HIM TO ACT CONVENIENTLY FOR ME.

THERE ARE OTHER POSSIBLE MISTAKES TOO.
FOR EXAMPLE, JUST BECAUSE HIKARU-KUN IS GOOD AT "LOOKING AND UNDERSTANDING"...
...WE MIGHT USE WORDS AND PICTURES TO MAKE HIM DO SOMETHING HE DOESN'T WANT TO DO.

OH, I DID THAT YESTERDAY!
IN THE END, HE WENT OUTSIDE AND GOT IN TROUBLE.
I UNDER-STAND.
I FEEL REALLY BAD FOR THE CHILDREN.
I MADE MY ROUND OF MISTAKES WITH THEM.

YOU KNOW HOW TEACHERS AND PARENTS ARE USUALLY THE ONES GIVING CHILDREN INSTRUCTIONS?
SO WE TEND TO HAVE THE UPPER HAND, AND THE RELATIONSHIP BECOMES ONE-SIDED.
BUT TRUE COMMUNICATION IS AN EXCHANGE OF FEELINGS.
IF WE DON'T GIVE THEM THE OPPORTUNITY TO EXPRESS THEMSELVES, AUTISTIC CHILDREN WON'T COMMUNICATE WITH US.

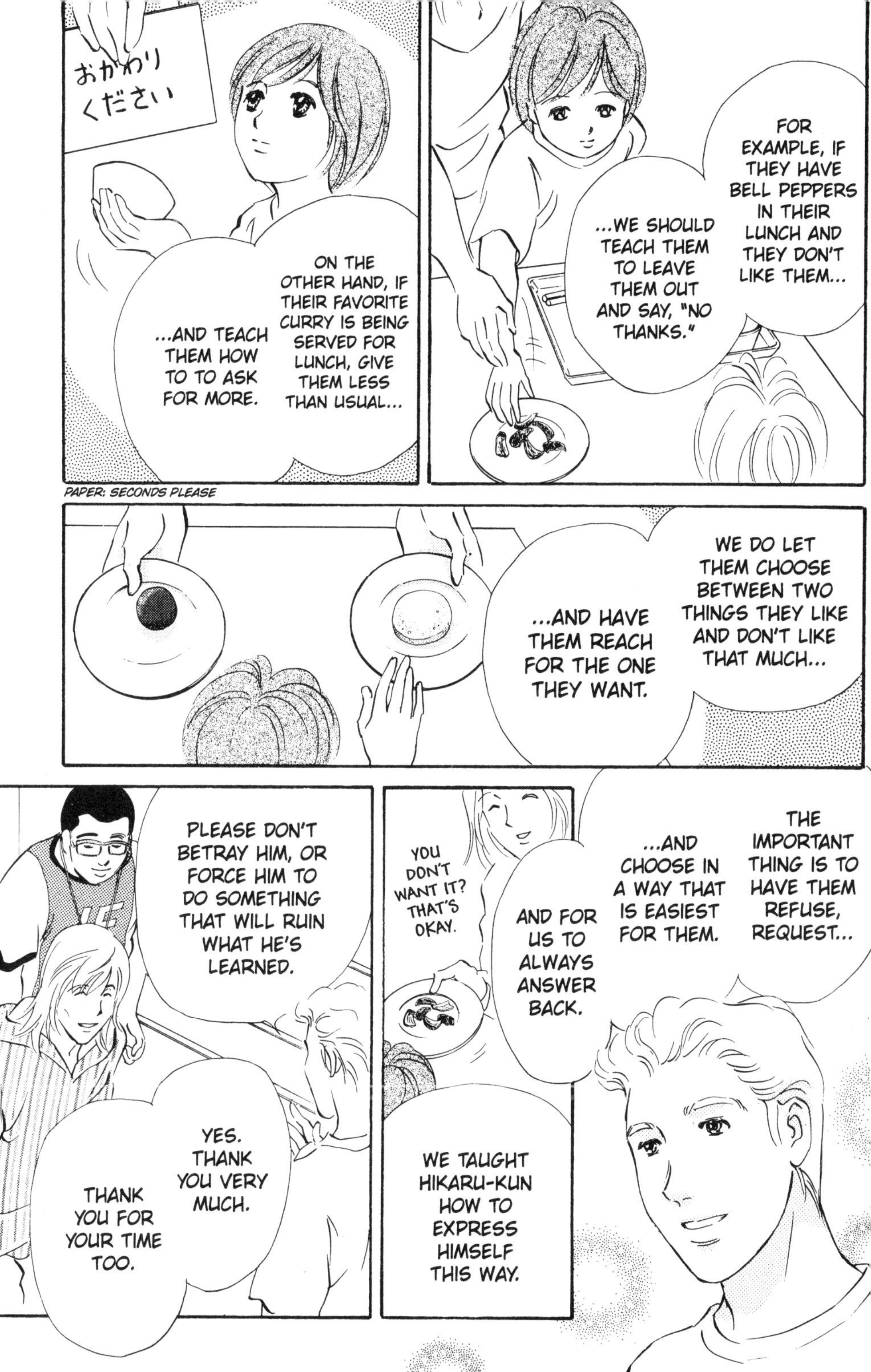
FOR EXAMPLE, IF THEY HAVE BELL PEPPERS IN THEIR LUNCH AND THEY DON'T LIKE THEM...
...WE SHOULD TEACH THEM TO LEAVE THEM OUT AND SAY, "NO THANKS."
おかわりください
ON THE OTHER HAND, IF THEIR FAVORITE CURRY IS BEING SERVED FOR LUNCH, GIVE THEM LESS THAN USUAL...
...AND TEACH THEM HOW TO TO ASK FOR MORE.
PAPER: SECONDS PLEASE
WE DO LET THEM CHOOSE BETWEEN TWO THINGS THEY LIKE AND DON'T LIKE THAT MUCH...
...AND HAVE THEM REACH FOR THE ONE THEY WANT.
THE IMPORTANT THING IS TO HAVE THEM REFUSE, REQUEST...
...AND CHOOSE IN A WAY THAT IS EASIEST FOR THEM.
AND FOR US TO ALWAYS ANSWER BACK.
YOU DON'T WANT IT? THAT'S OKAY.
WE TAUGHT HIKARU-KUN HOW TO EXPRESS HIMSELF THIS WAY.
PLEASE DON'T BETRAY HIM, OR FORCE HIM TO DO SOMETHING THAT WILL RUIN WHAT HE'S LEARNED.
YES. THANK YOU VERY MUCH.
THANK YOU FOR YOUR TIME TOO.

I'D LIKE TO LEARN MORE ABOUT AUTISM, BUT WHERE CAN I GO FOR INFORMATION?
I WOULD TOO.
ME TOO!
THERE'S A NEW FACILITY CALLED SUNSHINE HOUSE, TWENTY MINUTES AWAY FROM SHICHIGATSU-CHO ELEMENTARY. THEY DO SEMINARS THERE.
I GET CALLED IN TO LECTURE TOO. PLEASE ASK THEM ABOUT IT.
WE WILL!

WE SHOULD TRY WHAT WE JUST LEARNED.
HIKARU-KUN LOOKS TIRED...
...SO LET'S HAVE HIM CHOOSE BETWEEN EATING WITH EVERYONE IN THE CAFETERIA AND EATING ALONE IN THE ROOM.

GOOD IDEA. WE SHOULD HAVE HIM CHOOSE IF HE WANTS TO TAKE A BATH ALONE OR WITH HIS CLASSMATES.
YES!

YOU GUYS LOOK LIKE YOU'RE HAVING FUN.
WE'RE PLAYING OLD MAID.
WE PLAY IT DURING RECESS, SO WE THOUGHT HE'D BE USED TO IT.
THAT'S TRUE. THANKS.
OH, YOU CAN SEE ALL HIS CARDS.
WE CAN TELL HE HAS THE OLD MAID.
HIKARU SEEMS TO BE MORE INTERESTED IN COLLECTING NUMBERS THAN WINNING THE GAME.
SIGN: SHICHIGATSU-CHO DAY CARE
七月町保育

SO HIKARU-KUN IS ENJOYING HIS TRIP?
THAT'S GOOD.
I WAS SURPRISED WHEN I HEARD THAT.
IT'S ALL THANKS TO HIS TEACHER, THE SUPPORT TEACHER, AND HIS CLASSMATES.
AND AOKI-SENSEI, WHO TRANSFERRED TO SHIMADA ELEMENTARY IS THERE ADVISING THEM TOO.
EVERY-THING'S DIFFICULT BEFORE IT BECOMES EASY...
I REMEMBER THE FIRST TIME HIKARU-KUN WENT ON A FIELD TRIP...
IT WAS OUR FIRST TIME WITH AN AUTISTIC CHILD TOO, SO I WAS WORRIED.
BUT WHEN HE GOT ON THE BUS, HE WAS REALLY QUIET. HE JUST LOOKED AT THE SCENERY OUTSIDE THE WHOLE TIME.
HE LIKES TO RIDE IN VEHICLES.
THEY'RE TAKING CARE TO ADJUST TO HIKARU'S CHARAC-TERISTICS.
AND THEY MAKE SURE HIKARU ISN'T TRYING TOO HARD, AS WELL.

HE RODE A PONY AND SWAM IN THE OCEAN.
THIS IS A PICTURE THE SUPPORT TEACHER SENT ME.
WOW, HOW AMAZING.
HIKARU-KUN IS ABLE TO DO ALL THIS NOW?
I'M REALLY HAPPY FOR HIM.
うるうる
TEARY
WE HAVE A NEW GIRL WITH AUTISM IN OUR CENTER.
SHE'S FITTING IN PERFECTLY WITH THE OTHER CHILDREN.
SIGN: TURTLE BRUSH
亀ずし
IT'S HARD TO BELIEVE WE ONCE HAD TO CALL A FIRE TRUCK TO GET HIM DOWN FROM THAT SIGN.
OH, AZUMA-SAN...
THE YEAR WE SPENT WITH HIKARU-KUN IS PRECIOUS TO US TOO.
YUMIKO-SENSEI...
...THANK YOU FOR YOUR KIND WORDS.

I'M SURE I'LL BE TRANSFERRED NEXT YEAR.
SHOULD I REQUEST TO WORK AT A WELFARE FACILITY?
YOUR DINNER IS READY.
KANON WANTS TO DO IT TOO!
SFX: SQUIRT SQUIRT
ぶちゅ ちゅ
YAY! YAY!
WOW, YOU'RE SO GOOD!
KANON, IT'S HARD TO EAT IF YOU SIT ON MY LAP.
TEE HEE!
LOVE

WHEN THE CATERPILLAR HAD EATEN HIS FILL OF THE FEAST...
...HE BECAME SLEEPY AND TOOK A NAP.
AND WHEN HE WOKE UP...
...HE TURNED INTO A BEAUTIFUL BUTTERFLY.
BOINK
WHOA...
MOMMY, WHERE'S BROTHER?
HE'S AT A SLEEP-OVER.
FLAP FLAP
WHERE'S DADDY?
HE'S STILL WORKING.
I MISS THEM...
NOD
ZZZ ZZZ
KANON...

EVEN IF SHE FIGHTS WITH HIM EVERY DAY, SHE STILL MISSES HER BROTHER.
HEE HEE.
SMACK
ぷちゅ
PHEW. MASATO SAID...
...HE WOULDN'T BE THAT LATE TODAY.
I'LL WORK WHILE I WAIT FOR HIM.
SIGN: PUB PUKU-CHAN
AWNING: PUB PUKU-CHAN
LANTERN AND CURTAIN: PUKU-CHAN
居酒屋
ぷくちゃん
居酒屋 ぷくちゃん
ぷくちゃん
ぷくちゃん

DAMMIT. THAT BALD BASTARD USUI...
...HE'S ALWAYS BEEN ON MY BACK.
COMPUTER TECHNOLOGY CHANGED SO MUCH, YET HE DOESN'T KEEP UP WITH IT.
INSTEAD, HE JUST GETS BETTER AT KNOCKING OFF PEOPLE WHO GET IN HIS WAY.
I CHOSE A PLACE IN KOSHIKAWA, NEAR YOUR HOUSE, SO YOU COULD SLEEP IN A LITTLE LONGER.
URGH.
CAN I HAVE ONE MORE?
YOU SHOULD STOP, AZUMA-SAN.
I DON'T KNOW WHAT HAPPENED, BUT YOU'RE DRINKING TOO MUCH.

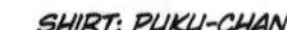

HMMM?

COME ON.

IT'S REALLY TIME TO STOP WHEN SHE SAYS SO.

OKAY?

PUKU-CHAN...

...I WAS TRANSFERRED TO KOSHIKAWA. I'LL BE IN CHARGE OF A WAREHOUSE.

SO I WON'T BE ABLE TO COME HERE MUCH ANYMORE.

EH? REALLY? I'LL MISS YOU DEARLY.

I'LL GIVE YOU A DISCOUNT TONIGHT THEN. TRY TO COME WHEN YOU CAN, OKAY?

I GUESS IF BOTH OF YOU INSIST, I HAVE TO LISTEN...

CAN I GET THE CHECK?

THANK YOU.

I'LL WORK HARD CLEANING EVERY DAY.

SLIDE

I NEED TO DRINK SOME MORE. MAYBE I'LL GO TO ANOTHER ONE.

Later Elementary Years ㉒ / FIN

Later Elementary Years

Episode 23

IT WAS THE SECOND NIGHT OF HIKARU'S SCHOOL TRIP.

GOOD MORNING.

HIKARU-KUN... IT'S STILL NIGHTTIME.

HIKARU COULDN'T SLEEP THAT WELL.

LET'S GET UNDER THE BLANKET AND CLOSE YOUR EYES

I WONDER IF HE WAS AWAKE BECAUSE HE WAS NERVOUS THE ENTIRE DAY?

ON THE OTHER HAND, KANON WAS FAST ASLEEP.

EVERYONE SPENT THE NIGHT DIFFERENTLY.

OKAY, I SHOULD WORK WHILE I WAIT FOR MASATO.
HE SAID HE WOULDN'T BE THAT LATE.
CLICK CLICK CLICK
カタカタカタ…

SIGN: NANDAKANDA STREET
南田神田通り
WOBBLE
I NEED TO DRINK MORE. I'LL GO TO ANOTHER STORE.

THIS IS YOUR LAST CHANCE.
GO TO BAHRAIN OR A SUBSIDIARY WITHIN JAPAN.
I NEED YOUR DECISION IN TWO HOURS.

GOOD, YOU'LL TRANSFER, EH?
I CHOSE THE OFFICE NEAREST TO YOU.
YOU'LL BE GOING TO KOSHIKAWA STARTING NEXT WEEK.
THAT BALD BASTARD USUI...
...HE THINKS HE GOT RID OF ME, BUT I'M GOING TO FIGHT.
SIGN: PLEASE DO NOT SMOKE WHILE WALKING. POLE: THIS IS A SMOKE-FREE ZONE.
I CAN'T LOSE MY JOB NOW...
WOBBLE
...FOR THE SAKE OF SACHIKO, HIKARU, AND KANON.
NO MATTER WHAT ABUSE I TAKE...
...I'M NOT GOING TO QUIT!

SIZZLE
......
OWWWW!
スナック
HAHAHA...
USUI...
YOU BAS-TARD!

HEY!!
DON'T YOU SEE THE SIGN RIGHT NEXT TO YOU!?
やめましょう。
SIGN: PLEASE DO NOT SMOKE WHILE WALKING.
FOO
OH, PLEASE. I HAVE AN ASHTRAY WITH ME.
MIND YOUR OWN BUSINESS.
SFX: TAP TAP
WHAT!?
GRAB
YOU JUST BURNED ME. IT IS MY BUSINESS!!
POW
THUD
TOKU-SAN!!

TOKU-SAN?
SPIN
HOW DARE YOU HIT ME, YOU YOUNG PUNK!
I CAN'T SEE WELL.
SPIN
IT'S NOT USUI?
STOP IT, TOKU-SAN. YOU CAN'T TAKE HIM.
DON'T STOP ME!
WOBBLE
DAMN IIIT!
AAARGG
GRAB
CRASH

STOP IT.
YOU...
PLEASE STOP IT!
WOBBLE
WOBBLE
HEY, MY SIGN!
CALL THE POLICE!
SIGN: TOMITA
WE HAVE TO GET OUT OF HERE, TOKU-SAN. IF THE POLICE COME, YOU'LL REALLY BE FIRED.
THAT YOUNGER MANAGER IS GOING TO GET RID OF YOU FOR SURE.
SIGN: SMOKE-FREE ZONE
STAGGER STAGGER
UGH...
WHO'S TOKU-SAN?
I THOUGHT I SLUGGED USUI.

WOOO
WOOO
WOOO
YES, THAT'S RIGHT.
THIS MAN AND ONE OTHER PERSON WERE FIGHTING AND DID THIS TO MY SIGN.
YEAH, I SEE IT'S A BIT DENTED.
SIGN: SMOKE-FREE ZONE / CHIYODA DISTRICT
SIGN: TOMITA DRUGS
WHAT DO YOU MEAN, "A BIT?"
THIS IS THE SIGN I WORK HARD TO PROTECT.
BUSINESS IS TOUGH ENOUGH, NOW THAT THERE'S THAT BIG DRUGSTORE CHAIN ON THE MAIN STREET...
...BUT THIS GUY AND THE OTHER GUY...
WHERE IS THIS OTHER GUY?
HE RAN OFF WHILE I WAS CALLING YOU.
......

HIC...
HE'S COM-PLETELY DRUNK.
LET'S TAKE HIM BACK TO THE STATION.
WE'RE GOING TO INTERROGATE HIM, SO CAN YOU COME WITH US?
OF COURSE! I'M GOING TO MAKE HIM PAY.
WOO
WOO
......
OH MY, IT'S ALREADY 1:30.
SFX: BEEP BEEP BEEP
I SHOULD TEXT HIM TO COME HOME SOON...
OKAY, SENT.
BUZZ
HE SAID HE'S NOT GOING TO BE THAT LATE.
OH, HE REPLIED.

MASATO?
Hello, is this the Azuma residence?
My name is Aida, and I work for the Nandakanda Police Station.
Your husband was drunk and got into a fight with a passerby.
We're holding him here.
WHAT!?
MASATO'S AT THE POLICE STATION!?
A FIGHT? NO WAY...
AND IS MY HUSBAND OKAY?
HE DIDN'T GET HURT, DID HE?
He did cut his mouth, but it's minor.
警視庁南田神田
His fight broke a store sign.
He'll be charged with property damage.

SIGN: NANDAKANDA POLICE STATION

CAN I TALK TO MY HUSBAND?
IF I GO THERE, WILL I BE ABLE TO SEE HIM!?
I'M AFRAID NOT.
HE'S NOT SORRY FOR WHAT HE DID. I'M NOT SURE IF HE CAN GO HOME TOMORROW EITHER.
TOMORROW!?
NO...MY HUSBAND DOESN'T GET VIOLENT WHEN HE DRINKS!
I THINK THIS IS SOME KIND OF MISTAKE.
HE'S KIND TO HIS CHILDREN AND A GOOD FATHER.
ANYWAY, HE CAN'T LEAVE TONIGHT.
I'LL CONTACT YOU AGAIN TOMORROW.
IF YOU HAVE QUESTIONS, CALL MY DEPARTMENT AND ASK FOR AIDA.
CLICK
ガチャ
OH...

PLEASE LET ME GO TO THE BATHROOM.

HIS WIFE HAS SO MUCH FAITH IN THIS GUY, BUT JUST LOOK AT HIM...

THIS WAY.

UGH.

I DIDN'T DO ANYTHING WRONG.

GO CATCH THAT BALDY!

SHEESH.

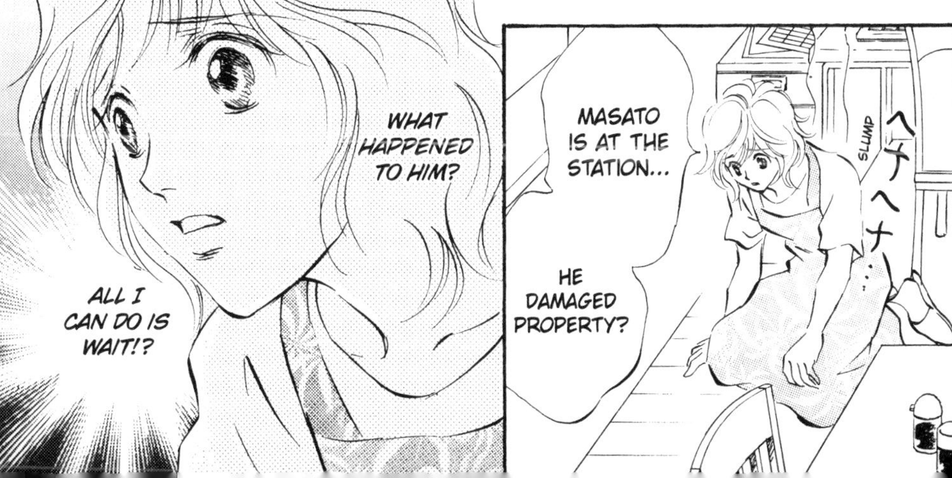

MASATO IS AT THE STATION...
HE DAMAGED PROPERTY?
SLUMP
WHAT HAPPENED TO HIM?
ALL I CAN DO IS WAIT!?

KURIBAYASHI-SENSEI E-MAILED ME TO LET ME KNOW THAT HIKARU'S HAVING TROUBLE SLEEPING.
BUT I DON'T THINK I CAN SLEEP TONIGHT EITHER.
I'M SURE MASATO'S CELL PHONE WAS TAKEN AWAY FROM HIM...
...BUT I'LL E-MAIL HIM ANYWAY.
BEEP BEEP
ピ ピ
ピ ピ ピ
PEEP PEEP PEEP
お父さん
何があったか
知らないけど
信じています
何時でも迎えに
行くからね
幸子
MASATO
I DON'T KNOW WHAT HAPPENED, BUT I BELIEVE IN YOU. I'LL GO PICK YOU UP ANYTIME, OKAY?
SACHIKO
OKAY, SENT...

南田神田通
SHEESH.
ブツブツ
MUMBLE MUMBLE
UM...
WHAT!? YOU SAW THE WHOLE THING!?
YES. MY BABY WAS CRYING, SO I CAME OUT TO THE STREET TO CALM HIM DOWN.
OH YEAH, HE'S ALWAYS CRYING.
I'M SORRY.
THE OTHER TWO MEN RAN AWAY. THEY WERE IN THEIR FIFTIES.
JUST AS THEY WERE PASSING BY THIS SIGN...
...THE MAN'S CIGARETTE BURNED THE HAND OF THE YOUNGER MAN.
WHEN THE YOUNGER MAN GOT UPSET AND STOPPED HIM...
...THE OLD MAN SAID THAT HE HAD AN ASHTRAY AND THAT THE YOUNGER MAN SHOULD MIND HIS OWN BUSINESS...
カチン
GRR

THEN THEY GOT INTO A FIGHT...
...AND THE OLD MAN PUSHED THE YOUNG ONE INTO YOUR SIGN.
IS THAT TRUE?
YES.
THIS IS THE CIGARETTE BUTT FROM THE INCIDENT.
WHY DIDN'T YOU TELL THE POLICE EARLIER?
......
I WANTED TO RETURN TO MY ROOM BECAUSE MY BABY STOPPED CRYING.
I THOUGHT IF I GOT INVOLVED, HE WOULD WAKE UP AGAIN.
BUT IT WASN'T THE YOUNG MAN'S FAULT, SO I CAME BACK.
THANKS. I'LL GO CALL THEM.
UM, WHAT'S GOING TO HAPPEN TO THAT MAN?
富田

DON'T WORRY.
I'LL MAKE SURE HIS NAME IS CLEARED.
I'VE BEEN COOPERATING WITH THE COMMUNITY...
...TO MAKE LIVING CONDITIONS BETTER AROUND HERE.
SO YOU CAN RETURN TO YOUR BABY.
YES!
AIDA-SAN, YOU HAVE A CALL FROM THAT DRUGSTORE OWNER.
OH, THANK YOU.
WHAT? A WITNESS? THERE SHOULD BE A BURN ON HIS RIGHT HAND?

STARE
Ah, I knew it.
YES, THERE IS A BLISTER FROM A BURN.
THEN HE'S THE VICTIM. PLEASE LET HIM GO.
I'LL DROP THE CHARGES.
YOU DON'T NEED HIM TO PAY FOR THE DAMAGES?
No, it's okay.
MY GRAND-CHILD WAS ONCE BURNED BY SOMEONE SMOKING WHILE WALKING TOO.
IT WAS HIS HAIR THAT WAS SINGED, BUT I STILL SHIVER AT THE THOUGHT THAT IT COULD'VE BEEN HIS EYES.
DID YOU KNOW THAT A LIT CIGARETTE CAN GO UP TO 600-1200 DEGREES CELSIUS?
NAG
NAG
YAWN
I'M GOING TO SLEEP NOW.

ブルル
BUZZ
がばっ
RISE
THIS IS AZUMA!
HUH? HE WAS RELEASED!?
YES, I'LL COME PICK HIM UP RIGHT NOW.
KANON, I'LL BE RIGHT BACK. SO SLEEP TIGHT.
I'LL LEAVE A PICTURE LETTER.
ブロ
VROOM

I KNOW THE DETAILS OF WHY HE GOT CAUGHT UP WITH THE POLICE, BUT...
...WHY DID MASATO....
...DRINK UNTIL HE LOST REASON?
IF SOMETHING IS BOTHERING HIM, I WANT HIM TO COME TO ME.
OR IS IT SOMETHING I WOULDN'T UNDERSTAND?
WRITE YOUR NAME HERE.
CHICKEN SCRATCH ...
SCRIBBLE SCRIBBLE
THESE ARE THE PERSONAL GOODS YOU VOLUNTEERED.
YOUR CELL WAS RINGING EARLIER.
'IGHT.

MASATO!
CLICK
ガチャ
もたもた
SFX: FUMBLE FUMBLE
SACHIKO ...
I'M SORRY...
NO, I'M GLAD YOU DIDN'T GET HURT.
LET'S GO HOME.
PLEASE WRITE YOUR NAME HERE.
OH... SURE.
I'LL HELP YOU DOWN.
THANK YOU SO MUCH.
警視庁南田神
I'M SORRY TO CAUSE SO MUCH TROUBLE.
NO PROBLEM.
TRY NOT TO DRINK SO MUCH.
DON'T MAKE YOUR WIFE WORRY.
SHADDUP! GO CATCH THAT BALDY BASTARD!
HONEY!!

UGH. I FEEL A LITTLE BETTER.
THAT COP SAID SOMETHING ABOUT MY CELL.
お父さん
何があったか
知らないけど
信じています
何時でも迎えに
行くからね
幸子
MASATO
I DON'T KNOW WHAT HAPPENED, BUT I BELIEVE IN YOU. I'LL GO PICK YOU UP ANYTIME, OKAY?
SACHIKO
SACHIKO...
ZSHHH
YIKES! EVEN HIS JACKET SMELLS LIKE ALCOHOL...

GULP GULP
ゴクゴク
PHEW
はあ
I FEEL MUCH BETTER.
KANON...
HIKARU'S ON HIS TRIP, RIGHT?
YEAH, HE'S COMING BACK THE DAY AFTER TOMORROW.
COME ON, WE SHOULD PUT SOMETHING ON THAT HAND.
OH... RIGHT.

SQUIRT
SQUIRT
I'M GOING TO BE WORKING IN THE KOSHIKAWA OFFICE STARTING NEXT WEEK.
KOSHI-KAWA...
IT'S A SUBSIDIARY WITH A SMALL WAREHOUSE.
HE WAS DEMOTED.
EVEN THOUGH HE WAS WORKING SO HARD IN THE WELFARE DIVISION.
HIS PERFORMANCE WAS GOOD TOO...
THAT'S WHY HE DRANK SO MUCH.

OKAY. THANKS FOR TELLING ME.
WE'LL PROBABLY WAKE UP AROUND THE SAME TIME THEN.
DON'T BE SILLY, SACHIKO, YOU DON'T HAVE TO CRY.
BUT IT'S FRUSTRATING ...
DON'T WORRY.
I HAVE SOMETHING IN MIND.
WE SHOULD GET TO SLEEP.
YEAH...
I FEEL SO GLOOMY...
LOOK, KANON KICKED OFF HER BLANKETS.

I HAD MANY SLEEPLESS NIGHTS.

BUT EACH TIME, THE SIGHT OF MY CHILDREN SLEEPING MADE ME FEEL BETTER.

KANON... HIKARU...

YOUR MOMMY AND DADDY...

...AREN'T GIVING UP JUST YET.

GOOD MORNING!

OH, YOU'RE ALL TOGETHER THIS MORNING.

HOW IS HIKARU-KUN ENJOYING HIS SCHOOL TRIP?

HE SEEMS TO BE HAVING FUN.

WE'LL SEE YOU LATER.
SQUEAL キャッ
SQUEAL キャッ
HIKARU'S FINALLY GOING TO SEA WORLD, EH?
YEAH. HE SAW THE DOLPHIN SHOW...
....AND I THINK THAT MADE UP HIS MIND TO GO.
SIGN: COME COME SEA WORLD
I HOPE HE HAS FUN.
かもかも シ～ワ～ルド

ザー
WHOOSH
CHEER
ワァ
JUMP
ピョーン
JUMP
ピョーン
HIKARU-KUN LOOKS SO HAPPY.
I'M GLAD WE CHOSE THE AISLE SEAT SO HE CAN JUMP UP AND DOWN.

WHOOSH
LOOK, IT'S SWIMMING BACK-WARDS!
SFX: BADUM BADUM
ドキ ドキ
SPLASH
SPLASH
SPLASH
WOW, THEY'RE SO SYN-CHRONIZED.
This ends the dolphin show.
The next show is...
CLAP CLAP

PAPER: THE DOLPHIN SHOW IS OVER / YES / NO
ゾロ FILE
ゾロ FILE
THAT WAS FUN.
LET'S GO SEE THE SEA OTTERS NEXT.
HIKARU-KUN LIKED IT SO MUCH HE'S NOT MOVING.
BOOK: STAMP HUNT BOOK, COME COME SEA WORLD
I'LL ASK HIKARU-KUN.
THE DOLPHIN SHOW IS OVER.
チラ GLANCE
IF WE STAY HERE, WE CAN'T COMPLETE OUR STAMP HUNT.
OH YEAH, THEY HAVE TO BE IN A GROUP, SO THEY'RE WAITING FOR HIKARU-KUN.
スタンプラリーノート
THE DOLPHIN SHOW IS OVER.
WHOA.

THE DOLPHIN SHOW IS OVER.

GOOD JOB.

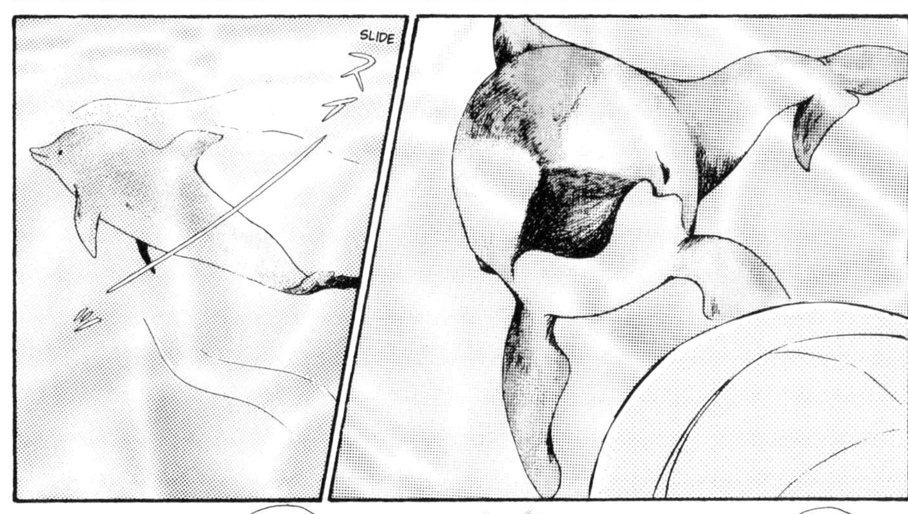

HIKARU WAS REALLY INTERESTED IN THE PENGUINS TOO.
GLIDE スイーーッ
PENGUINS ARE FAST IN THE WATER.
HOW MANY MORE STAMPS DO WE NEED?
FIVE MORE.
HEY, EVERYONE. HIKARU-KUN SEEMS TO WANT TO STAY HERE...
...SO GO AHEAD WITHOUT US.
I DON'T THINK HE WANTS TO SEE EVERYTHING.
AND HE'S NOT INTER-ESTED IN THE STAMP HUNT, EITHER.
WE'LL CATCH UP WITH YOU AT THE END.
SEE YOU LATER, HIKARU-KUN.
OKAY, THEN WE'LL GO SEE THE OCEAN SUNFISH.
OW...
I NEED TO GO.
I DON'T WANT TO TELL THEM, THOUGH.
I'M SURE THEY'LL NOTICE I'M GONE AND WAIT FOR ME, RIGHT?

THREE MINUTES LATER
DARN IT, THEY LEFT ME!
THE PEOPLE IN MY GROUP DON'T REALIZE IT WHEN I'M GONE, EH?
HOW SAD...
STAMP
ぽん
SIGN: SUNFISH
マンボウ
HEE HEE!
HUH? WHERE'S SANO-SAN?
GASP
ハッ
I DON'T SEE HER.
OH NO, WE SHOULD GO LOOK FOR HER.
DASH
バタバタ
SANO-SAN!
HOP
ぴょん
GIGGLE GIGGLE
ケタケタ

WANT TO GO NEXT?
どこへ行く？
HOO / HOO
IT IS A TUNNEL, AFTER ALL.
FALL

S-SANO-SAN!?
OH NO!

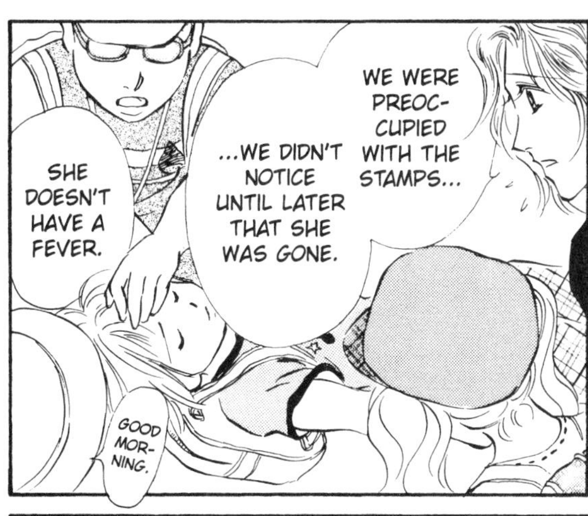
WE WERE PREOCCUPIED WITH THE STAMPS...
...WE DIDN'T NOTICE UNTIL LATER THAT SHE WAS GONE.
SHE DOESN'T HAVE A FEVER.
GOOD MORNING.

NISHIWAKI-SENSEI? THIS IS KURIBAYASHI.
SANO-SAN LOST CONSCIOUSNESS IN THE UNDERWATER WALKWAY.
PLEASE COME TO GET HER, AND BRING THE NURSE.

HOW IS SHE?
IT'S NOTHING SERIOUS.
NISHI-WAKI-SENSEI...
...DID YOU NOTICE SANO-SAN BEING ON A DIET DURING LUNCHTIME?
DIET?
OH!
SHE DID ALWAYS FINISH EARLY.
SHE HAD A LOT LEFT OVER TOO.
BUT SHE'S ONLY IN FIFTH GRADE!
I KNOW, BUT...
SANO-SAN, WE BROUGHT YOUR DINNER.
OH, THANK YOU. CAN YOU GO IN AND PLACE IT ON THE TABLE?
YES.
GASP

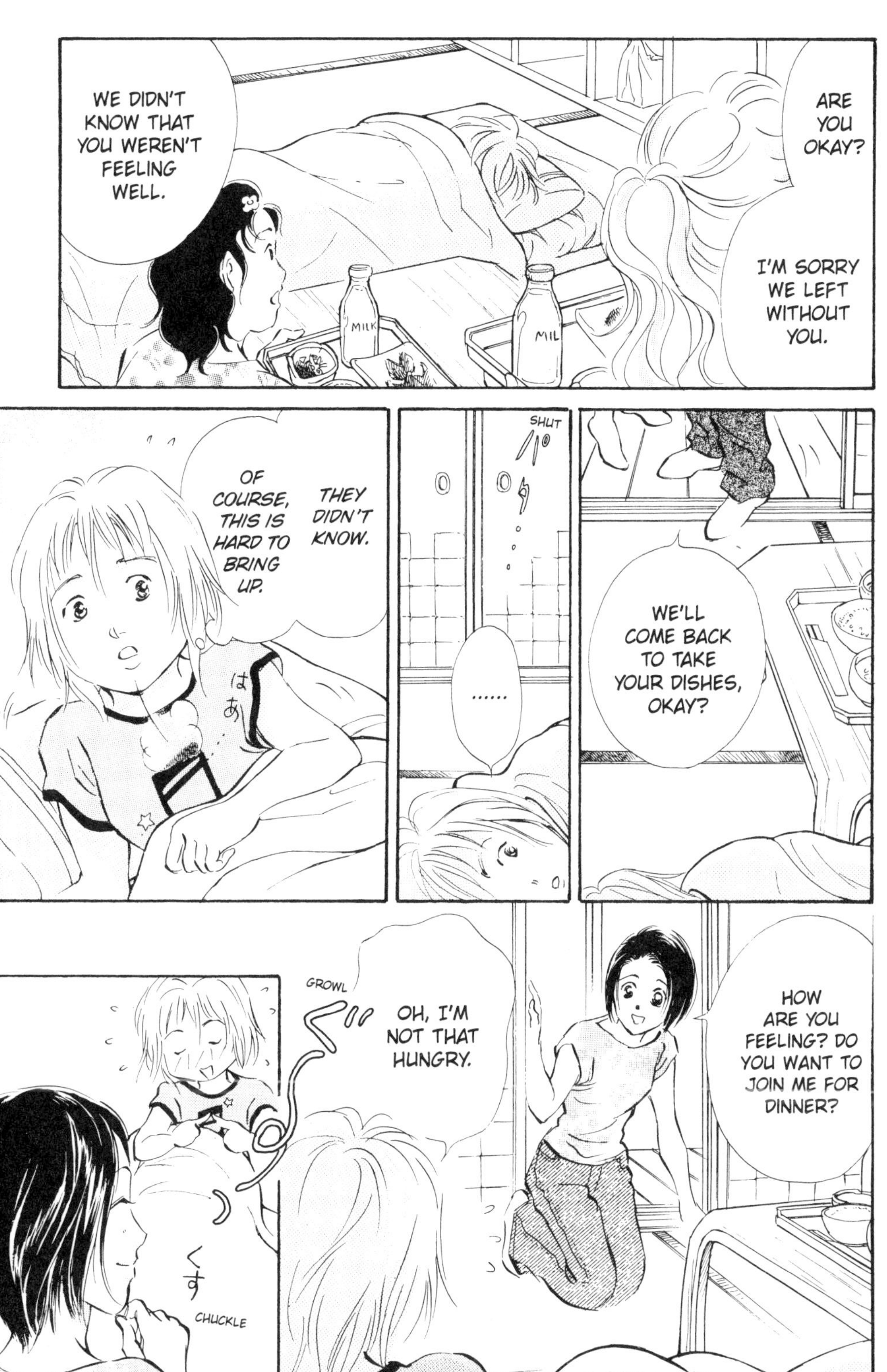
ARE YOU OKAY?
I'M SORRY WE LEFT WITHOUT YOU.
WE DIDN'T KNOW THAT YOU WEREN'T FEELING WELL.
WE'LL COME BACK TO TAKE YOUR DISHES, OKAY?
SHUT
......
THEY DIDN'T KNOW.
OF COURSE, THIS IS HARD TO BRING UP.
はあ
HOW ARE YOU FEELING? DO YOU WANT TO JOIN ME FOR DINNER?
OH, I'M NOT THAT HUNGRY.
GROWL
くす
CHUCKLE

ITADAKI-MASU.
YOU SHOULDN'T DIET WHEN YOU'RE STILL GROWING.
AND ESPECIALLY NOT DURING YOUR PERIOD.
HUH? HOW DID YOU KNOW?
I GOT MY FIRST PERIOD DURING A SCHOOL TRIP TOO.
SO I FIGURED.
DOESN'T IT MAKE YOU PANIC?
OH, SO YOU WENT THROUGH IT TOO...
DON'T WORRY, I WON'T TELL ANYONE.
OKAY...
...CAN YOU NOT TELL NISHIWAKI-SENSEI TOO?
OKAY, I PROMISE.
SO LET'S EAT.
SMILE
OKAY!
DID YOU KNOW?
WITHIN THE NEXT YEAR, YOUR BONES ARE GOING TO GET TWO TIMES BIGGER!
THAT MUCH?
THAT'S RIGHT. SO YOU NEED CALCIUM, PROTEIN, AND OTHER NUTRITION.

I DO WANT TO BE SLIM LIKE A MODEL TOO.
BUT FOR NOW, LET'S AIM FOR A BEAUTIFUL SKELETON.
PFFT!
YOU'RE FUNNY, SENSEI.
......
BUT I DO WANT TO BE PRETTY.
IF I WAS...
...I THINK SO MANY THINGS WOULD BE BETTER.
PEOPLE WOULD NOTICE WHEN I WAS MISSING.
YOU WERE LONELY, WEREN'T YOU?
BUT THE OTHER STUDENTS AREN'T PSYCHIC.
SO YOU HAVE TO TELL THEM, OR THEY WON'T KNOW.
YOU COULD'VE JUST SAID YOU JUST HAVE A WEAK BLADDER AND NEED TO GO TO THE RESTROOM. THEY WOULD'VE WAITED.

I DIDN'T REALLY THINK OF OTHER WAYS OF SAYING IT.
YEAH. I ONLY REALIZED HOW TO GET AROUND IT WHEN I WAS OLDER.
IT WAS EASIER FOR ME...
...TO TELL PEOPLE THINGS...
...WITHOUT SAYING THE THINGS I DIDN'T WANT TO SAY...
...THAN BECOMING PRETTY IN JUST ONE DAY!
HEE HEE!
YOU'RE SO FUNNY.
I WAS JUST LIKE HER WHEN I WAS IN THE FIFTH GRADE.
I WANTED TO BE WITH THE FRIENDS I GOT ALONG WITH ALL THE TIME.
SPLASH
BUT EVEN IF YOU DON'T GET ALONG WITH THEM AT FIRST...

...YOU MIGHT STILL END UP WITH A BUNCH OF FUN FRIENDS IN THE END.
IT'S A MOON JELLY. IT WON'T HURT EVEN IF IT STINGS.
JIGGLE
ぷるるん
AAAAGGHH
ぎゃあああ
SPLASH
バシャ
SPLASH
バシャ
THE OCEAN WATER IS SALTIER THAN THE SALT WATER I MAKE AT HOME.
SQUIRT
HOW'S THIS?
IT'S PRETTY.

KNOCK
KNOCK
SANO-SAN, HOW ARE YOU FEELING?
ARE YOU BORED?
WE BROUGHT YOU SEA-SHELLS.
AND A BEARD.
OH... THANKS.
IT'S PRETTY.
UGH, SHE HAD TO DO HOMEWORK.
DO YOU THINK YOU CAN MAKE IT TO TONIGHT'S BONFIRE?
YEAH, AS LONG AS I STAY QUIET.
I CAN'T TAKE A BATH BECAUSE I MIGHT FAINT AGAIN.
YOU'RE FEELING BETTER, SO YOU CAN GO BACK TO YOUR ROOM AND PRACTICE YOUR SKIT.
OH, OKAY. THANK YOU, TSUCHIYA-SENSEI.
OKAY. THEN LET'S WORK HARD ON OUR SKIT, OKAY?
WHAT'S HIKARU-KUN GOING TO DO?
I THOUGHT OF SOMETHING COOL. YOU KNOW WHAT...

HAVE YOUR SUCCESSOR TAKE OVER YOUR DUTIES BY THIS WEEK.

I ONLY HAVE A FEW DAYS.

I SHOULD DO WHAT I CAN.

SIGN: JAPANET CO.

カタ CLICK

カタ CLICK

THE LOGS THAT HAVE BEEN BUILT UP ARE WAITING TO BE LIT...

...TO BECOME THE FIRE THAT CHASES AWAY DARKNESS.

Later Elementary Years ㉓ / FIN

Later Elementary Years
Episode 24
MY SON, HIKARU AZUMA, IS AUTISTIC.
HE'S CURRENTLY ON A SCHOOL TRIP FOR FOUR DAYS AND THREE NIGHTS.
AS A MOTHER, I'M VERY WORRIED ABOUT HIM.
HIKARU ISN'T GOOD AT DEALING WITH CHANGES.
ONE NEW THING AFTER ANOTHER IS PROBABLY STRESSING HIM OUT.
BUT HE SEEMS TO BE ENJOYING IT...
...THANKS TO THE HELP OF HIS TEACHERS, FRIENDS, AND LOTS OF ENJOYABLE ACTIVITIES.

FRYING BOMBRU
MAGIC☆

SIGN: SHICHIGATSU-CHO DAY CARE CENTER

七月町保育園

OH, SO HIKARU-KUN'S FINALLY COMING BACK TOMORROW?

AREN'T YOU EAGER TO SEE THE EXPRESSION ON HIS FACE AS HE'S GETTING OFF THE BUS?

HEHE.

HE'LL PROBABLY LOOK THE SAME AS WHEN HE LEFT.

LOOK, MOMMY. A SUNSET.

YOU'RE RIGHT. IT'S PRETTY.

THERE WILL BE A BONFIRE ON THE LAST NIGHT OF THE SCHOOL TRIP.

I HOPE HIKARU HAS FUN...

IT'S PRETTY SMALL.
MATSUKO-SENSEI, WILL THIS HOLD FOR AN HOUR?
YES.
SPARKLE
I MADE IT WITH THE PROGRAM AND THE WIND IN MIND.
I SEE. AT MY LAST SCHOOL, IT WAS AS TALL AS ME.
ROAR
WE ADDED KEROSENE TO MAKE THE FIRE STRONGER...
...AND EVEN WHEN THE PROGRAM WAS OVER, IT DIDN'T GO OUT. SO WE POURED WATER OVER IT, BUT THE STEAM WAS SO INTENSE, IT WAS LIKE A VOLCANO!
SIZZLE
SIZZLE
HOW DANGER-OUS.
THAT'S LAME.

THE FIRE BECOMES BIG WHEN YOU USE CROSS-FIRE...
...ESPECIALLY WHEN YOU DOUBLE IT UP.
HEHEHEH, SINCE THIS IS FROM MY HOBBY...
...I PREPARED A TRICK AT THE END TOO.
MATSUKO-SENSEI'S BEEN CAMPING SINCE SHE WAS A STUDENT.
REALLY?
JUST WATCH. I'LL MAKE A BIG FIRE WITH THE LEAST AMOUNT OF FIREWOOD.
CANS: PINEAPPLE BOX: FOIL
IS THIS OKAY FOR THE TORCH TO LIGHT IT UP?
YES, THAT'S PERFECT.
I'M GLAD IT'S A CLEAR DAY.
THEY CAN SEE THE STARS TONIGHT.

SO GROUP 7 IS DOING THE "TANABATA" STORY?
AND TANAKA-KUN IS PLAYING VEGA?
IT'S NOT MOE-CHAN?
YES, I CONVINCED HIM TO DO IT.
THEN WE SHOULD TURN YOU INTO BEAUTIFUL VEGA.
LEAVE IT TO US!
YOU ARE DONE WIPING THE TABLES.
YOU WILL MEET GROUP 7 IN THE HALL.
EW, KANATA. WHAT'RE YOU DOING!?
DOESN'T HE LOOK PRETTY? HE LOOKS LIKE VEGA, RIGHT?

ポロ
TUG
AH!
BUT I DO LOOK LIKE VEGA.
HOW EMBARRASSING!
じ～っ
STARE
SO YOU'RE ACTUALLY HAPPY WITH IT?
SFX: GLANCE GLAMCE
チラ
チラ
サッ
GRAB
NO, HIKARU-KUN. YOU HAVE TO GIVE IT BACK.
WHAT ARE YOU DOING?
GIVE ME!
NO!
I WANT TO, BUT THIS IS SOMEONE ELSE'S, AND WE NEED IT.
OH NO, HE'S AT IT AGAIN.
THIS TIME IT'S THE OTHER SIDE.

HE PROBABLY WANTS TO HOLD IT.
IT'S SPARKLY, AND HIKARU-KUN LIKES SPARKLY THINGS.
YOU SHOULD JUST GIVE IT TO HIM.
HIKARU-KUN MIGHT GIVE UP FOR A LITTLE WHILE, BUT HE'LL TAKE IT AGAIN LATER ON.
PLEASE GIVE ME.
YOU'RE RIGHT.
YOU'LL PROBABLY LOSE AND END UP GIVING IT TO HIM.
AND IF YOU KEEP SAYING NO, HE MIGHT THROW A TANTRUM.
SFX: SHRIEK SHRIEK
UH, OKAY.
I DON'T WANT HIM TO COME GRAB IT DURING OUR SKIT.
キー キー
PLEASE GIVE ME.
HERE, HIKARU-KUN.
I PUT SPARKLY STICKERS I GOT AT THE DOLLAR STORE ON IT TOO.

......
青木
にこっ
SMILE
にこにこ
SMILE SMILE
I'M SORRY, SANO-SAN. YOU PUT A LOT OF EFFORT INTO MAKING TANAKA-KUN PRETTY.
I'LL TRY TO GET IT BACK LATER.
IT'S OKAY. HE'S SO HAPPY WITH IT.
I'LL GIVE IT TO HIKARU-KUN.
THANKS, YOU'RE A LIFE-SAVER.
OH NO... NOW HE GOT SOMETHING BY MAKING A FUSS.
WISH EY MADE SO THAT E HAS TO RETURN T IN TEN MINUTES.
I REMEMBER WORKING WITH AZUMA-SAN ON...
...HOW TO TEACH HIKARU-KUN HOW TO "GIVE BACK" THINGS.
SHE WAS DEALING WITH HIM TAKING STUFF AT HOME...
...SO WE FIRST TAUGHT HIM TO DISTINGUISH "HIS STUFF."
青木

AZUMA-SAN, I THINK THAT HIKARU-KUN TAKES HIS SISTER'S TOYS...
...AND GOES TO OTHER PEOPLE'S HOUSES TO PLAY WITH THEIR WATER...
...BECAUSE HE CAN'T DISTINGUISH BETWEEN HIMSELF AND OTHERS.
BUT AOKI-SENSEI, HE DOES UNDERSTAND WHICH ONE IS HIS FORK.
I ONCE GAVE HIM KANON'S FORK...
...AND HE CAME TO ME SAYING IT WASN'T HIS.
SO PERHAPS THERE ARE THINGS THAT HE CAN UNDERSTAND AS HIS, AND SOME HE CAN'T.
MAYBE YOU COULD TRY MAKING IT EASIER FOR HIM TO RECOGNIZE WHAT BELONGS TO WHOM.
MOUSE AND CAR: HIKARU PHONE AND MINIATURE: KANON
I DISCUSSED IT WITH MY HUSBAND, AND SINCE HIKARU COULD READ SO WELL, WE DECIDED TO WRITE NAMES ON ALL OF THE TOYS.
AS FOR PLATES, UTENSILS, AND TOOTHBRUSHES, WE BOUGHT DIFFERENT COLORS TO MATCH US INDIVIDUALLY.
GREEN FOR HIKARU, PINK FOR KANON, BLUE FOR MY HUSBAND, AND RED FOR ME.

JAR: KANON

BAG: MOM

CD: AOKI

WE TAUGHT HIM THAT ALL THINGS BELONG TO SOMEONE.

PLEASE ...

PLEASE LEND IT TO ME.

お母さん

PUNCTATUS

THIS BELONGS TO KANON.

LET'S RETURN IT.

IT'S KANON'S!

かのん

ONCE HE STARTED UNDERSTANDING THAT, WE WENT FURTHER, TEACHING HIM "LENDING" AND "RETURNING" THINGS.

THIS TOOK PATIENCE TOO.

WE TOLD HIM "UNTIL WHEN HE COULD BORROW," AND WHEN HE WAS ABLE TO RETURN THINGS ON TIME, WE PRAISED HIM.

BUT ALL OF THIS WAS POSSIBLE BECAUSE WE WERE IN A RELAXED ENVIRONMENT BACK AT HOME.

BUZZ BUZZ ザワ ザワ

I CAN'T WAIT FOR THE BONFIRE!

IT WOULD BE HARD TO APPLY HERE.

SHICHI-GATSU-CHO ELEMENTARY HAS A BONFIRE AFTER THIS.

WE NEED TO KEEP TRYING EVEN IF WE FALL BACK FROM WHAT WE TAUGHT HIM.

I JUST HOPE HIKARU-KUN ENJOYS AN ENRICHED LIFE FROM WHAT WE TEACH.

OH, AOKI-SENSEI. CAN I ASK YOU SOMETHING?
SURE.
THANK YOU.
IT'S ABOUT THE BONFIRE. IT'S A FIRST FOR HIKARU-KUN.
OH, THAT'S RIGHT.
I WAS TOLD BY AZUMA-SAN IF I SAY, "HOT, HOT!"
...HE WON'T GET NEAR THE FIRE.
BUT I JUST WANTED TO MAKE SURE.
HMM. ACCORDING TO MY EXPERIENCE...
...THERE ARE CHILDREN WHO LOSE THEMSELVES IN THE FIRE, THOSE WHO GET SCARED, AND THOSE WHO GET EXCITED.
EXCITED?
青木
THERE'S A FIRE AND PEOPLE START DANCING IN THE DARK.
IT DOESN'T MAKE SENSE TO THEM, AND IT'S A WEIRD SIGHT.

THERE'RE CHILDREN WHO CAN'T STICK AROUND FOR THE WHOLE HOUR.
WHEN I WENT TO A CAMP FOR AUTISTIC CHILDREN...
...WE ENDED THE BONFIRE IN THIRTY TO FORTY MINUTES.
OH, IS THAT SO?
IF HE CAN PARTICIPATE, I'D REALLY PRAISE HIM.
IF HIKARU-KUN CAN ENJOY IT, I'LL BE MOVED TO TEARS!
ACTUALLY, THE STUDENTS FROM GROUP 7 WANT HIKARU-KUN TO JOIN THEM IN THEIR SKIT.
!
THAT'S A BIG OBSTACLE TO GET OVER!
WELL, IT'S A VARIATION OF THE OTHER ACTIVITIES HIKARU-KUN DID IN THE PAST.
PRACTICING THE SKIT

BUT HIKARU-KUN'S BEEN WORKING HARD UP TO THIS POINT...
...SO WE DON'T WANT TO FORCE IT ON HIM.
THAT'S TRUE.
GATHER!
WE SHOULD LET THE STUDENTS DECIDE.
HIKARU-KUN'S DECIDING FOR HIMSELF TOO.
NISHI-WAKI-SENSEI.
WELL, HAVE A PLEASANT EVENING.

THIS WAY, HIKARU-KUN.
ちょん
TAP
HIKARU-KUN HAS A HARD TIME FOLLOWING YOU...
...BECAUSE YOUR HAIR'S UP IN BUNS.
AM I THAT PRETTY?
LISTEN, EVERYONE. IT'S THE LAST NIGHT OF THE TRIP.
LOOK AROUND YOU.
STAY BACK.
THE SUN HAS SET AND IT'S BECOME SO DARK YOU CAN'T SEE EACH OTHER.
LISTEN CARE-FULLY!
CREE CREE CREE
YOU CAN HEAR THE INSECT, RIGHT?
CAN YOU TELL ME WHAT INSECT THIS IS?
COCKROACH!
YEAH RIGHT, YOU DUMMY.
IT'S A CICADA.
CREE CREE
CREE

SNIFF SNIFF
SMELL THE AIR.
CAN YOU SMELL THE GRASS AND TREES?
DOESN'T IT SMELL LIKE A SUMMER NIGHT?
IT STINKS! YOU FARTED!
UGH...
I DIDN'T! IT'S NOT ME!
I BET IT WAS YOU!
DOESN'T MATTER WHO.
I'M SAYING THAT YOU SHOULD FEEL THE HUMIDITY IN THE AIR.
CREE CREE
IT'S NEGATIVE IONS.
AND YOU CAN SMELL THE PHYTONCIDE FROM THE TREES.
RUSTLE
RUSTLE
BOTH AFFECT YOUR PARA-SYMPATHETIC NERVES AND MAKE YOU RELAX.
THE ALPHA WAVES IN THE BRAIN INCREASES TOO.
CREAK CREAK
YOU'RE PRETTY SMART, YOUNG BOY!
RUSTLE
FIDGET FIDGET
OH YEAH. IT'S DARK, SO HE MUST BE SCARED.
GRIP GRIP
SHRIEK
I'M SURE THEY WON'T MIND THE PENLIGHT.
HIKARU-KUN, GORI-SENSEI IS TALKING.

DAZED
ぽえー
WHAT'S WRONG? DON'T YOU FEEL WELL?
HEY...
!?
I WONDER HOW IT FEELS LIKE TO BE IN LOVE WITH SOMEONE...
...SO MUCH THAT YOU CAN'T FOCUS ON ANYTHING ELSE?
THAT'S PROBABLY ...
...LIKE THE FEELING OF GOING TO KENDO PRACTICE WITHOUT DOING YOUR HOMEWORK.
LIKE PLAYING VIDEO GAMES WITHOUT EATING OR SLEEPING!
I SEE!
YEAH.
WRONG! WRONG! TOOOTALLY WRONG!

BUT WHY'S HE ASKING?
COULD IT BE THAT HE LIKES OOTA-SAN!?
NO WAY.
IT CAN'T BE.
IF WE DON'T DO ANYTHING, THE WORLD IS GOING TO BE ENVELOPED BY DARKNESS!
LET'S WORK TOGETHER TO SUMMON THE GOD OF FIRE!
THIS IS THE CHANT. WHEN I SAY, "AGNI, AGNI," I WANT YOU TO SAY "UHHO, UHHO."
AGNI, AGNI.
LOUDER, OR THE GOD OF FIRE WON'T HEAR YOU!
UHHO, UHHO!
HOW EMBARRASSING!
AGNI, AGNI!
UHHO UHHO!
IT'S TIME.
CLICK
AGNI, AGNI!
UHHO, UHHO!
OH, SOMEONE'S HERE.
IT'S THE GOD OF FIRE!

IT'S ONLY THE PRINCIPAL!
COLLAPSE
COLLAPSE
COLLAPSE
AND WE WORKED SO HARD TO CHANT FOR HIM!!
THE GOD OF FIRE HAS ARRIVED.
FIRE! BURN BURN BURN BURN!
I SEE.
WE WOULD LIKE TO TALK TO HIM, BUT SINCE HE SPEAKS FIRE LANGUAGE...
...I WILL TRANSLATE.
HELLO, STUDENTS OF SHICHI-GATSU-CHO ELEMENTARY.
I AM THE GOD OF NOKOGIRI MOUNTAIN.

I WILL NOW TALK ABOUT FIRE.
I'M HAPPY TO BE ABLE TO PARTICIPATE IN YOUR BONFIRE.
FIRE!
BURN BURN, ROAR!
FIRE IS IMPORTANT TO HUMAN CIVILIZA-TION.
THE DISCOVERY OF FIRE ALLOWED HUMANS TO PROGRESS.
HUMANS USE FIRE TO GET AWAY FROM THE COLD AND TO COOK.
HUMANS ALSO USE IT TO MAKE VARIOUS THINGS.
BUT FIRE CAN BE A DANGEROUS THING.
FIRES AT HOME AND FIRES FROM WAR CAN WIPE OUT HUMAN LIVES IN AN INSTANT.
BURN FIRE!
PLEASE USE FIRE FOR HAPPINESS AND PEACE.
BURN!
BURN, BURN.

NOW THE GOD OF FIRE WILL GIVE US A GIFT.
FIRE CHILDREN, COME UP.
FIRST, THIS IS THE FIRE OF FRIENDSHIP.
VOOSH
NEXT IS THE FIRE OF COOPERATION.
VOOSH
AND LAST IS THE FIRE OF HOPE.
LET'S BRING THE THREE FIRES TOGETHER AS ONE.
WHOA!
THE FIRE IS CLIMBING.

GOOD JOB BEING PATIENT. IT'LL GET BRIGHT SOON.
POOF
SNAP SNAP
THE NEWBORN FIRE IS STILL SMALL.
LET'S CHANT, "BURN, BURN" TO MAKE THE FIRE BIGGER.
CRACKLE CRACKLE
BURN~
BURN~
FIRE, PLEASE BURN~

CLICK
OH, WAIT, HIKARU-KUN.
STRIDE STRIDE
STRIDE
BLOCK
IT'S HOT, HOT. HOT, HOT.
HOT, HOT.
PAT PAT
LET'S STAY HERE AND WATCH.
HOT. HOT.
KURI-BAYASHI-SENSEI SENT ME AN E-MAIL LATER...
...AND TOLD ME THAT EVEN THOUGH HE WAS UPSET, HIKARU STAYED BEHIND THE LINE.
SHRIEK
HOT. HOT.
I'M SURE HE WANTED TO SEE THE FIRE UP CLOSE.
BUT HE PUT UP WITH IT.

HIKARU-KUN, IT'S ALMOST TIME FOR OUR SKIT.
WE'RE DOING "TANA-BATA."
HE WON'T MOVE AT ALL.
LET'S HOLD HANDS AND MAKE THE MILKY WAY.
HELP ME!
OH NO.
NOBUAKI, YOU CAN'T FORCE HIM. LET'S JUST GO.
HE PROB-ABLY WANTS TO WATCH THE FIRE.
THAT'S FINE.
NEXT UP IS GROUP 7, "TANABATA STORY."
THEN WE'LL DO IT WITH JUST US.
LET'S GO.
CHILDREN KNOW WHEN TO QUIT, DON'T THEY?
CHUCKLE
WELL, THEY CAN'T FORCE HIM IF HE YELLS, "HELP ME."

HERE YOU GO. CAN YOU READ THE LINES?
YES.
ON THE EDGE OF THE MILKY WAY, THERE WAS A BEAUTIFUL SEAMSTRESS NAMED VEGA.
KERCHUNK CHUNK KERCHUNK.
SHE WORKED HARD EVERY DAY TO WEAVE...
...AND MADE BEAUTIFUL, FIVE-COLORED FABRIC.
EEK, TANAKA-KUN IS DRESSED AS A GIRL!
VEGA, WHY DON'T YOU REST AND GO OUT SOMETIME?
NO THANK YOU, FATHER.
I LOVE TO WEAVE.
THE GUY AND THE GIRL ARE SWITCHED!
ギャハハハ
AHAHAHA
パッ
BUT THEY FIT THE ROLES WELL.
SFX: PFFT

CONGRATU-LATIONS!
THE FATHER WAS CONCERNED ...
...SO HE MARRIED HIS DAUGHTER OFF TO A CATTLEMAN NAMED ALTAIR, WHO LIVED ON THE WEST SIDE OF THE MILKY WAY.
ALTAIR WON'T GIVE ME ANY FOOD!
I'VE BECOME SO SKINNY.
MACK, MACK, MACK~
MISS MARY MACK, MACK, MACK~
BUT THEN THEY STARTED PLAYING EVERYDAY...
SUPER-FAST MARY MACK
COME ON IN.
SINCE VEGA WON'T MAKE FABRIC, MY CLOTHES ARE WORN OUT.
YOU'RE GOING TOO FAST!
WHIP
WHIP
STAR CHILDREN, KEEP THESE TWO APART!
YOU FOOLISH COUPLE!
わらわらわら
WHOOSH
WHOOSH
WHOOSH

ALTAIR-SAMA!!
WHOA
I FEEL SO BAD FOR THEM.
IF YOU PROMISE TO WORK HARD...
...THEN I'LL LET YOU MEET HIM ONCE A YEAR ON JULY 7TH.
OKAY. THEN I'LL WORK HARD FOR THAT DAY.
ME TOO.
YOU RECOVER FAST.
KERCHUNK CHUNK KERCHUNK.
IF IT RAINS ON JULY 7TH...
...BIRDS WILL SPREAD THEIR WINGS AND MAKE A BRIDGE OVER THE MILKY WAY.

CHEER
わあ
CLAP CLAP
パチパチ
I SEE...
SO IT'S A TALE TO TEACH THE KIDS TO BE MODERATE IN WHAT THEY DO.
AFTER THE SKIT IS DANCE TIME.
THE BONFIRE HAS GOTTEN BIG. JUST IN TIME FOR THE FINALE.
YOU DO THE HOKEY-POKEY...
THIS IS EMBAR-RASSING!
BUT YOU'RE AWFULLY INTO IT.
YOU PUT YOUR LEFT HAND IN~
YOU PUT YOUR BACKSIDE IN~
AHAHAHA
ぎゃははは

NEXT IS THE MOUSE MARCH!
HEY, KANATA.
GOT IT.
MOUSE, MOUSE, MOUSE.
OUR CITY HERO IS~
HIKARU WASN'T INTERESTED IN THE GAMES OR SKIT...
...BUT HE JOINED IN ON THIS DANCE WITHOUT MUCH RESISTANCE.
MOUSE~ MOUSE~
THIS MOUSE MARCH IS A DANCE HIKARU'S BEEN DANCING SINCE 1ST GRADE.
MOUSE~ MOUSE~
OH.
THE THREE FIRES WE RECEIVED FROM THE GOD OF THE MOUNTAINS BECAME...
...ONE BIG FIRE.
WE SAT AROUND THE FIRE AND ENJOYED IT.
TOMORROW WE SAY GOODBYE TO NOKOGIRI HOUSE.

LOOK AT THE STARS ABOVE!
LOOK UP AT THE SKY, EVERYONE.
WOW, I'VE NEVER SEEN THE MILKY WAY BEFORE!
OUR TRIP WENT BY SO FAST.
WE WENT HIKING, SWIMMING...
LET'S TAKE A MOMENT TO REFLECT ON THE TIME WE SPENT HERE.
STARE
THE FIRE IS DYING DOWN JUST FINE. I COULD MAKE A GOOD ONE.
WHAT IS SHE DOING? THIS LOOKS MORE INTEREST-ING.
IT'S SO HOT!
MY FORE-HEAD IS BURNING!
I'M READY, GORI-SENSEI.
LOOK!
A STAR FELL FROM THE SKY?
HUH? WHERE?

OVER HERE!
WOW, IT'S A STAR!
SWEET ...
THAT'S JUST THE LEFTOVER FIREWOOD SHAPED LIKE A STAR.
TEARY TEARY
WE KNOW. CAN YOU JUST SHUT UP!?
IT'S PRETTY.

A STAR.
TUG
OH...
HIKARU-KUN...
THAT'S RIGHT. IT'S THE SAME AS YOUR SHIRT!
NOBUAKI ALWAYS WEARS STARS.
HIKARU-KUN LIKES SIGNS AND SYMBOLS, SO HE KNOWS THAT.
REALLY? YOU THINK SO?
SFX: TUG TUG

IF THAT'S THE CASE, I'D BE SO HAPPY.
WE'RE GOING TO EAT MARSH-MALLOWS!
GET THEM FROM THE VOLUNTEER STUDENTS.
CHEER
HIKARU'S FIRST BONFIRE WAS A FASCINATING ONE.
IT SMELLS SO GOOD! ♡
IT'S DARK, NOISY, AND MAKES NO SENSE...
...BUT HE RECOGNIZED THE MOUSE MARCH.
I'M GLAD HIKARU-KUN DIDN'T HAVE A STRESSFUL TRIP HERE.

THE TASTY MARSHMALLOWS FINISHED UP THE NIGHT.
IT'S HOT!
MUNCH MUNCH
はふはふ
THANK YOU, NOBUAKI-KUN.
AND EVERYONE ELSE...
I'M HOME!
HI. BATH IS READY.
THANKS. IT WAS SO BUSY WITH HANDING OVER DUTIES AND SAYING GOODBYE TO EVERYONE.
TOMORROW'S MY LAST DAY AT MY CURRENT DEPARTMENT.
SO IT'S GOING TO BE MUCH BUSIER.

IT'S IMPOSSIBLE TO FINISH EVERYTHING IN TWO DAYS.
HE'S ACCOMPLISHED SO MUCH IN THE COMPANY, YET HE WAS DEMOTED.
HE'S GOING TO START WORKING IN A SMALL WAREHOUSE IN KOSHIKAWA NEXT WEEK.
MASATO ...
I HEARD THE PEOPLE TRANSFERRED THERE QUIT IN A FEW WEEKS.
I KNOW HOW MEAN THAT USUI-SAN IS, BECAUSE I HAD TO DEAL WITH HIM WHEN I WORKED AT JAPANET.
WHAT DO YOU WANT? I DON'T NEED THAT ANYMORE.
WHAT? BUT HE TOLD ME TO PREPARE IT AT THE LAST MINUTE.
NOW HE'S PICKING ON MASATO...
WHAT'S THIS? A BUNCH OF DISKS?
WHY DID HE BRING IT HOME?

IS HE GOING TO TAKE THIS TO A DIFFERENT COMPANY!?
HUH?
TAP TAP
SACHIKO, ARE YOU ACCUSING ME OF SOMETHING?
ACTUALLY, I WAS...
I MAY HAVE BAD BOSSES...
...BUT I DON'T HATE THE COMPANY.
I HAVE SOMETHING ON MY MIND.
YOU MIGHT WORRY, BUT I WANT YOU TO JUST BELIEVE IN ME FOR NOW.
OH, OKAY.
I'M SORRY.
KANON IS ALREADY SLEEPING?
I HAVEN'T SEEN HER MUCH LATELY.
HEE HEE.
YOU COULD SEE HER ON THE WEEKEND.
AND HIKARU'S COMING BACK TOMORROW!

IT HURTS.
HUH?
OH, YOU GOT SUNBURNED AND IT'S PEELING.
DON'T TOUCH IT.
HOLD ON. ONCE I FINISH THIS...
HE'S GONE!
I FORGOT HIKARU-KUN CAN'T "HOLD ON!"

HE CAME TO SEE HIMSELF IN THE MIRROR.
PANT
ハア
PANT
ハア
OH NO, YOU'VE TOUCHED IT SO MUCH IT'S BLEEDING.
STOP IT, HIKARU-KUN.
OH, I KNOW.
PAPER: X TOUCH NOSE. O NURSE.
X キズをさわる
○ 保健の先生
OKAY, THE MEDICINE IS ON.
LET'S PUT THE BAND-AID ON.
STICK
ペタ
にこにこ
SMILE SMILE

THANK YOU SO MUCH, TSUCHIYA-SENSEI.
NO PROBLEM.
SIGH
SMILE SMILE
にこにこ
HIKARU-KUN CALMS DOWN...
...WHEN YOU PUT A BAND-AID ON HIM.
HE MIGHT START PEELING AGAIN, SO LET'S KEEP THE BAND-AID ON FOR A WHILE.
Cut a little shorter.
TSUCHIYA-SENSEI, IS THIS OKAY?
THANK YOU. CAN YOU PUT THE SHEETS IN THE CART OUTSIDE?
WHO ARE THOSE STUDENTS?
I THINK THEY'RE HOMESICK.
THEY GET FEVERS OR STOMACHACHES...
...BUT ONCE THEY GET ON THE BUS AND ARE A FEW MINUTES AWAY FROM HOME, THEY'LL FEEL BETTER.
HAHA...

Every-one's here?
Then off we go!
GOODBYE, NOKOGIRI HOUSE!
BYE-BYE!
WE'LL PLAY BY THE ROCKS TODAY.
WOW, HE CAN GIVE THE PEACE SIGN.
I GUESS HE LEARNED IT DURING THE TRIP.
I CAN DO THE PEACE SIGN TOO.

IT'S SO MUCH FUN LOOKING AT THE WAVES.
WE CAN SPEND IT ANY WAY WE WANT.
BUT SUMMER VACATION IS WAITING FOR US! ♡
THE TRIP WAS SO FUN. I DON'T WANT TO GO HOME.
Dr. Ph.JL
YOU'RE SO BUSY.
AFTER THAT, I HAVE THEATRE WORK.
YEAH, I HAVE THE SUMMER CONCERT COMING UP, SO I HAVE TO REHEARSE FOR THAT.
KANATA, DO YOU HAVE WORK WAITING FOR YOU AT HOME?

I CAN'T PLAY WHEN I WANT TO.
SO I WAS THINKING OF QUITTING...
...BUT I CHANGED MY MIND. I WANT TO CONTINUE ACTING.
IT'S FUN TO BECOME SOMEONE ELSE.
THAT'S TRUE. YOU COULD EVEN BECOME A GIRL IN LOVE.
YEAH. EVERYONE LAUGHED AT ME, THOUGH.
I THINK THAT'S FINE!
THE VEGA YOU PLAYED IS PROBABLY GOING TO BE ONE OF YOUR BEST!
MY BEST...
I THINK YOU'RE GOING TO BECOME A GREAT ACTOR.
SANO-SAN...
I'M GOOD AT PREDICTING THOSE KINDS OF THINGS.

I CAN'T BELIEVE I SAID THAT.
OH... THANKS.
WOW, DID YOU SEE THAT, NISHIWAKI-SENSEI?
YEAH.
BEFORE, SHE'D NEVER SPEAK UP LIKE THAT WITHOUT HER FRIENDS AROUND.
SHE'S GOTTEN MORE CONFIDENT.
THESE PAST FOUR DAYS, I'VE BEEN THINKING...
...THE WAY CHILDREN TRY TO OVERCOME OBSTACLES IS SO CUTE.
SPLASH
I WANT TO WATCH OVER THEM AND CHEER THEM ON FOREVER.
'COS THEY'RE SO DARNED CUTE.
SENSEI...
OH, THERE'S THE BUS.
PHEW, I'M GLAD I RAN HERE AFTER MY WORK.
NOBUAKI!
I ♡ DOG

THE CHILDREN CAME OFF THE BUS WITH TIRED BUT SATISFIED FACES.
貸切
HE LOOKS MORE MATURE.
YOU THINK?
HIKARU ...
THE TRIP WENT BY SO QUICKLY.
WELCOME BACK, HIKARU.
IT WAS A LITTLE AWKWARD SEEING HIM AGAIN.

Later Elementary Years ㉔ / FIN

What is Autism?

by Tokio Uchiyama (Director, Yokohama Developmental Clinic; Assistant Professor, Otsuma Women's University)

Autism is considered a developmental disability. But what does that mean? The most commonly recognized facts about autism are that people are born with it, the symptoms appear during the developmental period, and it is a life-long disability. The word "autism" may bring to mind a person who closes him or herself off from the world as if in a shell, but autism is not about introverted or withdrawn children. It is not a psychological disability caused by the family environment or the manner in which the child is raised; rather, the root of the problem lies in a malfunction of the brain.

How do autistic children behave?

Autistic people experience what they see, what they hear, what they touch, and what they taste differently from most people. It is not that they cannot see or hear. They can see objects and hear sounds, but what they focus on is a little different from the norm. Because of this, they do not like to play with friends, make conversation, or guess what others are thinking.

All autistic people have a developmental disorder in three areas. These are: 1.) social skills, 2.) communication, and 3.) insistency.

The disorder as manifested in the realm of social skills is revealed from their lack of interest in other people and the way in which they interact with others. Autistic children prefer playing alone over playing with their peers. Even if they show interest in other children, they have a difficult time interacting with them; most of the time, they play by following along or copying the others. This lack of social skills can be seen even before the autistic child reaches one year of age. For example, the child may not reach out to the mother when she comes over or, when held, may turn away from her. Also indicative of this characteristic, autistic children often do not smile when played with. Most children twelve months or older have a tendency to point at what interests them and turn to smile to their mother. Autistic children, on the other hand, are slow to develop interests in other objects and people.

Autism also manifests itself in the realm of communication. Autistic children tend to be slow in linguistic development. Usually, one-year-old children will say "doggie" or "mommy." But autistic children will not say anything with meaning up through the first one-and-a-half years. Even if they do say something, it is a mere repetition of what they have heard a parent or a television commercial say. They will repeat words and phrases to themselves as though they are having a private conversation. Children with less severe cases of the disability may repeat the same things or ask what they already know. Not only do they have a speech disorder, but they also have a difficult time understanding what adults say. For example, if you tell them to "turn off the television and close the curtains," they may not understand because there are two instructions which confuse them. Autistic children also tend to not understand body language, including gestures and expressions.

Though they may have trouble with the gestures of others, autistic children tend to do many of their own repetitive gestures, such as waving their hand, twirling around, or rocking back and forth. This is the result of the third area affected by the disorder–insistency. For example, they wish to take the same route when going to kindergarten, wear clothes of the same color, or make sure all the doors are closed. When they are older, they may always read the train timetable or spend all day writing elevator model numbers in a notebook. They tend to show interest in things most kids would not. Furthermore, most autistic children have a hard time adjusting to change. If the school schedule changes or their recess is cut short, they struggle with it more than we can imagine.

In addition to the three areas mentioned above, they may also be sensitive to sound or never forget something they are taught once.

For autistic children, the world may be full of things they cannot comprehend. It is important for surrounding adults to understand the disability and make an effort to lessen their pain as much as possible so that they may live their lives comfortably.

My "With the Light..."
by Mariko Abe (Lawyer, Yuuki Law Office)

Hello, Pon-suke

August 1992. I was walking slowly on the bridge that goes over the Nakatsu River in Morioka City, Iwate prefecture. My contractions had begun earlier that morning, and I was walking to the nearest hospital to give birth.

My marriage was in its fourth year, and I was thirty years old. I'd been anticipating this first child dearly. I had struggled through a long period of infertility, and I knew that bearing a child was not everything to me as a woman. But when the child chose to reside in my womb and be born of me, I thought life overwhelmingly mysterious then. I was truly happy that I was going to be a mother.

The view from the bridge was amazing that day. The river, the green trees, the green grass. . . they were all moving beautifully. The contrast between the blue sky and the white clouds was bright. In the distance, the ridges of the Iwate Mountains were smooth, as though an ancient god were sitting there. I thought I would never forget this view. I decided that I would tell my soon-to-be-born child about how beautiful the world was and that "the day you were born, I was this happy." I gazed at that postcard-perfect view for a long time.

I went into the hospital in high spirits. When I heard my baby cry for the first time, I felt as if I wanted to thank everything that existed in the world. My baby was small and helpless. This was my first time meeting my son, Pon-suke.

Days of Struggle

Raising Pon-suke was not easy at all. This was because Pon-suke had a disability. I was told as much when he was two years and eight months old. He was autistic and his case was so severe that even the doctor would say, "This is pretty bad," to my face. Pon-suke cried day and night, and, if I let go of him even for a split-second, he would run off. I tried to teach him things, but he wouldn't even look my way. Though I talked to him until my voice grew hoarse, all Pon-suke would say back to me were commercial phrases and advertisement jingles. He was a picky eater, and, no matter how much effort I put into making his food, he would clam up and throw it on the ground. In reaction to adverse stimulation, Pon-suke would throw tantrums and scream.

Our house was a mess, and so were my husband and I. I never knew that people could cry out of physical fatigue. Of course, I did my best to understand my child's disability and make things better for him by reading books. But such situations do not improve in one night. My feelings were hurt every time my attempts to help Pon-suke failed; I felt betrayed and my once logical and kind personality faded. Maybe I took my frustration out on Pon-suke at that time. Looking back, I casually threw hurtful words at him. I spanked him almost to the point of abuse. During those times, I blamed Pon-suke for everything wrong in my life and tried to justify my actions.

The people around me tried to comfort me by saying things like, "He'll probably be able to talk when he's XX years old. My friend's child turned normal by XX years old when my friend tried really hard." But Pon-suke turned XX years old, and still he didn't improve. People would also say, "As long as he has his wits about him, he'll be fine," or "Why don't you focus on developing his artistic abilities?" But in Pon-suke's case, even those expectations were in vain.

People would point and whisper at day care events, "Oh, he's the one with the disability." I maintained a resolute attitude as a mother, but as I watched Pon-suke get out of line and run wild with the staff chasing after him, I was hurt and my nonchalant demeanor rejected the sympathy proffered by those around me. I was isolated and self-loathing, and I shut out everyone around me. I hit bottom when Pon-suke was five years old.

When I Saw the "Light"

The methods I learned from the facilities for those with learning disabilities saved me and my family. We learned to make visual aids that let Pon-suke know when activities began and ended, and we gave him a schedule that listed the day's activities in advance. Once we started implementing these methods, Pon-suke slowly started to improve. He was able to follow society's rules. And with Pon-suke's improvement, the family situation improved too. We were able to monitor our child's slow growth step by step and encouraged him. We were happy as parents to be able to do that. "We should do it again tomorrow," we'd say. Repeating days like this, I was able to regain my confidence as a mother.

It was also important to take a step back from raising a family by going out into society to regain my self-respect. While I was raising Pon-suke, I passed the bar and became a lawyer, engaging myself in supporting the disabled.

As a lawyer, I handled many cases of abuse. At the root of every case, much like my own, lay the frustration of the parents at what they perceived to be the betrayal of their love and expectations by their disabled children. I could understand it, but I also had to made sure that their actions were deemed unforgivable. I drilled infringement of children's rights into my head. And I vowed never to hurt Pon-suke again.

I started to think that my actions would not only help Pon-suke, but also help other children with the same disability. I believed that even if my time with Pon-suke would lessen, it would be well worth it.

It wasn't just me. There were many parents who regained self-respect by engaging in activities for their children, and often their child's disability was the force behind their fulfilling lives. If their children had not been disabled, they wouldn't have had to look so far into the future. But now, they work hard for their children's future–the near future of five years on and the far-flung future ten or more years ahead. Every time I see the people working hard throughout this country, I am assured that Pon-suke will be fine in the future.

Working Toward a Normal Life

The biggest goal of disability facilities is to create a society where the disabled can work where they live and lead a normal life. Because of the recession, the lack of funding is a serious problem, so the road to achieving that goal will be a long one. Also, the definition of a "normal life" also differs among people. Some believe in a society where a disabled individual can be him or herself, surrounded by people who understand their disability and can support them fully. On the other hand, some believe that an attitude which requires sacrifice and accommodation on society's part would impede the disabled person's growth and lead to lack of acceptance. The difference in these views is great; the struggle continues.

A parent does not know how long she can live with her child. But if I can be with Pon-suke when that goal is achieved, I would like to tell him, "I gave birth to you in a place with the most beautiful view of Morioka City. You can lead a happy life. I'm very glad I had you." And I would like him to relish his happiness even after I'm gone. . . hopefully in an environment surrounded by his supporters and loved ones.

My Son Is a Senior in College
by Masako Suzuki

My son is a senior in college, but he was diagnosed with autism when he was a child. He is able to attend college, so he does have high intelligence in certain areas (you call this high-functioning autism), but he also has the three characteristics of autism just like Hikaru-kun, which are "lack of social skills," "lack of communication skills," and "lack of imaginative skills." They have become less noticeable with age, but he continues to struggle with them.

I'd first like to talk about his lack of social skills. My son cannot act in a way that is most appropriate for the situation. He likes people but cannot interact with them well. Therefore, he does not have friends at college. He's better now, but up until junior high, he used to start talking to people he'd just met about the origins of geographical names. This was one of the things he was particularly interested in. He also used to go into different rooms of a house he was visiting and pull out maps from the bookshelves. There were many instances where little incidents like these would occur if the people around him were unaware of his disability.

In later elementary school years and junior high, I had him placed in the Special Education class so that others would understand his characteristics. Even when he entered high school and the college he currently attends, I made an effort to explain his disability to the school. I let them know how important it was for them to clarify rules to him and told them he was not defying their instructions out of disobedience, but rather because he could not understand them.

My son's lack of communication skills means that he does not understand abstract expressions or implications. I always come across times when I think, "That didn't make sense," when I talk to him. Even as I write this, he came to me and said, "I slept well." But then he continued, "But I had a hard time sleeping an hour ago." This gap in communication is not harmful, but once he starts interacting with others, it becomes problematic.

Until recently, my son was working part-time in a supermarket. He was able to stay on the job because his supervisors knew about his disability. But once they were gone, my son faced harsh criticism. Once, he was told to "look carefully" at his surroundings and he took the instructions literally. As he was looking around, he was scolded for standing around doing nothing. Another time, he was told to put away the empty pallets, which he did. But on a different occasion, he was told to not put them away. He came home despondent, saying that he was scolded for not making judgments according to the situation. When the poor economy hit his workplace, he was laid off. He had to stop working at the supermarket where he'd worked for three years.

His lack of imaginative skills is the most serious of his autistic characteristics. He cannot imagine a whole situation from partial information. He cannot understand what part of the whole he is looking at, or what his actions and the actions of others mean. Of course, his mind and actions are not flexible, so he cannot plan on his own. His interests become very narrow, and this is related to his particularity about certain things.

That is why this third characteristic is called "lack of flexibility in thought and action" or "particularity." My son has a particular interest in geographical names, cars, trains, countries, and weather predictions. And because he has good memory, he received good grades in elementary school, junior high, and high school. In college, he could write essays on specific topics such as "The State of Iraq." But on the other hand, if he was given a broad theme, such as "Genders Within Different Regions," he was unable to write on the topic. He would write, "Because women use their bodies, they live longer, which is why there are many old ladies in different regions," and would need "translation" support from me.

Our Experience in Britain

I found out that my son was autistic when he was in the third grade. We were in Britain at the time. Right after he transferred into a local school, he caused trouble, which led us to a series of tests and exams. He was placed in a special class for autistic students. Diagnoses and assessments involved a team that was made up of a pediatrician, a psychologist, an occupational therapist (OT), and a speech therapist (ST). The team spent two whole days thoroughly analyzing my son. My husband and I went into detail about his growth and development history, and we were present throughout the process. That is how we both understood the situation our son was in. This was our starting point in learning the different ways we could help and support our son.

The difference between the situation for autistics in Japan versus Britain is how many people get involved with you. In Britain, there are many specialists from various fields supporting one autistic person. There is a long history of social welfare, and there is a spirit of leaving no autistic child behind. The support is not aggressive, but it is not taken lightly either. There is research and practice behind their methods.

The school my son attended in Britain had many social workers coming and going. They would head to the quarters prepared by the school and hold many events to support the leisure time of the autistic students. Included in those events were "Youth Clubs" where they had woodworking, summer camps, and more. There was also an autism specialist/coordinator who made the interactions between communities go smoothly. At the school itself, when my son did an activity well, he would be rewarded with a chance to draw a city map in the break room or go to the mapped area by bicycle to confirm the streets. The teachers coming into the break room would be surprised at the detailed map he spent many weeks on and would praise him and cheer him on. The school was such a fun place for both my son and I. It made me happy that my son was popular and not regarded as a nuisance.

Understanding Autism

I really didn't expect this would happen at the time, but this experience got me learning about autism and supporting it as a lifework. (I'm sure the other supporting parents didn't expect this either). I started to translate books on autism, interpret for British research trips, and lend a hand to foreign specialists when they visited Japan. I learned many things through this process.

When I look at my son, I now notice that the three autistic characteristics are not stand-alone disorders but are intertwined. Someone once said it's a struggle because it is not three times as much, but to the power of three. Things we can do easily can't be processed by my son, and his brain seems to be taking different routes to process the information, hence his slow reactions or confusion. You might even think, "Huh? You can't even understand this?"

Recently, my son's acquaintances told him that he "has no common sense." Upon hearing this, my son went to buy a book quizzing the reader on "common sense" as an aid for young adults preparing to work in the real world. He is currently studying current events, proverbs, and honorifics every day. Because he wants to be accepted by his peers, he watches programs and sports on TV to "study." But even still, his wording doesn't always come out right and he gets ignored or laughed at. In the worst cases, he gets in a panic about getting criticized and breaks a glass. When this happens, his processing capability escapes from him too. It is necessary for the people surrounding him to understand and support his autism at times like these.

Supporting Autism

For autistic children whose disability affects their everyday life so much, they need as much support from others as possible. Parents need to comprehend the situation of their child. To do this, a thorough diagnosis is needed. The child's school must to understand and support the child. And when the child goes out into the real world, there needs to be a system that supports his or her way of life.

For people with autism like my son, this world which prioritizes efficiency is a difficult place to live. But look on the bright side; the adults who know my son say he is kind and innocent, that he is a good person who would never betray anyone. I think a brighter future is in store for all of us if we create a world where autistic people can live comfortably. It would enrich our lives as well.

I Love This School: The Special School Parent and Child Experienced by Masako Suzuki (published November 1993 by Budou-sha, Tel. 03-3234-1450)

Translation Notes

Golden Week, page 14

Golden Week is another name for the period of time from April 29 to May 5 in Japan. Because four national holidays occur during this period of time, many Japanese people take the week off.

Vultan Alien, page 92

Vultan Alien is a monster from the special effects show *Ultraman*. He has scissors for hands.

Love-love Umbrella, page 154

The doodle you see on the wall here is a love-love umbrella, which is the Japanese equivalent of drawing a heart and putting your and your beloved's initials inside.

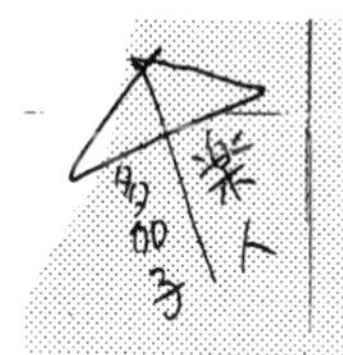

Takoyaki, page 173

Takoyaki is a grilled ball with a piece of octopus in the middle. It is made on a grill shaped in half-circles. You whisk some flour, water, and egg and pour it into the hot grill. You then put a piece of octopus, some cut up green onion and grill for a bit. The hardest part is flipping over the mix to make a ball. You use a takoyaki pick, which is similar to an ice pick but thinner. It is a popular stall item at festivals, where Hikaru is pictured on the splash page.

Udon, page 177

Udon is a white, thick noodle. Like porridge, it is a popular dish to make when one is sick because the broth is soothing and warms up the body and also because the ***udon*** noodles are easy to digest. Of course, people like to eat it even when they are not sick. Among the types of ***udon*** from different regions in Japan, those from Sanuki are known to taste the best.

Akiko nee-san (big sister Akiko), page 249

Reference to *Kyojin no Hoshi*, literally "Star of the Giants," a classic sports manga featuring a boy named Hyuma going through rigorous training to become a professional baseball star like his father. ***Akiko*** is Hyuma's kind and caring older sister and is like a mother to the motherless boy. She supports Hyuma and is often depicted as watching over him from behind the scenes. Sachiko is doing something similar to Hikaru in this scene, hence the comparison to ***Akiko nee-san***.

Koshihikari rice, page 290

Koshihikari is a brand of rice made in the Niigata prefecture of Japan. Relatively expensive, this rice is the most popular brand of rice and is also considered the most delicious. The latter part of the brand name– *hikari*–means "light" or "to shine"; ***Koshihikari*** rice grains do actually shine when cooked.

Cell phone e-mail addresses, page 298

In Japan, text messaging is called e-mailing, and each cell phone uses a specific e-mail address instead of their cell phone numbers.

Pop idol pictures in Harajuku, page 300

Harajuku is the place to buy candid and posed pictures of pop idols. The stores are usually swamped with young teenagers buying pictures of their favorite stars.

Mamakari, page 310

Mamakari is another name for *sappa*, which are herrings. Tomoya-kun is playing with the words of switching out "mama" with "papa."

Sato Family Dinner Table, page 315

This is a parody of an actual show in Japan called the *Ito Family Dinner Table*. It was a show that featured many household tricks collected from viewer postcards and e-mails. The show ran from October 1997 to March 2007.

Three Dango Sisters, page 328

Mr. Nishiwaki is making a reference to **"Three Dango Brothers,"** a famous song that was popular in Japan in 1999.

Waterboys, page 334

Mr. Kuribayashi is looking at Kanata and Nobuaki and making a reference to ***Waterboys***, a Japanese film about a high school synchronized swimming team comprised of boys. Featuring a number of up-and-coming pop idols, the film was a huge hit in Japan, and spawned a TV series as well.

Nokogiri House, page 335

Nokogiri is the Japanese word for "saw." Tomoya-kun makes the connection with another tool, a hammer.

Fukujinzuke, page 336

Fukujinzuke are pickled vegetables most commonly served with Japanese curry. They are usually dyed red to add color. ***Fukujinzuke*** includes vegetables such as daikon radish, eggplants, and cucumbers that are finely chopped and pickled in a mixture of soy sauce, sugar, and mirin (rice wine). They are slightly sweet in flavor.

Omurice, page 381

Omurice is a Japanese dish that is comprised of stir-fried rice inside a folded-over egg omelette. The stir-fry inside includes rice, chicken, vegetables, and it is flavored with ketchup or demiglace sauce. After enfolding the rice with the egg, it is topped again with ketchup or sauce.

Kendo, page 398

A sport similar to fencing. People use bamboo swords and wear protective gear in practice.

Ashtray, page 424

Portable ashtrays are available in Japan for smokers to carry around. They come in different shapes and sizes. The one this man is holding is a pouch type that opens if you pinch the sides.

Tanabata, page 469

Tanabata is a festival held annually on July 7. It is to celebrate the meeting of the stars Vega and Altair, who are separated by the Milky Way. They are allowed to meet once a year on July 7.

Autism, page 508

In Japanese, the word for ***autism*** is written literally as "self-closing syndrome" or "cloistered syndrome." For this reason, many in Japan mistake the disorder as being a personality disorder.

Other Books of Interest from
Hachette Book Group USA

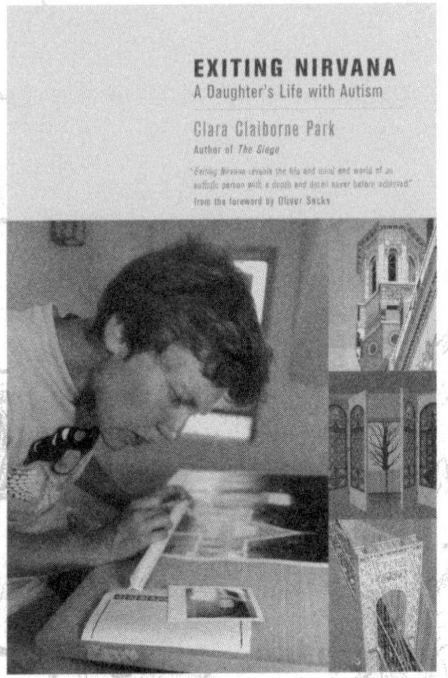

EXITING NIRVANA
A Daughter's Life with Autism
Clara Claiborne Park
Author of The Siege
from the foreword by Oliver Sacks

Exiting Nirvana
A Daughter's Life with Autism
by Clara Claiborne Park

"Jessy's autism is incurable, but her story is nonetheless one of triumph. . . . Together *The Siege* and *Exiting Nirvana* constitute what may be the best-documented case history of an autist. Without doubt it is the most readable."

— Megan Rutherford, *Time*

"As much as *Exiting Nirvana* succeeds in bringing us into the world of autism, perhaps its greater accomplishment is in making us reconsider whatever we thought we knew about what it means to be human in the first place."

— David Royko, *Chicago Tribune*

The Siege

A Family's Journey into the World of an Autistic Child

by Clara Claiborne Park

"Beautiful and intelligent. . . . One of the first accounts of autism, and still the best."
— Oliver Sacks, author of *An Anthropologist on Mars*

"*The Siege* has much to tell us about how different we are from one another and how alike; about the limits of teaching and the possibilities of a family's love."
— Brina Caplan, *The Nation*

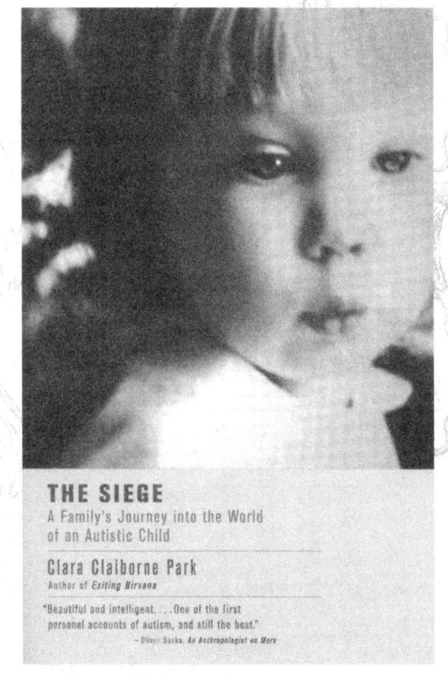

Back Bay Books
Available wherever paperbacks are sold

With the Light

Raising an Autistic Child
(Hikari To Tomoni)
Volume 3
by Keiko Tobe

English Translation: Satsuki Yamashita
Lettering: Alexis Eckerman
Logo Design: EunKyung Kim

First published in Japan in 2004 by Akita Publishing Co. Ltd., Tokyo.
English translation rights arranged with Akita Publishing Co. Ltd.
through Tuttle-Mori Agency, Inc., Tokyo.

Volume number(s) of Japanese edition: 5 and 6

Yen Press
Hachette Book Group USA
237 Park Avenue, New York, NY 10017

Visit our Web sites at www.HachetteBookGroupUSA.com
and www.YenPress.com.

Yen Press is an imprint of Hachette Book Group USA, Inc.
The Yen Press name and logo are trademarks of
Hachette Book Group USA, Inc.

First Yen Press Edition: September 2008

ISBN-10: 0-7595-2384-3
ISBN-13: 978-0-7595-2384-5

10 9 8 7 6 5 4 3 2 1

BVG

Printed in the United States of America

Reader's Note

The orientation of this book is not a printing error. Keiko Tobe's ***With the Light:*** *Raising an Autistic Child* was originally created and published in Japanese which one reads right-to-left as opposed to left-to-right as in English. To preserve the natural flow of the story and art, this original orientation has been preserved for the English language edition of the book.

Please turn the book over and begin reading from the "back" where you will find additional tips as to how to easily progress through the panels and balloons of the book if you have never before had occasion to read manga (Japanese comics).

Once you start, you will quickly lose yourself in the latest installment of this moving story.